Poverty and Progress

RICHARD G. WILKINSON

Poverty and Progress

An ecological model of economic development

Methuen & Co Ltd
11 New Fetter Lane
London EC4

First published 1973
by Methuen & Co Ltd
11 New Fetter Lane London EC4
© *1973 by Richard G. Wilkinson*
Printed and Bound in Great Britain by
Richard Clay (The Chaucer Press), Ltd
Bungay, Suffolk

SBN 416 08660 8 hardbound
SBN 416 77600 0 paperback

Contents

Acknowledgements	*page* vii
Preface	ix
1 Introduction	1
2 Cultural evolution	9
3 Ecological equilibrium	18
4 Disequilibrium and the stimulus to development	53
5 The structure of development	90
6 The English industrial revolution	112
7 Innovation and technical consistency	138
8 American economic development	147
9 Industrial societies: production and consumption	173
10 Explanations of underdevelopment	197
Postscript	217
Index	221

Acknowledgements

The author and publishers would like to thank the following for permission to compile the text figures in this volume from the following sources:

Ajia Keizai Kenkyusho for statistics from S. Ishikawa, *Economic Development in Asian Perspective* (1967); Cambridge University Press for statistics from B. R. Mitchell and Phyllis Deane, *Abstract of British Historical Statistics* (1962); T. H. Hollingsworth and Anthony Sheil Associates Ltd for statistics from T. H. Hollingsworth, *Historical Demography* (Hodder & Stoughton, 1969); Macmillan & Co Ltd and St Martin's Press Inc. for statistics from C. Clark and M. Haswell, *The Economics of Subsistence Agriculture* (1970); E. H. Phelps Brown and Sheila V. Hopkins for statistics from 'Seven centuries of the prices of consumables, compared with builders' wage rates', *Economica*, XCII (1956); Routledge and Kegan Paul and Humanities Press Inc. for statistics from M. Young and P. Willmott, *Family and Kinship in East London* (1957); the Science Museum for statistics from *Synopsis of Historical Events: mechanical and electrical engineering* (1960); Weidenfeld and Nicolson for statistics from E. A. Wrigley, *Population and History* (1969).

Preface

For the layman who is fortunate enough not to have been exposed to some of the more obtuse academic thought on economic development, most of this book will, I hope, seem little more than common sense. Most of the components are commonplace in one or other discipline of the social sciences. What is new is that the pieces have been put together in a way they have not been before, so that they yield a radically different perspective on the subject matter. Many of the criticisms which will be levelled against the model are likely to reflect interdisciplinary conflict as people see how ideas accepted in other disciplines affect their own, but given the necessity of adopting a unified approach to the subject matter, this is unavoidable. For people already familiar with several disciplines, there will be fewer surprises.

It seems likely that the main body of knowledge that we have to bring to bear in understanding any social situation will always be the informal, intuitive knowledge, which we call common sense. We have each accumulated a remarkably sophisticated understanding and pattern of expectations of how people will behave in different situations which are not enshrined in any formal theory. Although the social sciences have a great deal to offer us, their theories must be used as adjuncts to our main body of informal knowledge, rather than as something to stand in its stead. The development economist or social worker who approached practical problems in the field believing that the main analytical tool he had at hand were the theories he had learnt, would be less effective than most non-specialists. I have tried to set forth the model in this book in such a way that it will unfold in company with a commonsense approach to the problems of development. Unfortunately, oversimplifications and definitions which can easily be lifted out in isolation and misapplied cannot always be avoided, but I have tried to clarify the meaning and use of concepts in relation to specific situations rather than spelling out universal definitions which detract from clarity and lead to intransigent thinking.

It is of course easy enough to misuse almost any model. This one indicates three distinct sources of change: the breakdown of ecological equilibrium, the demands of technical consistency and the development of new forms of need as the real costs of living are changed. In each real-world situation the reader will have to decide which of these causes is operative. None of them will on its own explain all change. In this, and probably many other respects, I depend upon the reader's co-operation.

Sometimes the apparently commercial world of publishing seems readier to supply the support and encouragement needed for new research than our universities are. The work involved in developing the theory set out in this book would have been difficult – if not impossible – within the restrictive framework of a Ph.D. degree. The approach to the subject seemed a radical departure from established lines of thought, I was unproven, and the material was strewn indiscriminately across the boundaries of the disciplines into which the social sciences are divided. I owe a great deal to my publishers who, from the beginning, gave me moral as well as some essential financial support, and to the open-mindedness of their academic readers.

Though Professor F. J. Fisher cannot be held responsible for the ideas developed in this book, they would not have come to mind when they did had I not had the benefit of his teaching at the London School of Economics. His lectures and classes were a constant source of new insights, confined, only for the sake of argument, to sixteenth- and seventeenth-century English economic history. It is of course a little embarrassing to write at all when someone of his ability has so far limited himself to a few brief essays, but perhaps this situation can soon be remedied. I am particularly grateful to Professor Fisher for his willingness to give his time to those who seek his advice and for his valuable criticism of my manuscript. Professor Eric Jones, Professor Peter Mathias and Dr Andrew Sherratt have also read my manuscript and made valuable criticisms. I am only sorry not to have known earlier than I did that Dr Sherratt was working in archaeology along broadly similar lines to mine. Eric Jones has the rare ability to offer constructive criticism, advice and references designed to strengthen even the parts of an argument with which he disagrees. My references to his published work in agricultural history give no indication of the impressive range of topics in which he was able to offer help. Jim Potter gave me some key suggestions and references on how I might start work on my interpretation of American development for chapter 8. Professor A. H. John, both as my former tutor and also more recently, has answered my questions when I encountered particularly knotty problems. All the material I have used is taken from other people's published work and my task would have been impossible without it. I regret that these debts are too numerous to mention except in footnotes.

Richard Wilkinson

1 *Introduction*

The main ideas in this book took shape in opposition to what seemed – initially – from the student's position – to be the prevailing academic view of economic development. Together they are intended to provide a new approach to what is now a well-worn subject. As the volume of published literature expands one becomes extremely hesitant to add to it, but there are times when both the established body of theories, and the assumptions which underlie them, are ripe for change. The need for a new vantage point on development has been stressed increasingly frequently, particularly by economists. Two such appeals appeared recently in a volume of essays on growth economics. T. W. Swan mentioned the danger that growth theory may become 'merely jejune mathematics', and said:

> We all know that in models of economic growth we can produce stagnation crises, Malthusian traps, inflation barriers, take-off instability situations, even trade cycles, at the drop of a symbolic cliché. The trouble is that any one of quite a lot of clichés will do. We also know that if we were asked to think about a five-year plan for India we would not look to economic theory for ready answers: we would need to learn a great deal about India, about people, about practical techniques . . . Can we conceive of the existence of a theory of economic growth (long-run dynamics if you like) which would neither be too closely tied to a particular historical situation nor resemble a game of entrepreneurial blindman's buff, but would provide some relevant insights? – not a description of reality but (as Joan Robinson says) 'a device for sorting out our ideas'?[1]

Amartya Sen was thinking along similar lines when, in an introductory essay, he wrote 'the weakest link in the chain

[1] T. W. Swan, 'Golden ages and production functions', in Amartya Sen (ed.), *Growth Economics* (Harmondsworth, 1970), p. 203.

is the set of empirical theories of growth that underlie the logical exercises. Possible improvements of policies towards growth that could be achieved through a better understanding of the actual process of growth remain substantially unexplored.'[1]

The weakness of any mathematical model of the real world is almost certainly in its underlying assumptions – unless someone has simply got his sums wrong. These assumptions are of course the body of empirical theories on which any model rests, but instead of being dealt with as such, they are usually derived from the unstated personal 'world view' of the author. This book is concerned with laying out a new foundation of explicitly empirical theories of development.

It should not be necessary to apologize for having taken an interdisciplinary approach to this subject. Too often inquiry in the social sciences is hampered by sectarianism. When confronting such formidable problems it is essential that one should be free to draw on all the available evidence. It is manifestly unscientific to impose arbitrary limits on the variety of evidence that can be brought to bear on a theoretical problem. Subjects must be defined by the problems they tackle rather than by the types of evidence they are willing to consider. Economic development is a process which clearly ignores the divisions between the social sciences, and in doing so it sets the pace for those who wish to study it.

But as well as having something to gain from the various disciplines in the social sciences, the study of economic development also has something to offer them. These considerations have imposed certain stylistic demands on the way material is presented. In particular, because of the increasing need to choose between dipping into a great deal of published material or reading rather less more thoroughly, an attempt has been made to make each chapter into a slightly more coherent unit than it might otherwise have been. Hence the occasionally repetitious sentence to give the theoretical context of a section.

*   *   *

[1] Sen, op. cit., p. 33.

Few of the elements of change which contribute to the process of economic growth can properly be called growth. Apart from the monetary aggregates such as national income, population size is almost the only real factor which could be said to grow. Otherwise, economic development is made up of an enormous number of diverse changes in kind. Consider for a moment some of the more obvious changes as they would have affected an ordinary Englishman before the industrial revolution, after it, and in the present day. In pre-industrial England he would typically have been an agriculturalist, living in a house built of timber and local stone from which he would have walked to work. His clothes would have been woollen, linen and leather, with leather boots or shoes. More often than not he would have eaten bread and cheese, sometimes eked out with fresh or salted meat and vegetables, washed down with beer. Almost all social life centred on the village. In the late nineteenth century, after the initial stages of industrialization had passed, most Englishmen lived in towns. Many houses were jerry-built brick buildings; most people would still have walked to work but a few travelled by train or bicycle. Cotton cloth had replaced linen and sometimes wool for many garments, tea would have replaced some of the beer that was drunk earlier, and most people's food was more varied, though often less fresh than before. What entertainment there was, was to be found at music halls and drinking clubs. Today many urban workers live in concrete blocks of flats, they travel to work by public transport, their clothes are made from artificial fibres, and rubber and plastics are increasingly common in footwear. A wide variety of well-preserved food is available from all over the world. Watching television has become the dominant leisure-time activity. It is this process of change, affecting every aspect of life, which constitutes what we call economic development. We must start out from these real practical changes, not from economic development as it is abstracted, idealized or imagined. General *a priori* and metaphysical judgements of the nature of these changes (such as the belief in progress), which are used to circumvent any proper examination of them, must be discarded. The problem is to find a theory that explains the actual practical changes which have taken place. Too often economic theory bypasses the whole issue by assuming that all innovations can be subsumed by concepts such as a growing national income. The advantage of using those blanketing concepts as tools of economic analysis is that they hide more than they reveal. Many changes have no appreciable positive effect on national income, and even those which do are revealed only as unexplained bulges beneath the blanket.

The approach to economic development with which this book is concerned is basically very simple. The development of clothing materials will serve as an illustration. The easiest way of clothing oneself is to make use of the skins of animals that are eaten. This is the most primitive method. When the supply of leather becomes inadequate to meet the population's growing needs, people are forced to develop textiles from natural fibres such as bark, flax, wool and cotton. The necessity of spinning and weaving these fibres greatly increases the work required to produce clothing. As the population grows and the pressure on the land increases, artificial fibres are developed from mineral resources leaving the land for more specialized food production. Once again the manufacturing process becomes more complex and difficult. Similar sequences of change have occurred in other fields many times over. The changing ecological circumstances, centering on the relationship between population and resources, force societies to exploit their environment in new and often more difficult ways. Development is delayed not by lack of capital or inventive ability, but because new techniques often seem – at least in their initial stages – more onerous, or the product is regarded as an inferior substitute for the old. We now regard plastics as an inferior substitute for leather in shoes and handbags, and primitive societies of hunters and gatherers no doubt thought that much more work was involved in cultivating the crops they needed than in gathering those that grew naturally.

Development is primarily the result of attempts to increase the output from the environment rather than produce a given output more efficiently. Under the impact of ecological problems the productive workload tends to grow throughout.

More intensive peasant agricultural techniques often have a lower productivity per unit of labour than more primitive extensive methods. Mineral resources are less easily utilized than landbased ones, and transport becomes an increasing problem as local self-sufficiency breaks down. As the workload increases, societies bring additional sources of power to their aid, first animals, then wind and water power and finally mechanical sources of power. During industrialization the introduction of an efficient division of labour and the development of laboursaving machinery becomes a necessity as the workload reaches crisis proportions. In contrast with industrial societies, many smallscale primitive communities have managed to gain their subsistence with very little work. The long hours of leisure which were once possible in parts of the underdeveloped world must have been the source of the colonial European's belief that the indigenous populations of many countries were naturally lazy.

Development is needed when a society outgrows its resource-base and productive system. As the established economic system is proved inadequate and subsistence problems become more severe, societies are driven to change their methods. Development comes out of poverty, not out of plenty as many economic theories would lead one to suppose. Poverty stimulates the search for additional sources of income and makes people willing to do things they may previously have avoided. When for instance population growth and the division of land holdings makes units too small for subsistence, people are forced into towns to sell their labour or else they take up rural crafts to eke out a living. It is the population's increasingly exploitable situation which provides the basis for the growth of capitalist institutions.

On the other side of the coin are societies which have stabilized well within the means of subsistence available to them and so have avoided the problems which lead to development. Almost all living species have a choice between developing methods of population limitation or facing continuous starvation as their numbers are limited by the food supply. Natural selection seems to have led a great many species to

adopt the former strategy, and human societies, with the help
of social controls, have often done likewise. Many primitive
societies, particularly before contact with Europeans disrupted
their cultural systems, prevented population growth and
managed to live in equilibrium with their resources without
threat of hunger.

The next chapter puts this broad schema of economic development into the perspective of cultural evolution. It discusses the
constituents of the adaptive problem and the forms of adaptive
change.

Chapter 3, on ecological equilibrium, is conceptually
important because it deals with the converse of development –
i.e. the conditions for maintaining stability. Throughout most
of man's history, human societies have systematically avoided
outgrowing their productive system and running into new
ecological problems. Because so much of the evidence on early
methods of population control has long been forgotten by
modern anthropologists, some of it has been brought together
again in this chapter. Stability is sometimes reinforced by
judicious methods of resource management. Cultural practices
which help to prevent resources being overtaxed are included
in the discussion. Some evidence of the advantages of this
strategy may be gained from the abundance of food, the
standard of welfare and the amount of leisure achieved by some
primitive societies.

Chapter 4 shows in detail how change is initiated in societies
which have previously been in a condition of ecological
equilibrium. It shows how methods of population control have
broken down, and the emergence of subsistence problems has
led to the initial stages of change. The first half of the chapter is
based largely on anthropologists' reports of smallscale village
communities. The second half deals with the same subjects in
relation to largescale class societies, basing the discussion on
English economic history.

Chapter 5 is concerned with the basic dynamics of change. It
outlines the adaptive alternatives, changes in the resource-base
and the implications of basic changes on the requirement for

labour. The general course of agricultural development as the intensity of cultivation is increased forms the main subject of the earlier part of the chapter.

Chapter 6 is a case study of the English industrial revolution and its historical roots. Economic trends and technical innovations are placed in their proper ecological perspective. The build-up of problems which society had to deal with is traced out so that one can see why particular changes came when they did. The chapter covers the traditional subjects of the industrial revolution without reference to standard economic theory.

Chapter 7 is an attempt to sort out technical change in the context of technical interrelations. In particular it is intended to show the physical constraints on the flow of technical innovations designed to increase efficiency. It provides a formal framework in which to analyse the spreading impact of an initial disturbance on a stable technological system.

Chapter 8 is a case study of economic development in America to contrast with the English experience. It was chosen because the basic ecological and resource situation during American development appears so radically different from what it was in England that it may have been expected to provide an important test of the theory put forward.

Chapter 9 starts off from the apparent contradiction between common experience and a theory which seems to suggest that industrial societies would be characterized by hard work and poverty. It deals briefly with the actual changes in the *per capita* workload and with the nature of poverty; it goes on to show how new economic needs, created by the impact of industrialization and urbanization on people's lifestyles, provide the stimulus to higher levels of consumption. In effect, the real cost of living is increased by industrialization.

Chapter 10 returns to the problems of underdeveloped countries and contains the only explicit criticisms of other theories of development. It suggests that the fundamental problems of underdeveloped countries in need of development are more likely to be technical than strictly economic.

The relevance of the model of economic development put

forward here is not confined to societies with a particular set of economic institutions. It is extra-cultural. Because it is set in the ecological framework of cultural evolution, it goes some way towards defining the adaptive tasks which the cultural system as a whole has to perform. It deals essentially with the relationship between human needs and the environment. When the economic system can no longer bring these two together satisfactorily it shows how individuals are motivated to change the economic system. In this sense it is a human theory: it is not highly abstracted and removed from the feelings, experiences and problems facing real people. It shows in terms of their needs why they do one thing in one period and something else in another, and also why – in different economic systems – the growth of need makes new activities profitable.

Another claim which could be made for the ecological model of development is that it leaves no place for the patronizing attitudes towards pre-industrial societies so commonly reflected in the literature on development. Instead of making the easy assumption that underdeveloped countries are simply inefficient versions of the more developed ones, populated by people who have somehow failed to achieve anything better, each economic system is seen in the context of the particular problems it is designed to deal with. Contrary to the traditional view, it could easily be argued that industrial societies distinguished themselves historically by their lack of stabilizing controls capable of keeping their productive systems out of serious trouble.

2 *Cultural evolution*

The concept of cultural evolution may seem a remote starting point from which to tackle the main issues of economic development. Development, however, is composed of a series of adaptive responses to the changing ecological situation. The theory of cultural evolution provides a framework which implies that change takes place for specifically adaptive reasons, solving problems that crop up between man and his environment. A brief discussion of cultural evolution will reveal some of the basic dynamic characteristics of longterm economic development as well as indicating the background of later ideas.

Man's pattern of living is a product of the particular cultural system in which he grows up. His behaviour is primarily determined not by genetics, but by learning and intelligence. Each generation is the recipient of a body of knowledge, tradition, institutions and material culture accumulated by previous generations. These, subject to the minor modifications he makes to them, constitute man's mode of existence: his means of gaining a living from his environment, his basis of social organization and intercourse. As genetic control of behaviour has weakened, so cultural variations have become increasingly important. Man has become a creature of culture to the extent that lifestyles vary from one part of the world to another, and from one historical period to the next.

Once man's behaviour and mode of existence are determined primarily by his culture, then he is able to make adaptive changes to meet his environmental conditions by modifying his culture. He is no longer dependent on genetic mutations and biological evolution as his only adaptive mechanism: he has extra-somatic possibilities. Stone toolmaking may date back over 2 million years, but it may not have been before the advent of Neanderthal Man (say 100,000 years ago), with a brain at least as large as our own, that the evolution of cultural systems replaced biological evolution as man's most important means of making adaptive changes. The evolutionary advantages of possessing the capacity for culture are not simply that it provides for the development of a more sophisticated mode of existence and adaptation. When new adaptive problems are encountered, cultural innovations can be purpose-built to deal with new situations, while, in contrast, biological evolution must wait on the process of natural selection of random genetic mutations to produce an adequate response.

This process of evolutionary adaptation – whether biological or cultural – is a process by which species develop an ability to exploit a particular ecological niche. Each species monopolizes a particular way of life and method of gaining its supply of food. It must have access at one or other trophic level to the flows of energy and to the life-maintaining materials which circulate in the biosphere. It must be able to compete successfully for its position in the total community of living organisms which form an important part of its environment. It has been suggested that the capacity for culture is itself an ecological niche;[1] but in reality it provides a means of exploiting different ecological niches. Cultural change is a means of changing from one niche to another. When man changes the source of food and raw materials he depends on, when he finds ways of increasing his resistance to diseases and parasites, or develops forms of protection against inclement climatic and geographic conditions, then he may be said to have changed his ecological niche.

If the adaptive function of culture is its *raison d'etre*, then the implication seems to be that most of the individual elements of cultural systems must be explained in terms of their contribution towards this function. But culture is not merely an inter-

[1] See for instance C. Loring Brace, *The Stages of Human Evolution* (Englewood Cliffs, N.J., 1967), chapter 8.

mediary between man and his environment. Man's social life and all other aspects of his behaviour are also culturally determined. A society's culture is a hotchpotch of different elements, designed to perform different tasks, satisfy different needs and cater for different groups of people within the population. It is not an integrated harmonious system designed to achieve a single unifying objective. But among these sometimes strained cultural interactions, some elements take precedence over others. Both individuals and societies will give priority to the maintenance of subsistence activities at a level at least adequate for survival. This is a cultural imperative. The importance of basic production gives it a key role in initiating cultural change. If the demands which basic production imposes on society change, then the rest of the cultural system will have to change to meet them. The demands of production have a pre-eminent position which allows them to ride roughshod over other elements of a culture. It is in this sense that economic life plays a more basic or formative role in cultural development than other elements. To the extent that a society's culture is an integrated system, it will be integrated around the demands imposed by its adaptive function.

Most fundamental within the adaptive context is a society's technology. Productive tools and equipment are designed to exploit a particular set of resources and transform them into the articles we need. Any process of adaptive change, particularly a shift from one ecological niche to another involving changes in the resource-base, will necessitate technical change. As the 'leading edge' of culture, the technology may initiate a process of change which could force the rest of the culture to re-assemble round a new productive system.

If economic development is to be seen as a process of cultural evolution it immediately raises questions of the direction of evolution. All sorts of anthropocentric and teleological ideas of progress have been read into the process of evolution. Man is used to putting himself at the top of the evolutionary tree – as the highest form of life – and emphasizing human characteristics such as intelligence as the criteria for progress. In a similar way people in industrial societies emphasize various features of their societies as marks of cultural progress. However, in evolution there are no criteria except adaptation. Intelligence was never an end in itself: it developed because of its adaptive advantages.

It is important to distinguish between two different forms of adaptation: improved adaptation within a fixed environmental context, and adaptation to meet changes in the environment. The first is a process which tends to work itself out after a period of increasingly fine adaptation to the environment. A fixed environmental context provides a fixed set of selective criteria. Survival of the fit leads to the establishment of a fairly stable genetic population capable of dealing with its habitat. In this situation a new period of rapid evolution will only be ushered in by a change in the environmental context. As the selective criteria are changed new features are selected as advantageous while others are put at a disadvantage.

The same pattern holds true for cultural evolution – not by analogy, but because cultural and biological change have the same function. In terms of survival, improved adaptation to a fixed environment is likely to be a process which makes life easier, and allows for the development of a more integrated cultural system. Changes in the environmental context are – in contrast – likely to seem threatening or disturbing to the established system. Many anthropologists working on cultural evolution have however failed to make the distinction between these two forms of adaptation. They have discussed cultural change only in the limited context of primitive societies adapting to fixed climatic and geographical conditions, rather than as a truly dynamic process.[1] The fault lies in failing to see how a cultural system runs into changing environmental problems which generate further cultural change.

To understand the process of cultural change we must examine the components of the adaptive problem situation which it faces. Initially it appears as if each culture defines its own adaptive problems. By determining a society's mode of

[1] See for instance contributions to Andrew P. Vayda (ed.), *Environment and Cultural Behavior* (New York, 1969).

existence a cultural system puts that system into a position where it is more likely to run into some adaptive problems than others. An industrial society which uses large quantities of minerals is more likely to face problems of mineral shortages than an agricultural one is. But to say that culture itself poses the adaptive problem is misleading: the fundamental adaptive problem is posed by the genetic structure of man and his natural environment. A culture, as a means of achieving adaptation, is capable of specifying particular adaptive problems only in so far as secondary problems are derived from the major adaptive strategy adopted by the culture. This means that to analyse the make-up of the adaptive problem situation we must start not with culture, but with the extra-cultural elements which pose the initial adaptive problem.

Biological man and the natural environment provide the basic setting: i.e. the means and ends which must be brought together. Although they are determinants of culture they are not entirely extra-cultural factors. Biological man contains genetic characteristics which represent adaptations to particular cultural ways of life. Because man has lived by hunting and gathering for very much longer than he has lived by agriculture or industry (all except for the last 3–8,000 of say the last 100,000 years), one might expect him to have some inherited characteristics which suit him to that way of life. Likewise, the natural environment has been more or less transformed by man working according to the dictates of particular cultures. But although culture has left its marks on both biological man and the environment, these two elements must be regarded as providing the extra-cultural conditions within which any culture must work. In terms of cultural changes during historical time – measured perhaps in centuries – biological man has to be regarded as a fixed element which all cultural systems must come to terms with. Similarly, even a culturally modified environment imposes not only a set of geographical conditions but also the rules – or natural laws – by which man may modify them.

For biological man, behaviour is an intermediary between internal feelings and external objects. A culture's task is to provide ways of using the external environment to satisfy physical and mental needs. Man's feelings of pleasure and pain, appetites and aversions, motivate him to fulfil his various needs through the behavioural channels his culture has taught him. Some of the feelings of pleasure and pain relate to imbalances in the metabolic processes of our bodies – hunger, thirst, tiredness and so on – but others are obviously more complicated. Culture serves not to teach us the complete set of objects and situations from which we can gain satisfaction, but instead focuses our attention on a specific subset which it defines as legitimate and consistent with its overall adaptive strategy. What is regarded as good food in one society may be regarded as inedible in another.

The key to man's adaptability is the maximization of the universe of objects and behavioural situations which are potentially satisfying to him. This gives culture the greatest possible choice of adaptive strategies. The obvious precondition for achieving this situation was that the genetic influences on our behaviour should be minimized, and made as unspecific (in terms of their attachment to specific objects in the external world) as possible, leaving the maximum room for learning and intelligence. Animals and insects which have instincts that lead them to build nests in particular ways from particular materials, or which escape from confined spaces not on the basis of an intelligent look at their problem, but because of an instinctive tendency to move towards light, have more sophisticated but more restrictive instincts than we have. Man appears to have only the most simple, basic and open-ended survival instincts. Culture fills the gap with a particular adaptive system which serves to relate man to man and man to his environment in such a way that he is provided with the social and material conditions necessary for him to live and reproduce. Working on the basis of man's limited genetic propensities for activity, a cultural system must shape the behaviour of a multiplicity of individuals so that it forms a consistent whole, favourable to the survival of the society. Thus the most sophisticated behavioural system is built on the simplest instinctive base.

The natural environment provides the other half of the adaptive problem. Environmental conditions decide not only what resources are available to the productive system, but also under what conditions they are supplied. The climate and soils determine what crops can be grown and what must be done to grow them. The occurrence of minerals and the way they are deposited affects the course of industrial development and the particular extractive technology which must be used. The kind of terrain, its rivers and harbours, affect the development of transport, the position of towns, and the formation of trade routes. The climate affects the type of clothing and shelter man needs, whether they have to provide protection against wind, rain, sun or cold.

Unlike biological man, the environment cannot be regarded as a constant factor throughout the time periods we are interested in. It undergoes changes caused both by its own natural agencies and by man's actions. Climatic change, although a long slow process, probably played an important part in the Neolithic revolution. As the last Ice Age receded man found himself faced with a different distribution and different types of fauna, flora and soils. These and other factors changed the complexion of the adaptive problem and led to the replacement of the hunting and gathering way of life by shifting agriculture. Apart from natural processes of change, the environment has often been changed artificially and intentionally to benefit man – for instance by turning forest, arid or marshy areas into agriculturally productive land. Changes of this kind are really part of the solution to the adaptive problem. However, man's actions have frequently had unintended repercussions on the environment which have created new adaptive problems. The current concern with environmental pollution is one instance of this. As it becomes more serious we may expect it to elicit remedies, just as the pollution of urban water supplies has led to the introduction of sewers and treated water supplies. The most important category of artificial but unintended environmental changes are those which follow from the overtaxing of particular natural re-sources: either using up vegetable resources faster than they can be replaced, or working out deposits of mineral resources. Not only is this one of the most common sources of change in the adaptive problem situation, but because it directly threatens the particular adaptive strategy which the culture has chosen, it is one of the most important. The culture must find either an alternative source of supply or a substitute for the scarce resource.

The variable which usually plays the decisive role in determining how fast a society uses up the resources which its culture depends on is the size of the population. Of course, in the ecological equation, population size is the quantitative dimension of biological man. It decides the amount of labour which is available and the quantity of food and other materials needed; it is in fact the most important determinant of the scale of cultural operations which relate man to his environment. But as well as having a quantitative impact on the cultural system the size of the population also has a qualitative impact: adaptive strategies which are practical at one level of operation may be impracticable at another. Limitations on the supply of resources can mean that quantitative change necessitates qualitative change. The 'carrying capacity' – or population size which can be supported on a given area of land – is a function of the kind of productive technology which is used. To increase the carrying capacity of any territory a new adaptive strategy, based on a new technology, will have to be introduced. Much of the historical development of agricultural techniques the world over appears to be a series of attempts to increase the carrying capacity of the available land area in response to population pressure. But this is encroaching on the subject matter of chapter 5.

Like every other animal species, man has the biological potential to increase his numbers very rapidly. Population numbers will increase unless either the environment imposes positive checks in the form of epidemic diseases and food shortages, or the cultural system contains checks such as contraception, abortion, pressure to delay marriages, etc. This potentially volatile element in the adaptive problem situation has played an extremely active role in cultural evolution.

Several important points have emerged from this brief discussion. Cultural change has taken the place of biological evolution as man's chief adaptive mechanism. At the forefront of the adaptive process are economic and technical innovations, capable of forcing change on the rest of the cultural system. Although improved adaptation within a settled ecological context may seem to be a vehicle for general cultural progress, the cultural responses to a changing problem situation often seem to threaten progress. In the context of cultural evolution, the intermittent character of economic development is understandable. Stability is achieved when the culture is adequately adapted to a particular ecological niche; further development only takes place in response to some alteration in the adaptive-problem situation. The most likely causes of such an alteration are population change and the unintended consequences of man's actions on the environment. The make-up of biological man is so nearly a constant over the sort of time periods we are interested in that it would be a good methodological rule not to invoke increases in intelligence, individualism or inventiveness to explain development, unless we can give cultural explanations for such increases.

3 *Ecological equilibrium*

At first man multiplied so fast as to make the earth too crowded.
Kari, the Thunder-god, slew some of them to reduce the number
of mouths to be fed, but this proved insufficient. Eventually Death
was instituted to relieve the situation.

A Semang Myth.[1]

This chapter deals with the essential preconditions for the
stability of cultural systems. It develops the concept of a stable,
well-adapted culture, existing in an equilibrium situation. This
concept is needed primarily to provide part of the analytical
framework for looking – in later chapters – at the process of
adjustment and change going on in most contemporary
societies. Just as the economist analyses price movements as if
they were movements between theoretical equilibrium prices,
so the concept of a cultural system in an equilibrium situation
will be used to provide a theoretical limiting case for a study of
the process of adjustment itself. The picture of a stable, well-
adapted society which we are concerned with, is of a society
which has settled into a known and proven way of life which
allows it to deal with all eventualities without innovation. It
must have found solutions to all significant problems and have
established itself in such a way that it does not have to face new
and unprecedented situations. It will be shown that a fundamental element in achieving this situation is the development
of a balanced relationship with the environment. But more
important than establishing the preconditions for this kind of
stability, is showing that cultural evolution tends to develop

[1] W. W. Skeat and C. O. Blagden, *Pagan Races of the Malay Peninsula*
(London, 1906), volume II, p. 184.

these conditions – that the concept of a cultural system existing in a stable equilibrium situation is not based on theory alone. Evidence will be produced to suggest that a variety of historic and prehistoric societies have developed these preconditions and have come sufficiently close to such a situation to serve as examples of it.

In terms of coping with the most fundamental adaptive problems, a society must meet two requirements before it can stabilize: it must of course have developed an integrated productive technology, but it must also have found ways of ensuring that a balance is maintained between its demand for natural resources and the environment's ability to supply them. Every society and every technological system has the potential to expand beyond the limits of its resource-base. If for the moment a society's ecological niche is defined in terms of the particular group of natural resources which the productive system is designed to use, then it can be seen that each niche has a definite size as determined by the quantities of resources available, or rather, by the level of resource use *which the environment can sustain under given conditions*: it is possible for a productive system to outgrow its ecological niche. The development of a productive system is a process of adapting to a *particular* ecological niche, of exploiting and processing a specific set of natural resources. It entails developing particular kinds of technology. Once this has been achieved the question is whether or not it is possible to avoid threatening the whole structure by outgrowing the niche. Thus we can see that before a society can stabilize it must solve both a qualitative and a quantitative problem. In this chapter we will assume that the first has been solved – that the society has established a viable, integrated productive system, and is left only with the quantitative problem of establishing a balance between its demand for resources and the supply which the environment can sustain.

In this form the problem is exactly the same as that faced by animal species, and perhaps a similarity between problems would lead one to expect some similarity in solutions. Every animal is equipped to exploit the particular set of plants or other animal species which provide its food, just as every productive system is designed to exploit a particular group of resources. Because its potential rate of reproduction is very high, every animal population must find some way of avoiding the dangerous consequences of overhunting, overgrazing or overfishing its essential food source.

All animals, including man, depend upon organic materials – either plants or other animal species – for their food. In addition man's fuel resources (wood, coal and oil), all his clothing materials (wool, cotton, linen and modern artificial fibres made from oil) and many other materials including paper and plastic are all organic. By comparison, the inorganic materials such as metals and some of our chemicals play a smaller role, and still depend on organic fuels for their purification. Organic resources are *reproducible*: they depend on the environmental cycle of 'life processes' which derives its energy initially from the sun. Whether it is a matter of the rate of reproduction of various plants and animal species, or the laying down of matter which will form fossil fuels, organic resources are available as a continuous but limited *flow*. Inorganic resources on the other hand appear as limited *stocks* which are not renewed in the course of natural processes. From the point of view of a study of ecological relationships however, it is probably more useful to treat man's use of fossil fuels as if they were non-renewable stocks: they are laid down too slowly to make much practical difference to how long they will last. But the use of other organic resources must conform to the conditions of their supply. If they are overexploited their ability to reproduce themselves will be impaired and they will become progressively scarcer. Part of what appears at any time to be the available food supply must always be left untouched; it must be treated as a capital stock from which the next season's crop will be raised. Each animal or plant population can be exploited to yield what is called a 'maximum sustainable crop'. If less than this amount is taken wastage occurs; if it is exceeded, future yields will decline. By taking just this amount a predator species would be able to maintain its numbers at the highest possible level; if it started to take more than this amount it would be eating into its 'capital stock' and would face progressive starvation and a decrease in its numbers in the future.

Given the dynamics of this system, one would expect that the overexploitation of resources would be a major problem for most species. But in practice overhunting, overfishing and overgrazing appear to be extremely rare in the natural world. As Wynne-Edwards has said:

> Where we can still find nature undisturbed by human interference . . . there is generally no indication whatever that the habitat is run down or destructively overtaxed. On the contrary the whole trend of ecological evolution seems in the very opposite direction, leading towards the highest productivity which can possibly be built up within the limits set by the inorganic environment.[1]

Natural populations tend to establish themselves in an *ecological equilibrium* situation. Rather than overexploit their resources, they build up a pattern and a rate of resource use which the environment can sustain indefinitely. Without this, the stable, well-balanced 'climax communities' of flora and fauna which ecologists describe could not exist.

The concept of an ecological equilibrium is meant to cover any combination of a method and a rate of resource use which the environment can sustain indefinitely. It may refer to a situation in which the population restricts its demand for resources to a level which the environment can supply naturally, or it may refer to a balance struck on the basis of particular cultural patterns of resource management by which the environment's production of particular renewable resources is artificially increased. In this context the 'carrying capacity' of an area of land is of course the largest population which can be maintained on it in ecological equilibrium – given the prevailing method of environmental resource exploitation. Ecological equilibrium situations are defined to be consistent with cultural

[1] V. C. Wynne-Edwards, *Animal Dispersion in Relation to Social Behaviour* (Edinburgh, 1962), pp. 8–9.

B

stability from the point of view of subsistence and productive activities. If a society is in ecological equilibrium then it satisfies the *ecological* requirement for stability. It is not about to run short of the resources it depends on.

As we have already noted, every population has the potential ability to expand beyond the limits of its resources. If it is to be maintained within an ecological equilibrium it must develop mechanisms for limiting its numbers *before* resources are threatened. Any such mechanisms would have to act homeostatically to maintain the population at a level consistent with taking somewhere near – but not exceeding – the maximum sustainable crop of resources. If a population was checked only by starvation it would always grow up to the limits of the available food supplies; it would overexploit resources, eat into the capital stock and damage the ability of resources to reproduce themselves. The presence of starvation in a population is an indication that the population is probably not in ecological equilibrium. Although Malthus's theory that starvation is the effective check on the size of populations still has an important following, it is rarely supported by observations of natural populations. Starvation does appear occasionally in both animal and human populations, but it only appears as a *normal* condition during unstable periods of transition in which traditional patterns have been disrupted. Examples will show that animal populations starve only during some exceptional disturbance to their food supplies, and that human populations starve only when a society is in transition – when traditional cultural methods of limiting population size have been broken down and new ones have not yet been established. If it is possible to talk of a 'normal' situation in the historic and evolutionary time scale, then the 'normal' situation is to live in ecological equilibrium and starvation is, by contrast, a rarity.

Malthus's theory can be fitted into this framework if it is regarded as a description of the society in which he lived. He was writing in exceptional times – at the outset of the English industrial revolution – and his theory describes the ecological problem facing a society in transition. His mistake was to present it as a law valid for all time. This was the inevitable result of his leaving it as a conjectural argument about the potential increase in population compared with food supplies, instead of going on to examine how populations actually dealt with this problem. The few observations he did make of primitive societies put his theory in serious difficulties – as we shall see later in this chapter. When later he watered down the theory to say that populations would be limited by starvation unless what he called 'restraint' was practised, he was from our point of view merely begging the question which we must tackle.

Our everyday observation of the few natural populations of birds and other animals which we may come across does not suggest that starvation is their normal condition. Even in underdeveloped countries starvation appears to have been a rarity before the disruptive effects of European contact. The persistence of the belief – in the face of the evidence – that starvation is the primary factor limiting the size of populations, may have something to do with its ideological connections. Free-market capitalism is often regarded as a 'natural' system because it seems to share with evolutionary theory the principle of the 'survival of the fittest'. It is easy to see both evolution and the free market as dependent on the competitive struggle of individuals, each for his own survival. The obvious implication of the theory of both systems is that the losers starve. But the principle of the 'survival of the fittest' applies as much to whole species and to groups of individuals, as it does to individuals within those species and groups. The development of the individual in directions which damage the group is checked by the force of *group selection* in evolution. If a high reproductive rate – and the consequent struggle between individuals for food as it becomes increasingly scarce – lessens the group's chances of survival, then group selection will tend to remove these characteristics from populations. But the ideological ramifications of the issue of group versus individual selection goes further than the controversy over population controls and starvation. The idea of individual selection as the sole determinant is presumably linked with the pessimistic view of an

unfettered 'struggle of each against all', and of a life in a state of
nature which was 'nasty, brutish and short' as people fought for
the means of subsistence. Group selection on the other hand is
linked with the more optimistic image of the naturally sociable
'noble savage' leading his idyllic life. But in reality both systems
of selection must operate together. Competition is regulated
within more or less socially acceptable forms.

Examples of the ways in which animal populations limit their
numbers will show how group selection has operated to
devise mechanisms for maintaining populations within ecological equilibrium. They will also serve as an introduction to an
examination of the same issue in human societies. Quite simple
experiments can be devised to show how some animal species
limit their populations. Insect populations can be kept in artificial environments – a bottle with a constant supply of food –
and their numbers counted at regular intervals. An experiment which involved putting different numbers of flour beetles
into containers holding different quantities of flour showed that
after a few weeks' breeding the populations in each container
had built up and stabilized at a density of around 44 per gram of
flour.[1] Numbers were limited by the tendency of the adult
beetles to eat the eggs as population density increased. It has
since been discovered that stabilization is also helped by a
decrease in the number of eggs laid by each female. Similar
experiments with grain weevils, which lay their eggs in wheat
grain, have shown that unless there are ten or twelve times as
many grains as the female needs to lay in, she begins to lay
progressively fewer eggs.[2] Experiments with guppies have
shown a similar pattern.[3] Fish were put into two identical
aquaria, a single pregnant female in one and a mixed group of
fifty in the other. Both tanks were supplied with more than
enough food. The mixed group of fifty guppies not only pre-

[1] Royal N. Chapman, 'The quantitative analysis of environmental
factors', *Ecology*, IX (1928), pp. 111–22.
[2] D. S. MacLagan and E. Dunn, 'The experimental analysis of the growth of
an insect population', *Proceedings of the Royal Society*, LV (1936), pp. 126–39.
[3] C. M. Breder and C. W. Coates, 'A preliminary study of population
stability and sex ratio of *Lebistes*', *Copeia* (1932), pp. 147–55. (As reported
in Wynne-Edwards (1962), op. cit., p. 543.)

vented their population increasing by eating all the fry as soon as broods were hatched, but they also reduced their own numbers to nine by cannibalism. At that point their population stabilized. In the other tank with only one fish, the first brood had a 100 per cent survival rate, but this rate was progressively reduced in subsequent broods. The adult female thinned out the young as they grew larger until this tank's population also settled at nine. Experiments with more complicated animals reveal similar patterns of population limitation: house mice supplied with a limited quantity of food bred successfully up to the limits of their food supply with an average of nine out of ten of their young surviving. As the food shortage began to be encountered the proportion of young surviving from the next few litters was more than reversed, but this was followed by a six-month period when the mice stopped breeding altogether.[1] Mice, like rats, rabbits and a number of other mammals, have been found to reabsorb young embryos into the uterus – an ability which provides an alternative to miscarriage as a means of population control. In a population of wild rabbits it was found that 64 per cent of all conceptions had been reabsorbed in this way.[2]

Most species, as well as being able to control the numbers of eggs or young produced, also practise some form of infanticide: birds will sometimes break their eggs, kill fledgelings or desert their nests; other animals will eat their young. Most of us are familiar with some of the evidence of these practices, though perhaps without recognizing its significance. Where unwanted eggs and fledgelings are not eaten they can sometimes be found lying around broken and dead. The tendency of cats to eat their kittens when they are disturbed is also well known. But usually several methods of population control are used in conjunction with each other. A population of great tits, which normally nested in a limited number of holes in trees, were suddenly

[1] Robert L. Strecker and John T. Emlen, 'Regulatory mechanisms in house-mouse populations: the effect of limited supply of food on a confined population', *Ecology*, XXXIV (1953), pp. 375–85.

[2] H. V. Thompson and A. N. Worden, *The Rabbit* (London, 1956), pp. 112–13.

given more nesting boxes than they could use.[1] The result was that almost three times as many pairs bred as before, but the effect on total population numbers was offset by a decrease of nearly two eggs in the average clutch size, and a fall in the proportion of pairs raising a second clutch in the season to a quarter of what it had been. The population equilibrium was maintained in spite of a dramatic change in the breeding pattern.

Wynne-Edwards has described some of the social conventions animals have developed as additional methods of regulating their populations in relation to their food supplies.[2] Direct competition for food – with all its damaging implications – has been replaced, he says, by competition for such things as socially recognized territories or breeding sites which are sufficiently limited to check population before food supplies are threatened. Species of birds which have territories defend them only over the breeding season; territorial behaviour among ground-feeding birds serves as a powerful mechanism to relate the size of the breeding population to the available resources. Studies have shown that birds will vary the size of their territories according to the productivity of the area, as might be expected.[3] Some species of birds, particularly those whose feeding area is hard to define territorially, such as sea birds and birds which feed in the air on flying insects, nest in socially recognized colonies. Failure to gain a place in the colony prevents a bird from breeding but does not necessarily exclude it from the community. Some of these colonial breeding grounds represent extremely old traditions among the birds which use them; as Wynne-Edwards says,

> We have in Britain a number of ancient Viking names such as Lundy – 'isle of puffins', and Sulisgeir – 'gannets' rock', both

---

[1] H. N. Kluyver, 'The population ecology of the great tit, *Parus m. major L.*', *Ardea*, XXXIX (1951), pp. 1–135. (As reported in David Lack, *The Natural Regulation of Animal Numbers* (Oxford, 1954).)

[2] Wynne-Edwards, op. cit.

[3] G. R. Miller *et al.*, 'Responses of red grouse populations to experimental improvements of their food', and Richard T. Holmes, 'Differences in population density and food supply of dunlin on arctic and subarctic tundra', both in Adam Watson (ed.), *Animal Populations in Relation to their Food Resources*, British Ecological Society Symposium, X (Oxford, 1970).

dating from the 8th–10th century A.D., and still perfectly appropriate a thousand years later. Long standing breeding places of seals and turtles are similarly known by old descriptive names in various parts of the world.[1]

It is difficult to do justice to the evidence which is available of the ways animal populations limit their numbers: examples are too numerous. But the evolutionary disadvantages of overpopulation are clearly demonstrated; even in experiments where food was supplied artificially in superabundance, reproduction was checked homeostatically to prevent overpopulation in relation to other environmental factors. Unless these limitations on breeding reflect the advantages of avoiding the problems consequent on overexploiting resources, it is difficult to see how they could be interpreted as anything other than genetic malfunctions. Perhaps the most dramatic illustration of the need to maintain an equilibrium relationship between population size and resources is the behaviour of migrant animals. The advantage of migratory behaviour is that it allows an animal to develop an improved pattern of resource exploitation, using different resources as they come into season in different areas. But a great many migrant animals return to their birthplaces to breed year after year, not just to the same general area, but to the same nest or stream. This allows the established communal mechanisms to maintain their homeostatic control of breeding. Methods of tagging or marking birds and fishes have shown that this sort of behaviour is widespread and not just confined to such well-known examples as the house-martin and the salmon.

The question of population controls must finally be decided by reference to the primary sources, but it will be found that the case for starvation is very hard to argue: Wynne-Edwards at the end of his section on experiments with rodent populations says that '. . . no adult mortality was ever caused in these experiments by actual starvation'.[2]

The most important mechanisms for limiting *human* populations are cultural. As with most aspects of human behaviour, the

[1] Wynne-Edwards, op. cit., p. 453. [2] Ibid., p. 505.

physiological and instinctive mechanisms for controlling reproduction homeostatically are weak and inadequate on their own: they can serve only as fall-back systems when cultural ones fail. Human populations are only adequately checked and starvation avoided in cultural systems which are sufficiently well adapted to have developed their own homeostatic controls. It is variations in the cultural system, not in man's physiology, which decide whether starvation occurs in human populations.

However there are remnants of physiological mechanisms for controlling reproduction in human beings, and these should be discussed before going on to deal with the variety of cultural mechanisms which have appeared in various societies. Just as neurosis induced in mice and other animals by overcrowding or other experimental conditions can interfere with reproduction, so it can with human beings.[1] It is well known that there are connections between emotional stress in women and both menstrual irregularity and the chances of miscarriage. Studies of women with records of spontaneous abortion have shown that they are more likely to have neurotic symptoms than a control group; any possible doubts as to which was cause and which was effect were cleared up when it was shown that therapy designed to deal with the neurosis successfully reduced the chances of another miscarriage, and also that the presence of neurosis was correlated with other experiences which could have been its cause.[2] Menstrual aberrations as well as male and female infertility can also be correlated with tension and stress.[3] Although the relationship between stress

---

[1] D. H. Stott, 'Cultural and natural checks on population growth', in A. P. Vayda (ed.), *Environment and Cultural Behavior* (New York, 1969), pp. 90–120.

[2] A. Nilsson, 'Psychiatric aspects of spontaneous abortion – i and ii', *Journal of Psychosomatic Research*, XIII (1969), pp. 45–51 and 53–9.

[3] H. J. Osofsky and S. Fisher, 'Psychological correlates of the development of amenorrhea in a stress situation', *Psychosomatic Medicine*, XXIX (1967), pp. 15–23; J. Johnson, 'Progress of disorders of sexual potency in the male', *Journal of Psychosomatic Research*, IX (1965), pp. 195–200; R. N. Rutherford *et al.*, 'The treatment of psychologic factors in anovulation', *Fertility and Sterility*, XII (1961), pp. 55–66.

and the reproductive functions will tend to inhibit births in any local or personal situations which the mother finds difficult, it will also act as a homeostatic mechanism, checking population growth whenever the cultural system itself is faced with a difficult situation. Any generalized upheaval or overpopulation causing food shortages will mean that more people are faced with the emotional difficulties of readjustment and the worries of poverty. But as well as mechanisms such as these, there are physiological mechanisms acting homeostatically in relation to the standard of living. Surveys have shown that stillbirths are a higher proportion of all births among poor people than among the well-off. A survey of births in Aberdeen between 1938 and 1944 showed that the proportion of stillbirths was three times as high among the registrar-general's social classes III, IV and V combined, as among classes I and II combined.[1] More recent studies have produced similar results for perinatal deaths generally – even when adjustments have been made for factors such as differences in the age of mothers or the numbers of children they have already had.[2] Of those babies born alive, a higher proportion born to working-class mothers are premature;[3] presumably this means they will be more prone to death from a variety of causes. A study of infant mortality which divided all classes of death into five categories: congenital, infectious diseases, bronchitis and pneumonia, diarrhoea, and all other causes, found that the death rate attributable to each category increased, the lower the social class.[4] Disease in general tends to act as a homeostatic regulator, taking a higher toll from a population living in bad conditions,

[1] D. Baird, 'The influence of social and economic factors on stillbirths and neonatal deaths', *Journal of Obstetrics and Gynaecology of the British Empire*, LII (1945), pp. 217–35.

[2] M. S. Feldstein and N. R. Butler, 'Analysis of factors affecting perinatal mortality: a multivariate statistical approach', *British Journal of Preventive and Social Medicine*, IX (1965), pp. 128–34.

[3] Alice Stewart, 'A note on the obstetric effects of working during pregnancy', *British Journal of Preventive and Social Medicine*, IX (1955), pp. 159–61.

[4] Barnet Woolf, 'Studies in infant mortality – Part 11', *British Journal of Social Medicine*, II (1947), pp. 73–125.

particularly if people are overcrowded or if their resistance is weakened by malnutrition. But on the adult population it can work very erratically; where it has its greatest homeostatic effect is on the infant mortality rate.

The importance of miscarriages and infant mortality on the effective rate of reproduction should not be underestimated. Professor Titmuss, working on figures for England and Wales covering the years 1936–8, said 'Ignoring induced abortion . . . at least one pregnancy in every 8 does not result in a live child aged one year.'[1] But that figure does not take into account losses of fertilized ova within the first month of conception before pregnancy has been recognized. Clinical evidence suggests that about one-third of all fertilized ova are lost at this stage and that the total loss from spontaneous abortion alone may amount to almost half the number of fertilized ova.[2] This suggests that the potential variation in fertility through the effects of physiological factors may be very large indeed. Perhaps such a weak and chancy link in the reproductive process provides a point at which minor variations in external conditions may intervene and become influential determinants of the reproductive rate. But however important the physiological checks on fertility may be, we know that they are insufficient to prevent the occurrence of starvation in a population. They can only reduce the pressure of population on resources and diminish the incidence of starvation.

If starvation is to be prevented, physiological checks on population size must be supported by cultural ones. But although physiological checks may be presumed to operate in all human populations, the presence and adequacy of cultural checks vary from society to society. The argument here is that adequate cultural checks only exist in well-adapted societies, or, in case that appears to be a tautology, they appear in traditional societies which have established themselves in a way of life

[1] R. M. Titmuss, 'Stillbirths and neonatal mortality', *Proceedings of the Nutrition Society*, II (1944), p. 40.
[2] William H. James, 'The incidence of spontaneous abortion', *Population Studies*, XXIV (1970), pp. 241–5.

undisturbed by European contact or other new influences. Unfortunately, 'pre-contact' societies are becoming increasingly hard to find. More and more of the societies which social anthropologists study tend to be societies in transition, disturbed from their traditional ways as they get caught up in the ever-widening net of the industrialized world. Our evidence of effective cultural methods of limiting population size has to be drawn from the diminishing group of relatively isolated, undisturbed societies, and from the early reports of other traditional societies which have now disappeared. It will be shown that the stability of these societies is based on an ecological equilibrium sustained by limiting population size. Starvation was avoided and resources were not overexploited.

In 1922 Carr-Saunders published his theory that human populations tend to be limited by cultural factors to a certain optimum size in relation to resources.[1] He thought that cultural systems had evolved elements which tended indirectly to limit population growth. These were such things as kinds of food and modes of life which increased infant mortality, periods during which there were taboos on sexual intercourse, prolonged breastfeeding, and pre-puberty intercourse which he believed caused a decrease in fertility later in life. But the practices which he thought were decisive in controlling population size were ones which had been developed specifically for that purpose such as abortion, infanticide and some of the taboos on sexual intercourse.[2] Because he believed that these were the decisive factors and that they represented a recognition of the population problem, he thought that they must have appeared first during prehistoric times as a result of the 'growth of the intellect'. However, the presence of infanticide among animal populations shows that it can be developed as a method of limiting population size without any conscious recognition of the problems of overpopulation. Carr-Saunders' work will probably remain for some time to come the most comprehensive survey of the methods which different societies have used to limit their populations. An appendix to his work

[1] Sir Alexander Carr-Saunders, *The Population Problem* (Oxford, 1922).
[2] Ibid., p. 242.

covering only primitive societies lists almost 200 which limited their populations, each with a reference to a reliable account of the practice of restrictions on intercourse, abortion or infanticide. More recent anthropological fieldwork would no doubt make it possible to enlarge this list, but as Carr-Saunders says, the evidence which it contains shows 'customs restrictive on (population) increase to have been so widespread, in the form either of abortion, infanticide or prolonged abstention from intercourse, as to have been practically universal'.[1] As well as dealing with the direct evidence of population limitation Carr-Saunders also discusses the state of health, longevity and food supply in primitive societies; he finds the evidence consistent with his theory that populations establish themselves at the optimum size – i.e. the size at which income per head is maximized, given the productive technology.[2]

Within the confines of the present chapter it is impossible to give more than the gist of Carr-Saunders' argument; but his work will be found to provide a thorough survey of the evidence available at the time, as well as containing a twenty-page bibliography. The examples used here to illustrate the ways primitive societies limited their populations within their resources are either cases which have come to light since Carr-Saunders published, or are taken from sources which he used.

The issue at stake is more than just whether primitive populations were self-limiting or limited by starvation. It involves throwing out the whole popular idea of primitive societies as societies which exist in a perpetual state of hardship, scarcely able to scrape up a bare minimum of subsistence, with large families, children suffering from malnutrition, and a low life expectancy. In so far as this *is* the situation in parts of the underdeveloped world today, it is a comparatively recent phenomenon. Contact with Europeans, and with their alien values and practices, has led to the abandonment of customs such as abortion and infanticide which once helped to prevent overpopulation. As early as the third quarter of the eighteenth

[1] *The Population Problem,* p. 483.   [2] Ibid., p. 200.

century a missionary in Paraguay claimed that Christianity had led to the abolition of abortion and infanticide among the Abipones.[1] Ironically the same missionary also remarked on how plentiful food had been as if the fact was unrelated to the existence of these practices: after describing the abundance of wild animals and plants which supplied all the food the people wanted, he exclaimed 'See the munificence of God even towards those by whom he is not worshipped! Behold a rude image of the golden age!'[2] The Abipones seem to have had a number of customs which would have tended to limit population. We are told:

> The mothers suckle their children for three years, during which time they have no conjugal relations with their husbands, who, tired of this delay, often marry another wife. The women, therefore, kill their unborn babes through fear of repudiation, sometimes getting rid of them by violent arts, without waiting for their birth. Afraid of being widows in the life-time of their husbands, they blush not to become more savage than tigresses. Mothers spare their female offspring more frequently than the males, because the sons, when they are grown up, are obliged to purchase a wife, whereas daughters, at an age to be married, may be sold to the bridegroom at almost any price.[3]

Whether or not the suggested causal connections are right, these people – like many others – had a taboo on intercourse while the mother was breastfeeding her baby. Here, where it lasted three years, it may be expected to have led to births spaced about four years apart. This spacing would have been increased by the practice of abortion, and infanticide would have caused the average age-gap between surviving siblings to be lengthened still further. In addition the Abipones apparently had a system of bride price which, like dowries, would have tended to raise the age at which people married and caused special delays during hard times when the husband, or his

---

[1] M. Dobrizhoffer, *An Account of the Abipones* (London, 1822), volume II, p. 99.
[2] Ibid., volume II, p. 112.   [3] Ibid., volume II, p. 97.

family, found it more difficult to accumulate the necessary gifts. The quotation shows many of the customs which we shall find typical of those operating in primitive societies generally. But during the discussion we should not lose sight of the important question of whether or not the checks on population growth in different societies are sufficient to ensure an adequate level of subsistence, and whether they can act homeostatically to maintain the population at a constant size within a situation of ecological equilibrium.

Sometimes population growth is limited explicitly to prevent the food supply from being threatened. For example Howitt says of the Mining aborigines of southern Australia 'The reason they give for this practice (of infanticide) is that if their numbers increased too rapidly there would not be enough food for everybody.'[1] Similarly, Turner says of the people of the Ellice Islands in the Pacific 'Infanticide was ordered by law; only two children were allowed to a family, as they were afraid of the scarcity of food.'[2] It seems that sometimes the population is controlled so effectively and the food supply is consequently so ample, that the relationship becomes obscured: one observer of the aborigine tribes of Queensland was able to say 'The motive for infanticide with these tribes could not be to save food in times of dearth, for the food supply was constant and plentiful.'[3]

Although there are many societies where people are fully aware of the importance of limiting population in terms of the food supply, there are also a great many societies where numbers are effectively regulated by populations conscious only of cultural or ritual reasons for continuing the all-important practices. But whatever the reasons people are conscious of, it is clear from quantitative estimates of infanticide and family size that population size is effectively controlled. Taking what seems to be a fairly representative sample of the estimates of the

[1] A. W. Howitt, *The Native Tribes of South-East Australia* (London, 1904), p. 748.

[2] George Turner, *Samoa* (London, 1884), p. 284.

[3] John Mathew, *Two Representative Tribes of Queensland* (London, 1910), p. 166.

rate of infanticide, we find that it is normal in many societies for some of the children born to each woman to be killed. Of the Narrinyeri aborigines of south Australia Taplin says 'more than one-half of the children born fell victims to this atrocious custom'.[1] Still in southern Australia, an estimate for the Dieyerie is that 'about 30 per cent were murdered by their mothers at birth'.[2] In an early account of the customs of the Sandwich Islanders we are told that 'parents seldom rear more than two or three, and many spare only one . . . from the prevalence of infanticide two-thirds of the children perished'.[3] In these examples – which are not untypical – and also in the one from the Ellice Islands, infanticide is clearly practised on a scale which could well have resulted in population stability.

In many societies there is a bias towards female infanticide which is doubly effective as a way of limiting population size. Rasmussen found that of the ninety-six Eskimo births on King William Island which he inquired into, thirty-eight girls (or 40 per cent of the total) were killed immediately.[4] This rate of female infanticide must have been exceptional as it would cause the population size to decrease. That it was exceptional is born out by the population's overall sex ratio which, for the Netsilingmiut Eskimos was apparently 109 women to 150 men.[5] Another example of the preference for female infanticide comes from the Yanomamo Indians who live on the borders of Venezuela and Brazil. Although they believe they kill equal numbers of male and female babies, the overall sex ratio of their population is 391 females to 449 males – and this is in spite of the fact that considerably more men than women are killed in inter-village warfare.[6] By practising abortion as well as

---

[1] George Taplin, 'The Narrinyeri', in J. D. Woods (ed.), *Native Tribes of Southern Australia* (Adelaide, 1879), p. 13.

[2] Samuel Gason, 'The manners and customs of the Dieyerie tribe', in Woods, op. cit. p. 258.

[3] William Ellis, *Narrative of a Tour through Hawaii* (London, 1827), p. 324–5.

[4] Knud Rasmussen, *Across Arctic America: Narrative of the Fifth Thule Expedition* (New York, 1927), p. 226.

[5] Ibid., p. 226.

[6] Napoleon A. Chagnon, *Yanomamo* (New York, 1968), pp. 74–5.

having taboos on sexual intercourse while a woman is pregnant
or nursing a child, live births among the Yanomamo tend to be
spaced five or six years apart.[1] When the effect of infanticide is
added to this, the average number of children brought up by
Yanomamo women works out at just over two each.[2]

Evidence on the limitation of family size is plentiful. For
instance, Bancroft says of the Nootka Indians of Columbia,
'Women rarely have more than two or three children, and cease
bearing at about twenty-five, frequently preventing the increase
of their families by abortions.'[3] In the Murray Islands 'After a
certain number had been born, all succeeding children were
destroyed lest the food supply should become insufficient. If
the children were all of one sex some were destroyed for shame,
it being proper to have an equal number of boys and girls.
Abortion was very common.'[4] Even when practices such as
abortion and infanticide are not actually recorded as common,
there is often evidence that they were. Skeat and Blagden for
example, in their work on tribes in the Malayan peninsula say
'The practice of abortion was well understood by the Jakun
women. . . . It was, however, very seldom practised, for if it
was discovered by the husband, he had the right to give his
wife a sound drubbing with a club. . . .' Further on however,
we are told that 'The average number of children born to a
Jakun is three'.[5] One can only assume that here, as in a variety
of other societies, the women dealt with abortions among
themselves and successfully concealed them from their own
men as well as from Skeat and Blagden. The situation seems to
be similar in relation to infanticide among the Sakai, a tribe
which lives in the same area. Deaths attributed to natural

---

[1] James V. Neel and Napoleon A. Chagnon, 'The demography of primitive, relatively unacculturated American Indians', *Proceedings of the
National Academy of Sciences*, LIX (1968), p. 684.

[2] Ibid., p. 683.

[3] H. H. Bancroft, *The Native Races of the Pacific States of North America*
(New York, 1875), volume I, p. 197.

[4] A. E. Hunt, 'Ethnographical notes on the Murray Islands, Torres
Straits', *Journal of the Anthropological Institute*, old series XXVIII (1899),
p. 11.

[5] Skeat and Blagden, op. cit., volume II, p. 24.

infant mortality vary from none among women who have only one or two children, to twelve for a woman who had sixteen children, with a norm of around three for women who have six children.[1] This is an important issue because the boundary between infanticide and natural infant mortality is not always distinct. When infanticide takes the form of strangling babies immediately they are born, throwing them into the bush, or anything similar, then there is no difficulty in distinguishing it from natural infant mortality. But if the mother does not want to keep a child she need not actually kill it, she may just not look after it properly, or she may give it particularly harsh treatment. Chagnon records a case of a Yanomamo mother who did not feed her baby.[2] She said it had got a bad case of diarrhoea some time ago and had stopped eating. He found that it would eat perfectly well, but that she was starving it. In a number of societies infanticide is practised in this way – simply by carrying babies around but not feeding them. Some cultures seem to provide a number of ordeals through which a mother is supposed to put her child; she can – no doubt – adjust their severity according to whether or not she wants to keep the child. These ordeals may involve anything from exposure to the elements to risking asphyxiation by holding the baby in the smoke from a fire as was done by the Jakun and several other societies in Malaya and elsewhere.[3]

To move on to other methods of limiting the population, a mother who wants to reduce her fertility can do so by lengthening the time she breastfeeds her baby. A study of the relationship between these two factors among mothers in eleven Punjabi villages, where it was normal to suckle a baby until it was well over a year old, found that mothers who fed their babies did not menstruate for an average of eleven months after giving birth. In contrast, mothers whose babies were stillborn or died in the first month, who did not lactate, tended to menstruate again only two months after the birth.[4] However,

[1] Ibid., volume II, p. 11.   [2] Chagnon, op. cit., p. 74.
[3] Skeat and Blagden, op. cit., volume II, p. 20.
[4] Robert G. Potter *et al.*, 'Applications of field studies', in Mindel C. Sheps

the true length of the average period of infertility is likely to have been a couple of months longer than those figures suggest: it has been shown that the first few cycles tend to be anovulatory.[1] There are apparently no studies intended to find out the effects of much longer periods of breastfeeding than the twelve or eighteen months which was practised in these villages. It may be that the period of infertility cannot be increased much beyond one year, but in many societies children are suckled until three, four or five years old. Nansen says that in Greenland 'mothers are often slow to wean their children. They often give suck until the child is three or four, and I have heard of cases in which children of ten or twelve continued to take the breast.'[2] Meyer says of the aborigines of Encounter Bay that 'children are suckled by their mothers for a considerable time, sometimes to the age of five or six years'.[3] Three years seems to be the minimum period which is commonly mentioned in the earlier reports. But the period of lactation has cultural associations which probably have a more important influence on the birth rate than physiological effects. One example from the Abipone Indians of the widespread taboo on sexual intercourse during lactation has already been given. The Coniagui of West Africa provide another: they have a taboo on intercourse during the two years or so that the women breastfeed their babies.[4] Johnston says that 'throughout Congoland . . . a husband shall not only cease cohabitation after pregnancy is well declared, but that he shall in any case absent himself from his wife during the whole period of lactation'.[5] He goes on to explain the prevalence of abortion

---

and Jeanne C. Ridley, *Public Health and Population Change* (Pittsburgh, 1966), pp. 377–99.

[1] I. C. Udesky, 'Ovulation in lactating women', *American Journal of Obstetrics and Gynaecology*, LIX (1950), pp. 843–51.

[2] Fridtjof Nansen, *Eskimo Life* (London, 1893), p. 152.

[3] H. A. E. Meyer, 'Manners and customs of the aborigines of Encounter Bay', in Woods, op. cit., p. 187.

[4] Monique Gessain, 'Coniagui women (Guinea)', in Denise Paulme (ed.), *Women of Tropical Africa* (London, 1963), p. 37.

[5] Sir Harry H. Johnston, *George Grenfell and the Congo* (London, 1908), volume II, p. 671.

and infanticide as a result of these taboos: 'As (the husband) is not restricted by monogamous principles these rules imply no hardship for him. But they prove intolerable for some wives, who in consequence either seek to rid themselves of mother-hood in order to remain with their husbands, or wean their children rapidly in order to kill them.'[1] This theory is very much the same as the one put forward by Dobrizhoffer for the Abipones, and shows the possibility of quite complex cultural subsystems for controlling population.

Many systems of population limitation depend upon taboos or other superstitious beliefs. The taboos on sexual intercourse during lactation are only one example. Among the Ibo of the Nguru area of Nigeria, babies born feet foremost were thrown into the 'bad bush'.[2] The same happens among the Bavenda.[3] The Bambwela of Zambia used to kill babies who cut their upper teeth before their lower ones.[4] Leith-Ross writing on another section of the Ibo tribe says that if a baby is 'inadvert-ently delivered inside the hut' instead of in the little yard immediately outside where it is supposed to be born 'it would be "abomination" and the baby would be thrown into the bush'.[5] At first it is difficult to see how such superstitions can act *variably* as circumstances require, to maintain the population homeostatically within equilibrium. Killing all breachborn babies or all those whose top teeth came through before the lower ones, would tend to remove a significant but constant proportion of all those born. The key to an explanation of how these practices do in fact provide a homeostatic mechanism for regulating population seems to be that superstition provides a person with a readymade idiom in which to justify to others the action that he or she may want to take.[6] Motives have very little to do with justifications. The process of justifying an action is a process of finding a way of making it seem acceptable

---

[1] Ibid., volume II, p. 671.

[2] Sylvia Leith-Ross, *African Women* (London, 1939), p. 60.

[3] Hutton Webster, *Taboo: a Sociological Study* (Palo Alto, 1942), p. 59.

[4] Ibid., p. 59.

[5] Leith-Ross, op. cit., p. 100.

[6] I owe this point – and so the basis for the argument which follows it – to Jacquie Sarsby.

to other people. If a woman wants to keep her baby Leith-Ross says that local midwives can turn it round before it is born so that it is not condemned as a breach baby.[1] Even if it is breach-born she can easily conceal the fact from others. However, should she want to get rid of it she can make use of the super-stition to justify doing so. Likewise, it would be extremely unlikely that a woman would 'inadvertently' give birth in her hut if she thought it essential that she should do so in the yard just outside, but if she did not want the child she could say she had it in the hut by mistake. When it is a matter of cutting the top or bottom teeth first, presumably it is sometimes debatable whether either came through first. But perhaps what clinches the argument are the examples of cultures which provide ways of warding off the evil effects of breaking taboos or going against superstition, and so leave people free to take whichever course they like. Among sections of the Bantu, if a mother breaks the taboo on sexual relations during lactation it is sup-posed to bring harm to her baby, but if she wants to she can get medicines to give her baby which ward off the ill effects.[2] Webster gives a description of how the taboo on children who cut their top teeth first may safely be broken.[3] The belief is that if such a child is kept, each time one of its milk teeth comes out someone would die. If the mother does not want to throw her baby into the river she can collect up the teeth as they come out and put them into the cloth she used for carrying the baby. When she has all the teeth she throws them from the cloth into the river and shouts 'Here is the tabooed child!' In this way patterns of taboo and superstition, together with other practices which help stabilize the population size, are endowed with an element of variability which will allow numbers to be made up if they should happen to fall too low, or decreased if they should become too high. The culture will tend to develop round norms consistent with normal population replacement.

A completely different approach to the problem of population

[1] Leith-Ross, op. cit., p. 160.
[2] A. T. and G. M. Culwick, *Ubena of the Rivers* (London, 1935), p. 375.
[3] Hutton Webster, op. cit., p. 60.

limitation and ecological equilibrium is to see what evidence there is that the means of subsistence available to different societies is adequate to meet their needs. It will be remembered that Carr-Saunders believed that population size in primitive societies tended to stabilize around an optimum where income per head was maximized. How near societies actually come to reaching this point need not, however, concern us too closely: we are interested primarily in the maintenance of ecological equilibrium as a precondition for cultural stability. The optimum population size is presumably influenced by a range of social and political factors as well as by economic ones, even if survival ability remains the ultimate consideration. Here there is no need to do more than show that the means of subsistence available to different societies met a criterion of regular sufficiency, that subsistence was not a constant problem and that starvation did not appear except during uncontrollable disturbances to the natural or cultural systems. Where these conditions exist, it is possible to say that population growth is adequately controlled and that the society is existing without problems in a situation of ecological equilibrium consistent with its continued stability.

Once more it is impossible here to give more than a few illustrative examples of the adequacy of the means of subsistence in various primitive societies. But they do at least prove the point for the societies from which they are drawn. Woodburn, for instance, says quite categorically of a group of hunters and gatherers in Tanzania, 'For a Hadza to die of hunger, or even to fail to satisfy his hunger for more than a day or two, is almost inconceivable'; he says that 'more animals could have been killed of every species without endangering the survival of the species in the area'.[1] The missionary's exclamations about the 'munificence of God' and a 'rude image of the golden age' when he saw how plentiful the food supply was for the Abipones of Paraguay has already been quoted.[2] Lee, in an essay dealing particularly with this problem of the sufficiency of the

[1] James Woodburn, 'An introduction to Hadza ecology', in Richard B. Lee and I. DeVore (eds.), *Man the Hunter* (Chicago, 1968), p. 52.
[2] See p. 33 above.

means of subsistence among a group of hunters and gatherers in south-west Africa, said, 'the habitat of the Dobe-area Bushmen is abundant in naturally occurring foods', so abundant apparently that the Bushmen needed only to 'collect food every third or fourth day'.[1] Ninety per cent of the vegetable diet was gained from hardly more than a quarter of the plant species which they regarded as edible, and they needed to hunt 'on a regular basis' less than one-third of the animal species which they regard as edible.[2] This tendency to recognize a large number of species as edible but only to use a small group of preferred species is quite common among hunters and gatherers. But variety of food resources is a safety factor in many primitive societies; it apparently enabled the Samoans to withstand the failure of their main crops without any real hardship:

> A crop of bread-fruit is sometimes shaken off the trees before it is ripe, occasionally taro plantations are destroyed by caterpillars; but the people have wild yams in the bush, preserved bread-fruit, cocoa-nuts, and fish to fall back upon; so that there is rarely, if ever, anything like a serious famine.[3]

But to return to the Bushmen, their longevity – in addition to what has already been mentioned – also provides evidence of the general sufficiency of their food supply. Lee says that 10 per cent 'were determined to be over 60 years of age, a proportion which compares favourably to the percentage of elderly in industrial populations'.[4]

Longevity is also an indication of good health. Deadly diseases were comparatively unimportant in primitive societies. They cannot be regarded as an effective regulator of pre-contact populations. Isolated, relatively self-sufficient societies are able to develop resistances to the indigenous diseases to which they are exposed so that their effects are relatively mild. New diseases are the danger: the devastating effect on the

---

[1] Richard B. Lee, 'What hunters do for a living', in Lee and DeVore, op. cit., p. 33.
[2] Ibid., p. 35. [3] Turner, op. cit., p. 107. [4] Lee, op. cit., p. 36.

American Indians and other populations of diseases introduced by Europeans is well known; so also is the effect of indigenous diseases on the European newcomer in various parts of the world. Many diseases seem to have been entirely absent in some isolated land masses. Davidson says for instance that Australia

> presents us with a spectacle of a continent, from the pathology of which entire classes of diseases, prevalent in other divisions of the globe, were, until comparatively recent times, completely absent. Thus the whole class of eruptive fevers – small-pox, scarlet fever, and measles – so fatal elsewhere, were unknown. Epidemic cholera, relapsing fever, yellow fever, whooping cough, and diptheria were equally absent, as was also syphilis.[1]

Leprosy was also absent. Observers frequently remark on the health of primitive populations; Schapera's comments on the South African Bushmen are fairly typical: he said 'The Bushmen in their own environment and leading their own mode of life seem on the whole to be a healthy and hardy people. Those communities in the north which have not been much in contact with civilization are said to be remarkably free from infectious, contagious and other diseases.'[2] Even during historical times in Europe it has been new diseases that have had the greatest impact. It was a new strain of Bubonic plague which hit the English population in 1348–9. But even in those societies where the incidence of disease is higher, its effects are too erratic and uncertain to provide a practical homeostatic mechanism to check numbers in relation to resources. The functionally developed cultural methods of population control provide the only adequate solution to a society's ecological problem.

Given that the populations with which we are concerned stabilize within an ecological equilibrium, it would be useful

[1] Andrew Davidson, *Geographical Pathology* (Edinburgh, 1892), volume II, p. 565.
[2] I. Schapera, *The Khoisan Peoples of South Africa* (London, 1930), p. 214.

to know whether they do so near the upper limits at which equilibrium can be maintained, i.e. near the carrying capacity, or whether they establish themselves well below the limits of resource use which the environment can sustain. There is some evidence that societies more usually approach the former than the latter condition. It has been found, for instance, that there is a close inverse correlation between the size of the tribal areas of Australian aborigines and the mean annual rainfall in each area.[1] The study was based on information from 409 tribes. Rainfall was used as an indicator of the productivity of each area in terms of the animal and plant life on which the aborigines depend. As tribal populations do not vary very greatly – the average size is about 500 people – the correlation has been taken as evidence that the area was occupied at close to its carrying capacity. Certainly one would not expect such a fit if tribal areas were very large in relation to their populations, but then perhaps the existence of defined tribal areas is itself an indication that resources are limited. The concept of property indicates a need to make a claim to limited resources.

Hunting and gathering societies are particularly illuminating in this context because it is probably safe to assume that if they practise any form of resource management, it is in response to scarcity. For example, Worsley says that the inhabitants of Groote Eylandt 'practise elementary conservation measures. Thus in digging out yams, a small proportions of the tuber will be left in order to ensure further growth next year';[2] this is an indication that some food plants are less plentiful than they might be – that the population is approaching carrying capacity in relation to those resources. Conversely, Woodburn says that

> With food of some sort always available, the Hadza give little attention to conservation of their food resources. When the women dig up roots, they do not attempt to replace any

---

[1] J. B. Birdsell, 'Some environmental and cultural factors influencing the structuring of Australian aboriginal populations', *American Naturalist*, LXXXVII (1953), pp. 171–207.

[2] Peter Worsley, 'The utilization of food resources by an Australian aboriginal tribe', *Acta Ethnographica*, X (1961), p. 174.

portion of the plant to grow again. When they gather berries, heavily laden branches are often torn from the trees and carried back to camp. . . . In hunting no attempt is made at systematic cropping. A man out hunting will shoot any animal he comes across. There are no inhibitions about shooting females . . . or immature animals.[1]

Resources must be plentiful to survive such wasteful use, and in fact Woodburn confirms that they are.[2] It is perhaps worth noting that here, where resources are plentiful, the Hadza 'assert no rights over land and its ungarnered resources'.[3] However if the signs are that the Hadza are well below the maximum potential limits of an ecological equilibrium, there is evidence from other societies which suggests that they stabilize much nearer the carrying capacity. In some areas there are examples of taboos designed to conserve resources by providing close seasons for particular animals and plants. Webster says that

In the Marquesian Islands, should the quantity of bread-fruit in a district be seriously diminished, the chief could taboo the trees for as long as twenty months so that they could recover their vigour. If fish were beginning to get scarce, a taboo might be laid on one part of the bay in order to allow fish to spawn without being disturbed.[4]

Another example is of the Guiana Indians who 'believe that if they kill too many of one kind of game the "bush spirit" of that particular animal may come and do them harm'.[5] A common arrangement which has the effect of preventing too much pressure on any one kind of animal or plant is the division of the tribe into a number of different totemic groups. Each group has a taboo against eating the particular totemic animal or plant with which it is associated, so that the full weight of the tribe's consumption is divided between a larger number of different species. In Australia there seem to have been totemic

[1] Woodburn, op. cit., p. 53.   [2] See p. 41 above.
[3] Woodburn, op. cit., p. 50.   [4] Webster, op. cit., p. 340.   [5] Ibid., p. 341.

groups covering almost every item in the aboriginal diet.[1] Here, as elsewhere, the totemic groups also performed various fertility ceremonies designed to make their totemic animals and plants more plentiful.

The ecological assistance which such a system of totemism renders to the society which practises it may be merely a by-product of something which has quite separate origins; on the other hand, there is a suggestion in legends concerning the origins of particular totemic groups that the ecological problem may have been at their foundation. Other aspects of totemism may have been built on to this basis. If this is so it shows the importance of the ecological problem's influence on culture. A legend quoted by Spencer and Gillen concerns the ancestors of the idnimita totem in an Australian tribe (*idnimita* is the name given to a type of edible grub). At one time 'there was nothing in the country but idnimita and a little bird called Thippathippa'. One of the ancestors decided to eat idnimita to keep himself alive. When he told the others what he had done, one of them 'jumped up and said, "I have been eating idnimita also; if I eat it always it might all die" '. The totem's ceremony for increasing the number of grubs was then performed and the grubs multiplied.[2] A second rather similar legend is also mentioned.[3] The two are suggestive of the origins of the taboos on a totem group eating their totemic animal or plant. But whether or not the ecological problem lies at the roots of totemism, totemism clearly includes elements which serve to spread the load of a society's consumption over a wider range of animal and plant species than would otherwise have been the case; these, together with the systems of close-season taboos and other conservation techniques, show that many societies stabilize their numbers near the upper limits of the range over which ecological equilibrium can be maintained.

Some of the evidence relating to the adequacy of a society's means of subsistence has often been misunderstood. It has

[1] Australian totemism is described in detail in Sir Baldwin Spencer and F. J. Gillen, *The Northern Tribes of Central Australia* (London, 1904), see especially chapters 5–10 and Appendix B.
[2] Ibid., pp. 324–5.   [3] Ibid., pp. 322–3.

frequently been assumed that if a visible surplus is not actually produced, this is evidence of an inability to produce it, and some have even argued that if a society fails to support a non-productive class, this is evidence that labour productivity is so low that it cannot afford to.[1] But before the work involved in producing a surplus becomes worthwhile there must be some need for a surplus. Demand for food is far from being insatiable and it is only rarely accumulated beyond possible need. When it is accumulated, it is usually because there is a need to store it between harvest time and consumption – a need which arises among hunting and gathering societies only if there is a part of the year not covered by the successive ripening of wild crops. Some societies never need to store food; they never have more than a few days supplies with them because there are always animals and wild plants ready for the taking. Their lack of stores reflects conditions of plenty rather than of scarcity, and in fact when primitive societies recognize a season of scarcity, it is often just a season for which they have to store food: it does not necessarily mean that there is an insufficient storable surplus from other seasons of the year to tide them over. If the criterion for scarcity is whether or not food has to be stored at harvest time to provide for other seasons, then our own society is poverty-stricken. This point is not a trivial one: it is suggestive of what economic development is really about – if we could only move outside the narrow confines of our particular cultural standpoint. The connotations of a 'hand to mouth' existence are sometimes incorrect. For hunters and gatherers it is a cherished luxury, as it was in the garden of Eden. Similar reasoning is often applicable to peasant societies which 'fail' to accumulate the capital surplus which many economists assume to be desirable.

We have already seen that some societies limit their populations *consciously* to prevent food shortages. Others, however, appear to limit them in relation to a scarcity of other goods associated with prestige and status which have nothing to do

[1] Melville J. Herskovits, *The Economic Life of Primitive Peoples* (New York, 1940), p. 359.

with subsistence. As Mary Douglas said in an article discussing population control, 'for human behaviour it can be more relevant to take into account the ceiling imposed by the demand for champagne or for private education than the demand for bread and butter'.[1] Competition for essential resources is replaced by competition for socially valued goods. If competition for scarce objects is used as the basis or incentive for population limitation, it is important that it is not competition for the essential food resources. The whole point of population limitation is to prevent essential resources from becoming scarce, and if some kind of social order and stability is to be maintained people should not have to deny each other the basic necessities of life. Wynne-Edwards says that even among animals, populations are limited in relation to scarce objects of 'conventional' competition which 'serve as dummies or substitutes for the ultimate goal that should never be disputed in the open – the bread of life itself'.[2] An example of such 'conventional' competition was the competition for a nest among an artificially limited number of recognized sites which tended to limit some bird populations.[3]

In many societies there is a sharp distinction between the way food and other goods are exchanged. If a society uses a form of money it can often only be exchanged for socially valued 'wealth objects'. Frequently food cannot be bought or sold within the village or tribe: sometimes it is distributed equally between people and sometimes it is subject to some sort of gift exchange. DuBois says of the Tolowa, Chetco and Tututni Indians of the North American Pacific coast,

> in the economic life of these tribes . . . their monies served as a medium of exchange primarily in the realm of prestige economy rather than subsistence economy. . . . The individualism and scheming parsimony . . . did not extend to subsistence . . . food was shared by the provident with the improvident within the village group.[4]

[1] Mary Douglas, 'Population control in primitive groups', *British Journal of Sociology*, XVII (1966), p. 267.

[2] Wynne-Edwards, op. cit., p. 13.   [3] See p. 26 above.

[4] Cora A. DuBois, 'The wealth concept as an integrative factor in Tolowa-

Among the Siane of New Guinea there are three distinct groups of goods: 'The notion underlying the basis of distribution of food is that of equal shares, a balanced reciprocity.' 'Luxury goods' are exchanged according to 'self-interest in a nearly free market situation', and the exchange of ceremonial goods is a political affair accompanied by 'strict accounting'.[1] Sahlins has dealt with this subject at a more appropriate length in his essay on primitive exchange.[2] Clearly these different exchange systems are another indication of the importance of the ecological problem. Among the societies which employ competition for scarce resources as an incentive to population limitation, we find that the competition is confined to a group of prestige goods and that subsistence goods are not disputed. An important by-product of such systems, which should not be passed over, concerns the homogeneity of societies. The more equitable the system for the distribution of food and other necessities, the greater the identity of interest within the society when faced with ecological problems. As Firth points out, the result of the Maori system of food distribution was that 'Starvation or real want in one family was impossible while others in the village were abundantly supplied with food'.[3] The impact of this becomes clear when the situation in these societies is contrasted in the next chapter with the inadequate methods of population limitation found in complex societies.

A society which is worth mentioning because it serves as the exception which proves these rules is that of the Trobriand Islanders. They compete against each other for status directly in terms of their basic food crops as well as other goods. But even so, they manage to avoid the dangerous position of struggling

Tututni culture', in R. H. Lowie (ed.), *Essays in Anthropology* (Berkeley, 1936), pp. 50–1.

[1] Manning Nash, *Primitive and Peasant Economic Systems* (San Francisco, 1966), pp. 48–51.

[2] Marshal D. Sahlins, 'On the sociology of primitive exchange', in Association of Social Anthropologists Monographs No. 1, *The Relevance of Models in Social Anthropology* (London, 1965), pp. 139–236.

[3] Raymond W. Firth, *The Economics of the New Zealand Maori*, 2nd ed. (Wellington, N.Z., 1959), p. 290.

to deny each other essential resources: they have stabilized so far below their territory's carrying capacity that each person can accumulate far more food than he can consume. They do not compete for scarce food, they compete simply to amass the greatest excess. In this way food is turned from the one vital resource into something which frequently has little or no utility value whatsoever. Malinowski says 'Great quantities (of yams) are produced beyond any possible utility they could possess.'[1] 'They will boast that . . . half of the yams will rot away in the store houses, and be thrown on . . . the rubbish heap at the back of the houses to make room for the new harvest.'[2] Presumably this kind of cultural system is rare because unless population size is stabilized sufficiently far below carrying capacity, there would not be enough land to cultivate yams on this scale. A less extravagant cultural system would allow a larger population to live in equilibrium.

All in all, it would be difficult to give a fair picture of the level of subsistence in pre-contact societies even if the information were available. The societies varied considerably, and any variation makes it possible to choose unrepresentative examples. This is a special danger when there is a need to offset the widespread belief that such societies were permanently on the brink of starvation. Sahlins thought it justifiable to label Paleolithic hunters as the 'original affluent society' to counter this impression.[3] But at least we are in a position to understand why Malthus had such difficulty applying his theories to some societies. Trying to discount reports that North American Indians did not seem to be starving, he said 'we must not fix our eyes only on the warrior in the prime of life: he is one of a hundred: he is the gentleman, the man of fortune.'[4] Malthus

[1] B. Malinowski, *The Argonauts of the Western Pacific* (New York, 1953), p. 173.
[2] Ibid., p. 169.
[3] Marshal D. Sahlins, 'Notes on the original affluent society', in Lee and DeVore, op. cit., p. 85.
[4] Thomas Malthus, *First Essay on Population* (London, 1798), pp. 42–3.

also tried to explain away reports of their relative equality in terms of subsistence goods saying that he thought it was the women and children who should be compared with the starving 'lower classes of the community in civilized states'.[1] It must be emphasized, however, that there is no argument against the application of Malthusian theory to the populations of changing and disturbed societies. Malthus does not make the necessary distinction between stable, coherent cultural systems and other, transitional cultures. This seems something of an oversight when we see that he was familiar with some of the evidence of the difference it makes: he says for instance 'it has frequently been remarked, that when an Indian family has taken up its abode near any European settlement . . . one woman has reared five or six, or more children; although in a savage state, it rarely happens, that above one or two in the family grow up to maturity'.[2] He also mentions the frequency of miscarriages in the 'savage state'.[3]

After looking at the evidence, the problem is not so much to believe that people in pre-contact societies did not starve, as to accept the suggestion that most societies allowed their numbers to grow anywhere near the carrying capacity. The evidence is that while some societies approached the carrying capacity of their territories, others maintained themselves in ecological equilibrium well below that level. But for all of them, the evidence from a wide variety of sources and on many different aspects of life shows that populations were indeed kept within the limits of ecological equilibrium, and that starvation was as rare in these societies as Wynne-Edwards says it is among natural animal populations. The significance of this situation is not only that resources were not overtaxed or subject to progressive scarcity; it is also that primitive societies were able to maintain a standard of living above the minimum. Their situation was one which could easily be worsened by the various forms of social and economic change which they might undergo. During economic development there is a constant dialogue between such worsening and the improvements which

[1] Ibid., pp. 41 and 43.   [2] Ibid., p. 40.   [3] Ibid., p. 42.

more intensive agricultural techniques or other forms of innovation have to offer.

We have seen that cultural systems do not just happen to settle into ecological equilibrium, but tend instead to develop ways of positively maintaining themselves in such a situation. The stable, coherent cultural systems which have been the subject of this chapter are sensitively balanced complexes, adapted to solve societies' ecological problems. Because the preservation of ecological equilibrium imposes constraints on human behaviour, it involves moral, religious, legal and other injunctions towards particular forms of behaviour and against others. Examples have been given of moral inhibitions on intercourse during lactation, of rules governing infanticide and family size, of taboos on collecting particular resources or on eating others, and of constraints in the form of what was regarded as 'proper' behaviour. The importance of the interrelationship between the social system and the problem of ecological equilibrium shows the necessity of considering social and economic change together.

Having examined the ecological preconditions for cultural stability we are now in a better position to see to what extent they existed in different societies, and whether particular changes will tend to build them up or break them down. The concept of stability within an ecological equilibrium also provides a satisfactory basis from which to go on to examine the process of adaptation, both in the technology and in the pattern of resource use, which takes place when these conditions are absent and a society outgrows its ecological niche.

4 Disequilibrium and the stimulus to development

Unto the woman he said, I will greatly multiply thy sorrow and thy conception; in sorrow thou shalt bring forth children; and thy desire shall be to thy husband. . . . And unto Adam he said, Because thou hearkened unto the voice of thy wife, and hast eaten of the tree, of which I commanded thee, saying, Thou shalt not eat of it: cursed is the ground for thy sake; in sorrow shalt thou eat of it all the days of thy life. . . . Therefore the Lord God sent him forth from the garden of Eden, to till the ground from whence he was taken.

GENESIS 3:16, 17, 23.

Having dealt with the cultural conditions necessary for the maintenance of ecological equilibrium we are now in a position to see that it is the progressive breakdown – or absence – of these conditions which stimulates a society into economic development. This chapter is the last chapter preparatory to the analysis of the course which development actually takes and of the forces which lie behind it. It is concerned only to establish factually what should be fairly obvious in the framework: that the breakdown of ecological equilibrium necessitates changes which are recognizably part of the process of economic development. But although the analysis of the pattern of change is the subject of later chapters, it would be worth sketching in the three main elements of development at this point: even a very brief introduction will make the examples of changing societies used in the following pages more interesting.

At the beginning of the last chapter it was said that different methods of exploiting the environment were adequate at different quantitative levels – or rates – of exploitation. It was shown how, principally through population control, a society

C

could limit its demand for the particular resources on which it is based to a level which the environment could sustain. A society which fails to do this, and moves out of ecological equilibrium, is allowing needs to arise within the system beyond the level which can be satisfied through the established technology and environmental relations. As basic resources become scarce, the growing needs which cannot be satisfied within the traditional framework provide the single most important spur to development. People are driven to change and to seek out a new way of life by the development of sheer poverty as the means of subsistence become inadequate. Sometimes scarcity does not appear initially in subsistence, but in the fuels and materials used in manufacturing processes. But whichever way shortage is first felt, it presents the same threat to a society's livelihood. Alternative sources of subsistence have to be developed: either methods must be changed to exploit traditional materials more intensively or new resources must be found to substitute for the old. All changes in the resource-base, technology or economic organization under this head represent attempts to raise the level of environmental exploitation. They are necessitated by the expansion of any given economic system beyond the bounds at which ecological equilibrium can be maintained.

Increasing the quantity of the means of subsistence, when population growth demands it, has no *a priori* connection with efficiency. Changes which are intended to raise the level of environmental exploitation may or may not require that more work be done to provide a person's means of subsistence. Of course the human implications of an economic or technical change go much further than the impact on working hours; a more important definition of efficiency would take into account the whole impact of technical change on the quality of human life. The point to be made here is that the desire to increase efficiency is independent of the need to increase the rate of environmental exploitation. Whatever the rate of exploitation, people will develop those methods and techniques appropriate to their environmental relations which seem to have advantages over others. It is an efficiency relative to their resource-base and particular ecological situation. Hunters will develop efficient ways of hunting, agriculturalists – given the land to population ratio – will develop efficient agricultural methods and so on. But presumably after a while improvements in methods get increasingly hard to come by, and a society's efficiency will tend to stabilize when it has adopted the best techniques that seem to be available to it. The system becomes fluid again only when the underlying resource situation becomes difficult because the society is moving out of ecological equilibrium.

It is important to emphasize that the problem of increasing the level of environmental exploitation and that of increasing the level of economic efficiency are quite separate issues. The motives for change and the form which change takes are different in each case. It may perhaps be useful to think of levels of environmental exploitation and of economic efficiency as measured on two separate axes against which every economic system could be represented as a point. (See diagram below.) A

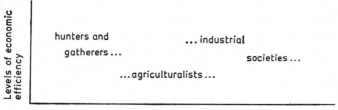

Dimensions of change in technical and economic development.

society in ecological equilibrium has its position stabilized in relation to both axes. By limiting its population it is not pushed out along the horizontal axis and, for the reasons mentioned in the last paragraph, its level of economic efficiency is stabilized on the vertical axis.

Most attempts to analyse economic development have been based on the assumption that development is mainly concerned with increasing economic efficiency; in contrast, the suggestion

here is that development is primarily a matter of increasing the
rate of environmental exploitation. Whenever the constraints
which maintain a society in ecological equilibrium break down,
the society will try to find ways of developing its technology to
increase the yield from the environment: the dominant movement is out along the horizontal axis. Changes in economic
efficiency are more complex upward and downward movements
reflecting the attempts of societies to deal with their ecological
problem as best they can. The stability achieved in the level of
economic efficiency is of course disturbed by any technical
changes introduced to increase the yield from the environment.
The level of efficiency tends to behave as the dependent
variable.

Movements along either of the axes in the diagram are not
made by smooth transformations. Technical change is lumpy;
the interdependence of technology tends to mean that it does
not behave as a continuous variable, but comes in discrete
packages. For example, as metals replaced wood for many uses
during the process of industrialization, workshops had to equip
themselves with completely different tools to handle the new
materials, and when significant improvements have been made
in car engines it becomes necessary to make corresponding
improvements in braking systems. This need for technical
consistency is more than a demand for physical compatibility.
As well as being shaped by simple physical practicality, it is also
affected by the relationship between mechanical and technical
efficiency on the one hand, and economic efficiency on the other.
It would for instance be possible to run some machinery without lubrication – provided one was willing to make frequent
replacements of worn parts; but in practice, mechanical,
technical and economic efficiency are all served if the development of machinery is accompanied by a corresponding development of lubricants. The lumpiness of technological innovation
means that both the speed and pattern of development are
erratic. If the course of development of a society was plotted
against the two co-ordinates in the diagram, it would appear as
an extremely uneven line. Major fluctuations would represent
such things as the exploitation of new resources which have

wide technical implications, and minor ones, less important innovations in method.

Within a stable society in ecological equilibrium, population growth is the most dangerous threat to continued stability. The growth out of ecological equilibrium brings almost every aspect of a society's technology and economy into question, but the detailed analysis of the way change works, in terms of the level of environmental exploitation, economic efficiency and technical consistency, will be the subject of later chapters. At this stage it is intended to show – by means of examples – merely that there are obvious overall links between the breakdown of ecological equilibrium and the need for change.

A society moves out of ecological equilibrium as a result of a disturbance to some part of the cultural system which acted to restrain the society within workable limits. Often historical and anthropological records do not show exactly how the delicate mechanisms maintaining a particular society in equilibrium were disturbed: perhaps all we know is that the society is currently suffering from population pressure on land and that the population started to grow soon after European influence became significant in the area. In a number of societies however there is clear evidence that they used to exist in an equilibrium situation which has, in one way or another, now been disturbed. After the society has moved out of ecological equilibrium, subsistence becomes a problem, economic conditions worsen and the society finds itself facing a number of difficulties which together indicate a mounting crisis. The most obvious repercussions are the real or potential threats to the standard of living which force people to explore alternative means of livelihood. Not only are we usually without information on the initial source of a disturbance to the cultural mechanisms for maintaining equilibrium, but in theory one can see that there are likely to be a very large number of points at which the system could be disturbed; one has only to look at the complex of social, economic and superstitious elements – mentioned in the last chapter – which played a part in maintaining equilibrium.

But wherever the disturbance starts, it appears that if it is to lead to economic development it must, somewhere along the line, damage the society's restraints sufficiently to cause conditions to deteriorate as the society moves out of ecological equilibrium. Most typically this involves breaking the restraints on population growth. The quantitative expansion of the traditional economy up to the limits of equilibrium ushers in the process of qualitative change. A few illustrative examples will give an impression of the variety of real forms represented by this schema.

Most of the examples used here are based on case studies of villages and small communities in the early stages of transition from their traditional way of life. Such smallscale studies are able to provide a more accurate picture of the pattern of change and the motives involved at the individual's level. After going through a number of these examples it will be possible to show that there are very close parallels between the patterns they show and the overall national economic development which took place for instance in Britain and Japan. Some differences, due to the difference in scale, are inevitable: although on the national level we would look for the growth of manufacturing, urban centres, commerce etc. as evidence of industrialization, the implications of economic development at the village level are different. Instead of developing their own local industry, there is usually a breakdown of local self-sufficiency. Villages become involved in the national process of industrialization by becoming more integrated in the national and international economy, by taking part in the wider division of labour, producing specialized crops for market and so on.

A study of a village called Hsin Hsing in Taiwan by Bernard Gallin shows a very common pattern of transition from a system of self-sufficient peasant agriculture, based on growing rice, sweet potatoes and soybeans, to a market economy producing specialized cash crops augmented by temporary wage labour in local towns.[1] Early this century the population in the

[1] Bernard Gallin, *Hsin Hsing, Taiwan: A Chinese Village in Change* (Berkeley, 1966).

area was 'sparse'.[1] Since then the population has grown at rates varying between about $1\frac{3}{4}$ per cent p.a. and $3\frac{3}{4}$ per cent p.a., roughly in line with the rest of Taiwan.[2] (2 per cent p.a. compounded would cause population size to double in thirty-five years.) The available land proved insufficient to support the population and we can safely assume that the society moved out of the ecological equilibrium based on its traditional methods at some time during this century. By 1957 the average amount of arable land per household had fallen to 1·6 acres.[3] Initially agricultural methods were intensified in an effort to meet the increased demands within the traditional framework. The irrigated area was increased till it covered 93 per cent of the cultivable acreage.[4] Three crops were often grown on the same land within a year, one sometimes being planted between the rows of the previous crop, just before harvest, as a way of increasing the length of the effective growing season. These changes meant people had to do more work per unit of output as well as bearing the costs of such things as fertilizers, but production failed to keep up with population growth. It was estimated that during 1957 the village's intensive agriculture provided only 65 per cent of the village income. The break with local self-sufficiency took two forms: one was the smallscale, but rapidly expanding, cultivation of vegetables for market (earnings from which are included in the 65 per cent), and the other was the tendency to temporary migration to work in local towns which earned villagers the other 35 per cent of village income. Most of the migrants go to Tapei where a few run small businesses, but many work as unskilled labourers, coolies, or pedicab drivers. Others find work in a local menthol oil factory or in the brickworks. In the late 1950s several women had started working in a sugar factory in the mountains, but more stayed in the village and earned additional income by making fibre hats. The hat industry was organized on a 'putting out' system like the domestic woollen industry in pre-industrial England; an agent distributed the bark fibre and collected in the finished hats. There can be little doubt that the rapid and

[1] Ibid., p. 29.   [2] Ibid., p. 29.   [3] Ibid., p. 36.
[4] Ibid., p. 48.

diverse changes in Hsin Hsing are the result of the breakdown of the sufficiency of the traditional subsistence economy and represent a search for supplementary sources of income. Gallin himself emphasizes repeatedly that the changes are responses to the land shortage produced by population growth.[1] It is likely that processes such as these are leading to the increased urbanization and industrialization of Taiwan generally.

D. H. Reader's study of a Zulu tribe – the Makhanya in South Africa, shows a society where the process has gone a little further.[2] Large areas of Zulu land were alienated from them when, in 1902, a commission was set up to demarcate areas for black and white occupation. Perhaps partly because of the European and Christian interference with Zulu social customs (traditional polygamous marriage is giving way to monogamous Christian marriage for example), the population has grown and pressure on resources mounted. By 1950 the population density in Makhanya country had reached 200 per square mile and not all areas were equally fertile.[3] There were already lean seasons when food had to be bought and the pasture showed signs of serious overgrazing. Reader says that the ideal way of life was still regarded as being the traditional pastoralism and shifting cultivation appropriate to the plentiful land supply of the past, although methods had had to be changed to meet the new situation. More intensive techniques involving ploughing had become almost universal. A few farmers used fertilizer and some grew a surplus for market. But here, as in the last example, the agricultural changes proved insufficient to solve the subsistence problem. Reader tells us that there was a 'steady deterioration of conditions in the Bantu areas of South Africa'.[4] Faced with the inability of the system to meet their growing need the Makhanya had no alternative but to sell their labour in Durban. Seventy-eight per cent of the male working population (15- to 55-years-old) worked in Durban during the week leaving the women to do most of the agricultural work.[5] (The proportion working in Durban was lower in outlying areas.)

[1] Hsin Hsing, Taiwan, pp. 38, 51, 120, 271.
[2] D. H. Reader, *Zulu Tribe in Transition* (Manchester, 1966).
[3] Ibid., p. 30.   [4] Ibid., p. 330.   [5] Ibid., p. 31.

Again there can be very little doubt that the Makhanya became migrant wage earners out of necessity rather than because they chose it as a way of life preferable to their traditional one: Reader says that

> the Makhanya, like other Bantu migrants, are prone from time to time to take long holidays (from industrial work) to 'rest' or 'plough'; and in this way they exhibit their fundamental longing for the rural way of life. When the need for money is again irresistible, they move relatively smoothly, though often reluctantly, back into the industrial world. . . .[1]

A couple more examples will help convey the picture of this pattern of change working in other types of societies. The development of an Indian village in highland Orissa, described by F. G. Bailey, shows the same pervasive pressure of growing necessity behind economic development.[2] This part of northeast India underwent an 'immense' increase in population during the nineteenth century.[3] During the short period for which there are figures, from 1891 to 1931 the density of population in the highland region as a whole increased from 83 to 103 persons per square mile.[4] In addition we are also told that during the past 100 years the population of the village itself has been increased by 'a large number of immigrants'.[5] Under these conditions of population growth the system of partible inheritance led – predictably – to the division of holdings into units too small to provide for 'the normal contingencies of the owner's lifetime'.[6] One of the results of this was that land became saleable and the landowning monopoly of the warrior caste, on which much of the social system was based, was broken. But what is more important to us is that by 1953 every household in the village had become at least partly dependent on a source of income other than agriculture. However, many of the non-agricultural occupations did not increase the village's total income but were concerned with the exchange

---

[1] Ibid., p. 332.
[2] F. G. Bailey, *Caste and Economic Frontier: a Village in Highland Orissa* (Manchester, 1957).
[3] Ibid., p. 6.   [4] Ibid., p. 9.   [5] Ibid., p. 47.   [6] Ibid., p. 48.

of goods and services within the village. Sources of additional income to the village as a whole included the export of cash crops such as oilseeds, lentils, ginger and turmeric. Some people worked for the Leaf Company which provided the outer wrappings for cigarettes, others traded in cow hides, and a few were government employees. The situation was summed up by O'Malley in 1941 who said:

> A largely increased population has caused pressure on the soil, which is acute in congested areas, where all cultivable land has been brought under the plough and holdings are incapable of expansion. There is no longer the same uniformity of interests* owing to the small size of holdings and the pressure of circumstances necessitating the adoption of different callings; one son, for example, may be an agriculturalist, another a mechanic, a third a clerk.[1]

A developing society which still shows the remains of its system of population control is Rusembilan, a Malay village in southern Thailand.[2] Their practice of abortion, and use of a doubtfully effective form of herbal contraception, linked with a system of bride price, is now insufficient to prevent population growth. The population has grown through natural increase and immigration. The clearance of new areas of jungle suggests that the community was expanding as early as the 1850s or 1860s. Presumably in the initial stages the clearance represented an expansion up to what were the limits of ecological equilibrium given the society's traditional methods. At some point people must have been forced to use more intensive agricultural techniques, but Rusembilan's final break with self-sufficiency did not come until the 1950s. Fraser says that 'until about 1950 Rusembilan had been entirely self-sufficient in terms of its rice production'.[3] However, by 1956, after the loss of 75 acres of rice paddy to a scheme involving the construction of a naviga-

---

* O'Malley was interested in the break-up of the joint family.

[1] L. S. S. O'Malley (ed.), *Modern India and the West* (London, 1941), p. 384.

[2] Thomas M. Fraser, *Rusembilan: a Malay Fishing Village in Southern Thailand* (Ithaca, 1960).

[3] Ibid., p. 59.

tion canal, only the largest and most productive family holdings were capable of growing enough rice for a family's rice subsistence.[1] Deficiency was practically universal, and people felt that 'making even a supplementary living by cultivating rice (was) becoming increasingly difficult. . . .'[2] Although land suitable for growing rice was scarce, the villagers were fortunate enough to have previously unused land suitable for growing other crops. The subsistence problem forced them to put this land to use, producing copra and rubber for world markets.

Once one has the concept of a society existing in ecological equilibrium there is no difficulty in accepting that the development of need is the real cause of economic development. The problem before was that the populations of underdeveloped countries were often regarded as having experienced the same level of unsatisfied need, or poverty, since time immemorial – without showing the rates of economic change which we have come to regard as significant. But as soon as one can see how cultural systems can establish themselves in an equilibrium situation in which unsatisfied needs are limited, it is easy to see how the pressure of need brought to bear on the economic system is subject to important variations. At this juncture it may be argued that the industrial capitalists who played a leading role in Western industrialization are, of all people, the ones least subject to the kinds of need discussed in this chapter. The explanation is that their role would have been impossible if the mass of ordinary people had already had adequate means of subsistence at their disposal. The general bulk of the population does not become exploitable until they no longer have the means (land and other productive resources) at their disposal to satisfy their own needs. Only in so far as people have unsatisfied needs will they be amenable to the twin roles of worker and consumer. Not only the methods and the technology but also the institutional organization of nineteenth-century capitalism was a response to the growth of need.

[1] Ibid., p. 64.   [2] Ibid., p. 67.

Although there are many studies, such as the four already mentioned, which show that the breakdown of an equilibrium system is fundamental to development, there are few which cover a long enough time span to show the complete process – starting with a description of the society in equilibrium, showing how it was disturbed and what was the initial course of development. Two societies for which we have reports which go some way towards providing the information we need are the Tikopia, a community in the Polynesian Islands, and the Vunamami in New Britain. The Tikopia were visited twice by Raymond Firth, once in 1929 and once in 1952.[1] During his first visit he was able to see the effects of European contact and Christianity on the traditional methods of population control: things were just beginning to change. Apart from practising abortion, Firth said that 'Contraception, celibacy and infanticide are resorted to consciously by the Tikopia as a reflex of the population situation'.[2] Responsible people were supposed to have only two children, and in families where there were more, only the eldest boy and girl were supposed to marry. But the influence of Christianity in the decade prior to 1929 had already begun to stimulate population growth. Since becoming a Christian, the chief had stopped giving the traditional ceremonial exhortation to people to limit their families by practising *coitus interruptus*. Contraception was ceasing to be 'part of the moral code of Tikopia, publicly inculcated with the weight of the chiefs and the religious values of the (ceremonial) occasion' which Firth says it had been.[3] Formerly men and women who remained unmarried had not been denied sexual satisfaction but had used *coitus interruptus* and abortion to avoid having children. The church threatened to bar anyone guilty of infanticide or abortion, and 'young people who (were) discovered to have had an intrigue (were) threatened by the Mission teacher and sometimes thrust into wedlock'.[4] By 1952 most of the traditional checks on population growth had disappeared. People had more children and all of them tended to marry. The situation was

---

[1] Raymond W. Firth, *Primitive Polynesian Economy* (London, 1939), and *Social Change in Tikopia* (London, 1959).

[2] Firth (1939), op. cit., p. 43.   [3] Ibid., p. 45.   [4] Ibid., p. 45.

regarded, especially by the non-Christian elders, as the result of 'improvidence' and 'a loosening of the sense of responsibility'.[1] Firth's description shows clearly how, in the case of the Tikopia, the initial source of disturbance to the system for maintaining the society within ecological equilibrium came from the proselytization of European social values under the auspices of the Christian church.

Although population was growing in 1929 the situation had not yet become critical; some people were becoming anxious about the future, but the threat was still 'potential rather than actual' and there was 'no real shortage of food'.[2] Between 1929 and 1952 the population grew by 35 per cent, from 1,300 to 1,750,[3] apparently creating 'acute pressure on food supplies'.[4] Unfortunately Firth's second visit to the Tikopia was immediately preceded by a hurricane which meant that the subsistence situation which he saw was worse than it otherwise would have been, but he was usually able to distinguish between the special effects of the hurricane and what was normal. In agriculture, the cultivated acreage was already incapable of significant expansion. People were shortening the fallow period of their garden lands and 'intensifying cultivation by planting short-term crops in the orchards. There was also a tendency to substitute easier growing and quicker maturing crops such as manioc and sweet potato for those demanding more care and maturing more slowly, such as taro.'[5] Firth also says that the Tikopia were keen to try out new plants but had found none which added to their production. He thought that as a whole their efforts had increased production but he feared that the shortening of the fallow and the changes in the balance of their diet would be damaging in the long run.[6] The Tikopia had no resources on which they could base significant production for trade, and the only way they could increase their incomes was by going abroad as temporary migrants to work on other islands. In 1952 the number of people working abroad ranged between 30 and 40 per cent of the effective male working population of Tikopia.[7]

[1] Firth (1959), op. cit., p. 157.
[2] Firth (1939), op. cit., p. 47.
[3] Firth (1959), op. cit., p. 53.
[4] Ibid., p. 47.   [5] Ibid., p. 156.
[6] Ibid., p. 156.
[7] Ibid., p. 115.

R. F. Salisbury's account of the Vunamami in New Britain is the other reasonably complete account of a small community going through the stages of transition we are interested in.[1] As recently as about 1875 Salisbury says that the population appears to have been in an 'equilibrium of low birth rate and low death rate' established 'as a means of stabilizing a relatively high standard of living'.[2] Apparently families were small and people married late. The society was stabilized well within the limits of its environment: 'the land could have supported a much larger population with ease'.[3] In the late nineteenth century the Vunamami lost some of their land to a missionary and more to other settlers. By the 1890s the encroaching coconut and cotton plantations were causing considerable resentment, and people from surrounding villages who had had their lands taken were coming to swell the Vunamami population. Conflicts between European and Vunamami concepts of property and land-use led to a European legal ruling in 1896 that the Vunamami would have to settle and plant their land within the following fifty years if they were to retain ownership of it.[4] On the initiative of one of their headmen the Vunamami started a conscious policy of increasing their numbers and planting coconuts on disputed land. By decree they lowered bride prices from 100 fathoms of shell money to 10, in order to encourage earlier marriage. Salisbury says the effect was dramatic. He says people married younger and that 'an annual increase of 3 per cent would fit the known figures for Vunamami populations'.[5] Through population growth and the loss of land, the amount of land available per person dropped from three and a half acres in 1875, to just over two-thirds of an acre in 1961. The response to these changes followed the pattern we are now familiar with. Although most of the Vunamami still cultivate subsistence gardens, they use the land more intensively and many use land some distance away where it is less scarce. In addition to copra and cocoa plantations, some of them grow

[1] Richard F. Salisbury, *Vunamami: Economic Transformation in a Traditional Society* (Berkeley, 1970).
[2] Ibid., p. 111.   [3] Ibid., p. 110.   [4] Ibid., p. 115.
[5] Ibid., p. 115.

garden crops for cash, but the largest part of village income comes from wage work either on local European plantations or as migrant labourers further afield.[1]

These two studies, of the Tikopia and the Vunamami, as well as providing remarkably clear illustrations of the sequence of events which lead to development, also give some indication of the variety of influences which do in practice cause societies to move out of ecological equilibrium. Symbolically the story of Adam and Eve outlines a pattern of events which is strikingly similar to the one just described. The garden of Eden symbolizes the hunting and gathering way of life, where food is there for the taking. The one condition for maintaining this idealizable state of affairs is to practise sexual restraint or some other means of population limitation. As soon as Adam and Eve break the symbolic sexual taboos, they are cast out of the garden and thenceforth have to till the ground.

So far we have dealt only with societies which fit particularly easily into the theoretical framework. The historical development of any of the modern industrial nations presents many more problems. Development does not seem to have sprung from a disturbance to a clearly defined stable equilibrium situation. This is largely because class societies – such as these – are much less likely to develop adequate social mechanisms for population limitation than classless tribes, village communities or chiefdoms are. One of the features found in many of the societies mentioned in the last chapter was the practice of food sharing. Within each society there was often relative equality as far as subsistence goods were concerned. Firth's statement that hunger was impossible in one Maori family while others had food to spare was quoted as fairly typical.[2] In class societies (which, from European feudalism to the Indian caste system, usually originated in territorial conquest), there is no longer a unified view of the society's subsistence problem: instead there are major inequalities between large groups of people. The rich upper classes have no need to limit their family size for fear of inadequate subsistence. This affects practices such as

[1] Ibid., pp. 91–2, 173.   [2] See p. 49 above.

abortion and infanticide which are, at best, necessary evils. If the upper classes find them unnecessary, then practising them will come to be regarded as an unmitigated evil. Because the upper class has a disproportionate influence on the society's ideology and law, frequently infanticide and abortion cannot be carried on openly but become illegal, undercover activities. Throughout the history of Western Europe abortion and infanticide have been carried on as surreptitious backstreet businesses. They certainly have not had the official backing and religious support which in some societies help to make them an effective means of population control. There is a lot of evidence to suggest that if these methods of population control could have been practised freely, population numbers would not have increased in many periods when they did. The prohibitions could, as suggested, be simply because these practices are abhorrent to those who are not forced to adopt them, but in societies where the ruling class could actually benefit from an increasing working population it may reflect a more fundamental divergence of interests. However, we do not need to go into this problem to see how common it is for the dominant value-systems of class societies to forbid methods of population control which are used elsewhere. The general tone of Christian thought is well known and we have already seen the impact of Christian missionaries from Europe on the methods of population limitation practised by the Abipones and the Tikopia.[1] But the position is even clearer in Muslim countries. The Koran contains a number of references to infanticide including the following two: 'slay not your children because of penury, We provide for you and for them'[2] and 'slay not your children fearing a fall to poverty, We shall provide for them and for you. Lo! the slaying of them is great sin.'[3] Societies which are denied the most direct methods of population control are forced to develop less direct and inevitably more tenuous methods. These less direct methods, such as controls on the marriage rate and so on, are often only partially effective; they

---

[1] See pp. 33 and 64–5 above.　　　　[2] The Koran, Surah VI: 152.
[3] Ibid., Surah XVII: 31.

are prone to intermittent breakdown and rarely seem to stabilize population size much below the upper limits of ecological equilibrium. It is this situation which provided the historical background to the developed nations.

Instead of moving from a clearly defined period of stability in ecological equilibrium into a clearly defined period of change, the industrial countries seem to have undergone slow but important change throughout their recent pre-industrial history. However, when the concept of a society in ecological equilibrium was introduced in the last chapter, it was suggested that ultimately it served as a theoretical extreme – or limiting – case for an examination of the process of change. In fact, of course, all societies are changing continuously in one aspect or another. What we are concerned to analyse are the variations in the rate at which societies make the innovations which constitute economic development. Whether or not a society is in ecological equilibrium as its population size and economic conditions fluctuate becomes a matter of degree. But it is in our understanding of this process of continuous change that the concept becomes important.

It was shown that the key factor in the maintenance of ecological equilibrium in any society was that population growth should be checked before it pressed on the limits of the environment. If periods of economic development are a response to population pressure, then as the rate of development is variable it must be shown that the pressure of population is variable. Where Malthusian checks are the only ones operative this condition cannot be fulfilled: the implication is that population is always pressing on the economic system and that numbers do – or do not – grow, simply in accordance with autonomous variations in the means of subsistence. But the evidence suggests, at least in relation to the longterm trends in the English pre-industrial population, that even a fluctuating population may be controlled primarily by cultural, social and other non-economic constraints. There is certainly no difficulty in showing that the population pressure on the English economic system varied over the centuries. Only in periods when all other constraints were weak did the population pressure mount until it encountered the Malthusian ceiling. It was during these periods of acute pressure that economic development was most notable.

Graph *a* on p. 71 shows the broad trends in the changing size of the population of England and Wales since medieval times. Although the earlier estimates must be less accurate than the later ones, the direction of the longterm movements is reliable enough for our purposes. There were two major periods of population growth before the modern expansion associated with the industrial revolution, but by modern standards both of these were periods of extremely slow growth. The average rate of growth during these periods was usually considerably below 1 per cent per annum. (1 per cent p.a. would cause numbers to double in seventy years.) Because the rate of population growth never approached the rates recorded in some societies (doubling in fifteen years), it must be concluded that growth was severely constrained throughout. The periods of growth are periods in which the constraints were marginally eased.

The relationships between population, real wages and prices were fundamentally different before the beginning of the nineteenth century from what they were afterwards. What follows concerns the earlier period. If Malthusian constraints were operative most of the time, one would expect that whenever there was a temporary improvement in real wages, population would immediately expand until wages returned to their normal level; and similarly, when there was a fall in real wages the population would decrease. Malthusian theory predicts that population movements will tend to iron out the variations in real wages. However, the graphs on p. 71 suggest that before the nineteenth century the tendency was for real wages and population to move in opposite directions. From the late fifteenth century to the early seventeenth century the population increased and real wages fell; the same is also true of the second half of the eighteenth century. From the Black Death until the mid-fifteenth century population fell and real wages rose, and during the second half of the seventeenth and first half of the eighteenth century population was stable while real

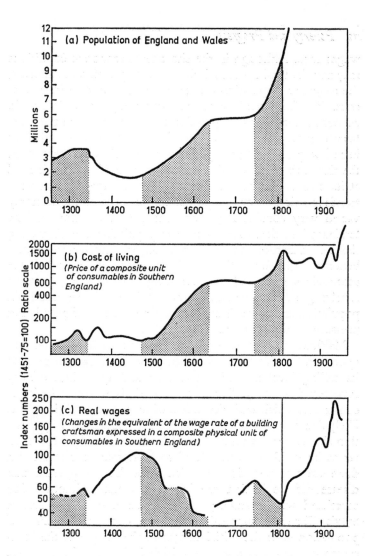

Sources:

Graph *a*: derived from E. A. Wrigley, *Population and History* (London, 1969), Fig. 3.3, p. 78; and T. H. Hollingsworth, *Historical Demography* (London, 1969), Fig. 10, p. 386.

Graph *b* and *c*: trend lines based on E. H. Phelps Brown and Sheila V. Hopkins, 'Seven centuries of the prices of consumables, compared with builders' wage rates', *Economica*, XCII (1956).

wages rose. Although in the short term economic conditions may have had an important influence on population movements, the longterm population trends show a remarkable independence. Far from tending to iron out longterm variations in economic conditions, population movements before the nineteenth century seem to have caused the most dramatic variations in real wages: during the population growth which centres on the sixteenth century real wages fell to two-fifths of their level at its outset. Not only the trends in real wages, but also the trends in prices show that population pressure on the economy varied very considerably from one period to another. The tendency for prices to rise whenever population does (including the period before 1300 but excluding the nineteenth-century breakthrough) shows the growing pressure of demand on the economic system and the increasing difficulties encountered satisfying it. The general similarity between the trends in population and prices indicates the *formative* role of population pressure on the economic system.[1]

Malthusian or neo-Malthusian checks may have come into operation for short periods when population growth reached its ceiling level around about 1300 and again in the early seventeenth century. But in other periods we must look for constraints which are independent of economic conditions. It is likely that disease would produce erratic fluctuations in population size rather than a consistent longterm trend except in so far as its incidence was related to economic conditions. But there are two periods for which it has been suggested that disease did lie behind the longterm trends without being correlated with changing economic conditions. The first is Sylvia Thrupp's suggestion that the continued decline of population after the initial impact of the plague in the fourteenth century was due to the high incidence of contagious diseases spread by the greater mobility of the population after

---

[1] The causal role of population growth behind the sixteenth-century price inflation was finally proved beyond possible doubt by F. J. Fisher, 'Inflation and influenza in Tudor England', *Economic History Review*, XVIII (1965).

the plague.[1] The second is Razzell's theory that the growth of population in the second half of the eighteenth century was the result of a decline in smallpox caused by very widespread use of inoculations against it.[2] There are a number of other explanations of the dominant population movements under discussion which, although not completely accepted, are supported by a good deal of evidence and cannot be dismissed on purely theoretical grounds. On the basis of evidence on the sex ratio of the population before and after the Black Death, J. C. Russell has suggested that female infanticide may have contributed to the levelling-off of growth before the plague and to the continuation of the decline after it. He says that between the middle of the thirteenth century and the plague, the sex ratio moved from equality to an average of four men to every three women.[3] The ratio was temporarily corrected during the plague – perhaps due to higher male than female mortality – but soon went back to its former inequality. The sex ratio among families of feudal tenants in the late fourteenth century shows 'an unmistakable deficiency in the number of female children'. Russell says that 'If the evidence is typical of the serfs it would indicate a rather rigorous control of numbers of servile children'.[4] It seems quite likely that the practice of infanticide, established initially during conditions of acute population pressure, may have been continued for a couple of generations before it was suppressed. It is possible that other methods of population control, also established in the pre-plague situation, continued in use after the plague and contributed to the lack of growth during the next two or three generations.

Recent work on parish registers has provided evidence of

---

[1] Sylvia L. Thrupp, 'The problem of replacement rates in late Medieval English population', *Economic History Review*, XVIII (1965), pp. 101–19.

[2] P. E. Razzell, 'Population change in 18th century England: a re-appraisal', *Economic History Review*, XVIII (1965), pp. 312–32. Reprinted in Michael Drake (ed.), *Population in Industrialisation* (London, 1969).

[3] Josiah Cox Russell, *British Medieval Population* (Albuquerque, New Mexico, 1948), p. 149.

[4] Ibid., p. 149.

social methods of population control during later periods. Wrigley has shown that in at least one village changes in the age of marriage, birth intervals and family size coincide with the national population trends to produce an increase in the sixteenth century, a levelling-off in the seventeenth and continued growth in the eighteenth.[1] At Colyton in Devon, the mean age at first marriage of women between 1560 and 1646 was 27·0. Between 1647 and 1719 it rose to 29·6; by the period 1770–1837 it had fallen to 25·1.[2] The average interval between births was four months longer in the second period than the first and, like the age of marriage, it decreased later.[3] Completed family size was reduced in the second period even among marriages which took place at the same age: for instance, for women who married between 25 and 29, the mean completed family size was 5·7 in the first period, 3·3 in the second and 4·5 in the third.[4] Many more such studies are needed before we can say with any confidence that changes in the age of marriage and forms of family limitation lie behind the changing longterm national population trends, but the balance of opinion among economic historians is moving towards a belief in the primacy of social constraints.[5]

From the trends in wages and prices we have seen that whatever the constraints behind the longterm population trends, they were independent of economic conditions except during brief Malthusian crises. The theoretical problem is to find

---

[1] E. A. Wrigley, 'Family limitation in pre-industrial England', *Economic History Review*, XIX (1966), pp. 82–109. Reprinted in Michael Drake, op. cit.

[2] Ibid., p. 86. [3] Ibid., p. 93. [4] Ibid., p. 97.

[5] Since the first draft of this chapter was completed Habakkuk has published a rather cautious recognition of the importance of social controls on population in England and Western Europe since 1750. While recognizing the importance of smallpox inoculations, he gives more emphasis to the declining age of marriage in the population rise of the industrial revolution period. See H. J. Habakkuk, *Population Growth and Economic Development since 1750* (Leicester, 1971). For evidence of the scale of infanticide in Europe between 1750 and 1850 see William L. Langer, 'Checks on population growth: 1750–1850', *Scientific American*, CCXXVI (1972), pp. 93–9.

variable factors capable of producing consistent longterm trends rather than erratic fluctuations. The general position may well be that societies have institutionalized mechanisms of population control which adjust only under extreme *economic* pressure but are sensitive to some independent cultural changes. This would explain the observed population trends punctuated by an occasional Malthusian crisis and yet would allow for the possibility of cultural disturbances to an ecological equilibrium. J. C. Russell pointed out that 'The institution of marriage is designed quite as much to prevent births as to encourage them and through postponement or even prohibition tends to restrict numbers of children'.[1] Systems of primogeniture as opposed to partible inheritance, the economic independence of the nuclear family in contrast to larger communal groups, are other examples of social institutions known to have had an important impact on population growth. A cultural conglomeration made up of a set of these institutions would restrict demographic behaviour within certain limits. This broad impact is then refined and adjusted slightly upwards or downwards by a set of norms which indicate more accurately how the institutions operate in terms of the age of marriage, attitudes to children, to sex, to economic independence, to the church's authority, to family limitation, etc. It may be that it is only when population has risen particularly high or sunk particularly low that economic pressure is strong enough to cause an adjustment in these norms. To a large extent changing population trends may reflect the conflicts between class ideology and the economic situation of the bulk of the population. This kind of system would produce the short-term fluctuations which we know occurred as a response to such factors as bad harvests, and would also produce consistent longterm trends by marginally altering people's decision-making; for instance, people under one set of norms would be more likely to tolerate a slight worsening in conditions rather than postpone their marriage than would people under different norms.

The economic effects of population pressure are clear. The periods of most acute population pressure – around 1300,

[1] Russell, op. cit., p. 162.

1600 and the late eighteenth century – were all periods of remarkable expansion and innovation as well as of unusual
poverty. This association should be predictable enough, but,
to dispel any lingering belief that economic development
is part of any simple continuum of improving living standards with societies developing naturally from good to better,
it may be worth sketching in the broad pattern of the
development associated with these periods of population
pressure.

A society established below the maximum level at which ecological equilibrium can be maintained is able to extend its
established economic system before having to innovate. The
area under cultivation can be expanded and the use of landbased resources can be increased before the society becomes
unable to support a larger population with traditional materials
and techniques. Only when any available slack in the resource-
base has been taken up is the pressure to innovate maximized.
During the population growth of the twelfth and thirteenth
centuries much new land was brought into cultivation. Wooded
areas were cleared and marshes and fens drained and reclaimed.
While it was still possible people increased agricultural production by extending the acreage under cultivation; only when
this became impossible were they forced to change methods in
an attempt to continue the increases in output by raising the
output per acre. However, there are signs that the average
fertility of arable land and the yields from seed actually declined
during the thirteenth century. The balanced system of medieval
agriculture had been upset. The expansion of the arable acreage
had not been matched by sufficient expansion of pasture and
animals to provide manure. The technical consistency had been
broken. Fallow periods had been shortened and poorer-
quality land had been brought into cultivation. Attempts to
increase yields per acre included liming and marling acid soils,
ploughing in straw ash, sowing more intensively and improving
and varying the kinds of seed used. But although agricultural
production increased, improvements did not keep up with
population pressure. Between the periods 1160–79 and 1300–19

wheat prices more than trebled,[1] and in many parts of the country the size of holdings diminished. As in the examples of individual villages in different parts of the modern under-developed world, population growth caused poverty and a need for supplementary sources of income. The response was what one economic historian has labelled 'an industrial revolution of the thirteenth century'.[2] Instead of growing coconuts or coffee for world markets, the woollen industry was expanded as the only source of additional income available to people in the economic conditions of the thirteenth century. The number of sheep increased, though – as already mentioned – not enough to balance the increased arable acreage, and English exports of wool rose by something like 40 per cent during the generation before about 1310. The growth of the rural industry shifted the emphasis of woollen production away from its older urban centres, where it had been under rigid guild control, into a new social and geographical situation which led to the introduction of fulling mills. The period saw significant expansion and in-novation in other basic industries including the mining and smelting of tin, lead and iron, salt production and pottery.

The population decline of the later fourteenth century saw some regression in agricultural methods but development continued during the population rise of the sixteenth century. During the sixteenth and early seventeenth centuries, especially after about 1560, agricultural methods were more carefully examined and discussed than at any time since the thirteenth century.[3] In the intervening years of lower population, much arable land had been converted to sheep pasture, but as relative prices changed under the impetus of population growth it became profitable to reconvert to arable. The margins of cultivation were pushed back to new limits and suggestions

---

[1] B. H. Slicher van Bath, *The Agrarian History of Western Europe, 500–1800* (London, 1963), p. 133.

[2] E. M. Carus-Wilson, 'An industrial revolution of the thirteenth century', *Economic History Review*, IX (1941); reprinted in E. M. Carus-Wilson (ed.), *Essays in Economic History*, volume I (London, 1954).

[3] Joan Thirsk (ed.), *The Agrarian History of England and Wales; volume 4, 1500–1640* (Cambridge, 1967), p. 161.

were made for making almost every part of the country productive, including even the hedgerows which some planted with fruit trees. As the last major additions to the cultivated area were made, the pressure to find ways of increasing output per acre increased. The problem was to increase the output of animals *and* crops, which, although they competed for land, were mutually beneficial when it came to increasing the productivity of a given area of land.[1] If the production of animal fodder could be increased then more animals could be kept and more manure would be available to increase the crop output. Improvement in crops and methods was a long, multifaceted process, starting in the late sixteenth century and culminating in the classical agricultural revolution of the late eighteenth century. Probably most of the increased output of the sixteenth century came from extensions to the agricultural acreage. When this source of growth had been used up, improvements in methods were still too slow to prevent the appearance of a Malthusian ceiling to check the increasing population. But even when population growth had been checked, population pressure remained – in the form of acute poverty – to act as a spur to further agricultural improvement. The introduction and spread of water meadows, better grasses for leys, more intensive rotations – including new fodder crops – and other improvements, brought a slow increase in living standards, which in turn favoured increased consumption of animal products and wheat over inferior foods. The shift in demand and the spread of improved methods combined to create a new pattern of regional agricultural specialization.[2] In the middle of the eighteenth century population started to grow again, redirecting and adding fresh impetus to the rate of innovation.

Just as the thirteenth century was notable for the development of industry such as it was, so also was the century of acute population pressure from about 1540 to 1640. It too has been

---

[1] E. L. Jones, 'Agriculture and economic growth in England, 1660–1750: agricultural change', *The Journal of Economic History*, XXV (1965). Reprinted in E. L. Jones (ed.), *Agriculture and Economic Growth in England 1650–1815* (London, 1967).

[2] Ibid.

characterized as an 'industrial revolution' and, although its historian, J. U. Nef, shunned that description, he did say that 'The growth in the importance of mining and manufacturing in the national economy was, it seems, scarcely less rapid between the middle of the sixteenth century and the Civil War than between the middle of the eighteenth century and the first Reform Act'.[1] The picture is one of general expansion accompanied by the introduction of new industries, widespread technical innovation and the substitution of new resources for old. Among the most important of the new industries was brassmaking based on a process in which copper was infused with zinc direct from unsmelted calamine. Brass became important not only for cannon, but was soon fundamental to a large section of the small metal trades. The same period saw the transformation of the iron industry from the traditional 'bloomery' technique associated with small forges to a large-scale industry employing massive blast furnaces. Many industries which used large amounts of fuel in heating processes, such as glassmaking, salt-boiling, brewing and brickmaking, responded to the growing scarcity of timber by switching to coal. The increased demand for coal for domestic and industrial use led to innovations in pumping and ventilating techniques as pits were sunk deeper. Overshot waterwheels became more common, not just for driving rag-and-chain or bucket pumps for mines, but in mills of all sorts. However, it was changes in the woollen trade which directly affected most people's lives. With population pressure mounting throughout the sixteenth and early seventeenth century, the export of raw wool was gradually transformed into a trade in finished cloth as more and more of the manufacturing process was taken over, as an additional source of income, by domestic workers in England. Up to the beginning of the seventeenth century the finishing processes were still done in the Netherlands, although the cloth was woven in England; but from then on there was an expansion of the finishing trades in England and merchants began to

[1] J. U. Nef, 'The progress of technology and the growth of large-scale industry in Great Britain, 1540–1640', *Economic History Review*, V (1934), p. 4. Reprinted in Carus-Wilson, op. cit.

export direct to the consumers. There can be little doubt that one of the most important reasons for this development – one of the central features of England's pre-industrial development – was the increasing population pressure on the land and growing poverty. English villagers, just like the people of Hsin Hsing, Taiwan, were forced to develop domestic industry as an additional source of income. Joan Thirsk has shown that the English woollen industry tended to concentrate in areas where inheritance customs led to the successive division of holdings in periods of population growth.[1] Villages which practised partible inheritance tended to be more densely populated than others; land holdings were smaller and people had to earn part of their income from weaving or other forms of domestic work. Thirsk quotes an account of an octogenarian Yorkshireman who in 1634 said that in his village the inheritance custom was to divide land equally between sons; he went on to explain that

> by reason of such division of tenements, the tenants are much increased in number more than they were, and the tenements become so small in quantity that many of them are not above three or four acres so that they could not maintain their families were it not by their industry in knitting coarse stockings.[2]

In areas where primogeniture prevailed, presumably the younger siblings with no means of subsistence in their native villages were often forced to join the growing numbers of wage earners and urban migrants.

The growth of towns and the increase in the proportion of the population relying on wages are important aspects of the economic development of this period. They serve as general indicators of the expansion of population beyond what could be absorbed within the framework of the rural economy, and provide a direct parallel to the appearance of urban migrants

[1] Joan Thirsk, 'Industries in the countryside', in F. J. Fisher (ed.), *Essays in the Economic and Social History of Tudor and Stuart England* (Cambridge, 1961).
[2] Ibid., p. 70.

and wage labour in the examples of the development of village communities. There are also important general indicators of the breakdown of the rural economy itself. Growing resource scarcities led to the development of trade in goods and commodities in which communities had traditionally been able to maintain a self-sufficiency. Local self-sufficiency was undermined as each region was forced by growing scarcity to take more notice of the differentials between its own resource endowment and that of other regions. The economic theory of trade suggests that each region put its main energies into those activities in which it had the greatest comparative advantage over other regions, while buying the things in which it was at a disadvantage. Certainly this period is well known for the increase in the numbers of merchants, middlemen and of trade generally. There was also an important expansion and development of land and water transport: packhorses continued to give way to wheeled transport, more rivers were made navigable and the coastal trade grew.

The population growth which started in the middle of the eighteenth century once more produced the familiar pattern of rising prices and falling real wages. Here we need only observe that it was accompanied by the agricultural and industrial revolutions proper, and that the latter was soon to reverse the movements in prices and real wages in spite of continued rapid population growth.

In English history there can be no mistaking the intimate connection between the periodic appearance of population pressure and economic development. Since the Norman conquest it seems that there have been three major periods of population growth leading to acute population pressure. Each one has, in its later stages, ushered in a period not just of agricultural expansion, but of agricultural innovation and industrial development as well. The connection is not one of association alone; we have seen – as yet very unanalytically – a little of the causal relationship between the problems created by population pressure and the forms which economic development has taken. The human motivational pattern was clear in the examples of smallscale communities, and there are sufficient indications that similar patterns appeared in many English villages. Should the argument need strengthening, a single paragraph will suffice to show that the pattern was repeated in the immediate pre-industrial period in Japan.

Japanese population grew during the seventeenth and early eighteenth centuries until it reached a Malthusian crisis level. Reduced to extreme poverty, population numbers levelled off under the impact of famine, frequent epidemics and the adoption of infanticide and abortion on a very large scale. In spite of the attempts of the Shogunate and feudal lords to prevent peasants from using abortion and infanticide, they were, according to Tsuchiya, the most important of the population checks: contemporary references to them seemed too numerous to mention.[1] As well as suffering the difficulties associated with population pressure, feudal tenants had to pay taxes which amounted to anything between 20 and 40 per cent of their annual income to maintain the feudal lords, the Shogunate and a 'vast army of vassals and retainers numbering upwards of 2 million'.[2] To alleviate the situation every attempt was made to increase agricultural production. All suitable land was brought into cultivation, the irrigated area was enlarged, greater quantities of fertilizer and manure were used and the variety of crops was increased. However, famines and hunger riots became common. Tsuchiya describes the rural community as 'utterly exhausted'.[3] Some people managed to add to their incomes by spinning or weaving, but many who could not make enough to live on sold their land and moved to the towns where, if they were lucky, they were employed by samurai, became small merchants, artisans or day labourers.[4] The scale of urban migration is indicated by the fact that during the late eighteenth and early nineteenth centuries Edo (Tokyo) was the largest city in the world.[5] Population pressure produced an

---

[1] Takao Tsuchiya, *An Economic History of Japan* (Tokyo, 1937), pp. 162–3.
[2] W. W. Lockwood, *The Economic Development of Japan* (Princeton, 1968), p. 4.
[3] Tsuchiya, op. cit., p. 164.   [4] Ibid., p. 164.   [5] Ibid., p. 193.

expansion of mining and industry including iron-smelting from iron-bearing sand.[1] But development was hampered politically by what Lockwood called an attempt to 'freeze society in a rigid hierarchical mold'. He says that 'through strict controls on travel and trade, as well as over freedom of occupation and enterprise, the Tokugawa regime sought to suppress the growth of any new forces which might threaten the feudal-agrarian foundations of the state'.[2] Considering the heavy taxation imposed by the Tokugawa regime and its attitude to population control, we could not agree that the regime suppressed the growth of the *forces* of change; what happened was that as these forces built up, change could only be prevented by the increasing harshness of Japan's ruling class. However, after the fall of the Shogun and the restoration of the emperor in 1868, Japanese 'modernization' was, as Lockwood says, like the 'bursting of a dam. It was the more violent because it brought the release of long-pent-up forces.'[3]

It is now time to start drawing a few theoretical strings together. The connection between the expansion beyond the bounds at which ecological equilibrium can be maintained and the appearance of economic development makes sense at the level of both the individual and society. At its simplest, the theory of economic development – or perhaps the lack of development – was summed up by a South African Bushman who, when asked why they had not taken up agriculture, said 'Why should we plant when there are so many mongongo nuts in the world?'[4] There is no need to labour to increase the productivity of the environment when the present level of subsistence is adequate. Though simple and apparently obvious, this approach places development in a completely new perspective. Development is here primarily an attempt to increase the amount of the means of subsistence which the environment can provide. Changes in efficiency are secondary and are subject to the constraints imposed by the problems of providing a particular quantity

---

[1] Ibid., pp. 173–4. [2] Lockwood, op. cit., pp. 4–5. [3] Ibid., p. 5.
[4] Richard B. Lee, 'What hunters do for a living', in R. B. Lee and I. DeVore (eds.), *Man the Hunter* (Chicago, 1968), p. 33.

e means of subsistence. In some periods economic
ency increases, in others it decreases. One of the reasons
in the past it has been assumed that development is
narily a process of making improvements, and increasing the
efficiency of the economic system, is that people presumably
make changes because they seem beneficial. That they are
beneficial in the contexts in which people find themselves need
not be disputed. But we have seen how people may be unwilling to accept changes while their society is in ecological
equilibrium and yet be willing to accept them later on when
they face subsistence problems. The appearance of subsistence
problems makes them willing to accept changes which previously seemed to require too much work or to suffer from other
prohibitive disadvantages. Population growth, in a society
established at a particular level of environmental exploitation,
leads to a steady worsening of the standard of living until
people are ready to accept any disadvantages which may go
with the changes in methods necessary to increase the supply
of the means of subsistence. Most of the changes are accepted
because they represent improvements in the supply of subsistence, not because they represent increases in efficiency for
societies with adequate subsistence. This point was made
explicit in a study of peasants' motives for changing their
methods of cultivation. Interviews with some 200 cultivators
in the Punjab and north-west Pakistan revealed that 92 per cent
of changes were made to increase production and only 5 per
cent because they were cheaper or easier – i.e. more efficient –
than the old ones.[1] (Changes involved cropping patterns, seed
varieties, fertilizers, numbers of livestock etc., and were
motivated by the need for more food, clothes and household
items.)

If some societies are not unwilling to sacrifice existing levels
of efficiency for increased production, others are unwilling to
sacrifice possible increases in leisure. That some societies show
what is called a 'leisure preference' has been the despair of many
development economists. Many societies have shown a

[1] Daniel W. Sturt, 'Producer response to technological change in West
Pakistan', *Journal of Farm Economics*, XLVII (1965), pp. 625–33.

tendency to use improvements in techniques which have reduced the amount of time necessary to produce their subsistence, to increase their leisure time. Economists who have attached a higher priority to increasing the output of goods would have preferred the extra time to have been used to increase production. A leisure preference is a clear indication of the relative sufficiency of a society's material means of subsistence and should be regarded as a feature of societies in ecological equilibrium. If a society is in equilibrium and has adequate subsistence then the leisure preference of its members will prevent increases in economic efficiency leading to what we would recognize as economic development. Only if a society is already out of equilibrium will it plough back increases in efficiency to achieve greater output and higher levels of environmental exploitation. A study which illustrates this point particularly clearly is Salisbury's monograph on the Siane of New Guinea.[1] The replacement of stone axes by steel ones had the effect of reducing the amount of time men had to spend on subsistence activities to less than two-thirds of what it had been.[2] They could already afford to leave most cultivation work to women, and instead of using any of their new-found spare time in subsistence or other economic tasks, the Siane spent it on additional ceremonial activities, fighting and leisure.[3] They were keen to take advantage of any possible way of increasing their *efficiency*, but because land was plentiful and subsistence adequate, increases in efficiency had very little connection with economic development.

There are two possible weaknesses in the chain linking the breakdown of ecological equilibrium and the creation of unsatisfied need with economic development. The first is that a stable society may develop a taste for goods over and above its traditional range – such as a desire for Western goods – which is powerful enough to stimulate the search for additional sources of income essential to economic development; the second is that some cultural systems may be able to contain the strains set up by inadequate subsistence and prevent the eco-

[1] R. F. Salisbury, *From Stone to Steel* (Melbourne, 1962).
[2] Ibid., p. 108.   [3] Ibid., p. 108.

D

nomic system from changing. To take the first point first, there is clearly no *a priori* reason why a sufficiently strong desire for new goods should not be created. New goods such as tobacco which cannot be regarded as substitutes for old did find their way into the pre-industrial English economy. The importance of 'rising expectations' and the demand for goods such as transistor radios is often emphasized in underdeveloped countries today. But several questions must be asked. Of course most people want things they have not got, but their wants are only important in the present context if they are prepared to do the work necessary to satisfy them. The demand for completely new consumer goods must rarely be strong enough not only to make people willing to work for them, but also to make people feel that methods of production must be intensified to provide access to the new goods. Certainly changing circumstances can generate important new practical needs, such as the need for transport to and from work in industrial societies, but where people's practical subsistence and social needs are adequately satisfied, can the remaining, necessarily whimsical desires for other goods really unhinge a traditional economic system? It seems likely that the role of such desires in stimulating economic development has been exaggerated. The underlying breakdown of ecological equilibrium tends to be overlooked because observers have not been aware of its significance. The result is that the adoption of Western goods is often seen as the cause of development rather than as part of the process – itself representing the integration of a small community into the national and international economy. As soon as economic development starts then pressing new needs – such as the need for education – will appear. (The development of these needs is discussed in chapter 9 below.) A few Western goods, far from having a disruptive influence, have been valued precisely for the contribution they make to the smoother running of the traditional system. But there are also a few cases where the demand for new goods has been at least indirectly instrumental in stimulating development: goods which compete with traditional goods as marks of social status and authority may have a disruptive effect on a social system and so lead to a weakening of the values and institutions which maintained the society in ecological equilibrium. However, the possibility that the desire for new goods could lead *directly* to higher levels of environmental exploitation cannot be excluded.

The second problem confronting the ecological approach to development is an important one. Many cultural systems clearly do find ways of preventing subsistence scarcities leading to economic change. Class societies contain varying degrees of working-class poverty. Whenever significant poverty builds up within a rigid class society and is contained by social rather than environmental constraints, the development problem becomes a political one. The problem is to see how the poor are prevented from making the economic system respond to their unsatisfied needs; in other words, to see how the system is maintained at too low a level of environmental exploitation for the society which it serves. One of the most obvious mechanisms contributing to this situation is a market economy which can make even the subsistence demands of some people 'ineffective'. The demand of a man without money has no influence on the economic system. The existence of his need does not affect the pricing and allocating behaviour of a market economy. People in a society where subsistence is not allocated according to the market mechanism may not get all they want, but at least their unsatisfied needs can influence the social process which controls future production levels. A second way in which adjustments in a market economy have been held in check is by the control of prices. If changing prices serve to allocate resources to meet changing market demand, then economic adjustment can be prevented by fixing prices at a stable level. The kind of legal and quasi-legal control of prices which existed in pre-industrial Europe and still exists in some primitive societies today must be regarded largely as an attempt to suppress economic change. In class societies where methods of population control are inadequate the threat to the *status quo* associated with moving out of ecological equilibrium must be suppressed. A ruling class whose position would be weakened by economic development will endeavour to maintain the *status quo* against growing need using whatever social, political and economic means it can. The fight for development then becomes a class conflict along Marxist lines in all these spheres. The Japanese example is a case in point. Acute poverty was contained for a while by the Shogun's attempt to 'freeze society in a rigid hierarchical mold'.[1] Rapid development waited on the fall of the Shogun.

The general character of the stimuli to development discussed in this chapter can be summarized by reference to a society where they are conspicuously absent. The Pakot, a Nilotic tribe in western Kenya who are primarily herders but also practise a little agriculture, have been studied as an example of a society which has resisted all attempts to change its traditional culture.[2] Europeans, and the British colonial administration in particular, have tried to get the Pakot to change their herding and agricultural methods because it was believed that the land suffered from overgrazing and that there was a threat of soil erosion. But whether or not this view was correct, the environmental deterioration had not yet affected the Pakot: they were able to keep more cattle than they needed and Europeans were constantly surprised by how their 'healthy, fat cattle . . . contrasted sharply with the seemingly sparse grass'.[3] The Pakot did not want to plant new crops which would have decreased the threat of soil erosion because they required more labour than traditional crops.[4] Where possible the Pakot ignore the government's attempts to change their ways; elsewhere they counter its moves 'with passive resistance or active obstructionism'. They cling to their own culture, methods and beliefs, of which they are proud, they reject European clothes 'and remain unconvinced of the alleged benefits of government schooling and Christianity'.[5] Schneider says that 'The Pakot's determined resistance to British pressures is based upon their satisfaction with their traditional culture and their feeling that it is superior

---

[1] See p. 83 above.

[2] Harold K. Schneider, 'Pakot resistance to change', in William S. Bascom and Melville J. Herskovits (eds.), *Continuity and Change in African Cultures* (Chicago, 1958), pp. 144–65.

[3] Ibid., p. 156.   [4] Ibid., p. 154.   [5] Ibid., p. 160.

to and more desirable than Euroamerican civilization. . . .
Their herding life provides all they need and all they want, and
they have found almost nothing in Euroamerican culture that
will entice them to abandon their old ways.'[1] This type of
cultural pride and conservatism is a common feature of
societies in ecological equilibrium; it reflects a lack of unsatisfied
needs in the cultural system which it serves to protect. But if
the colonial government's prognosis of overgrazing and soil
erosion is correct and the Pakot have expanded beyond the
limits which their environment can sustain – given their productive methods – then the end of their traditional culture is in
sight.

[1] Ibid., p. 160.

5 *The structure of development*

> ... it is one of the eternal verities of history that as societies become wealthy they are no longer able to afford pleasures that were well within their reach when they were poor.[1]

In the last chapter it was shown that the primary stimulus to economic development came from the growth of material needs beyond the maximum level which could be satisfied within the existing environmental relations. The established productive system was rendered inadequate by population growth or some other change which upset the balance between supply and demand in the resources it depended on. In this chapter it will be shown that the main features of longterm economic development, including changes in the resource-base, the division of labour, the development of trade and industry, increasingly intensive agricultural methods and many other aspects of a society's changing productive activity, are all predictable responses to the growth of need. They cannot be understood as attempts to increase economic efficiency. The notion that economic development is a process of increasing efficiency dies hard, but it will be shown that development is accompanied – as often as not – by a decrease in the real efficiency of societies.

In its broadest ecological context economic development is the development of more intensive ways of exploiting the natural environment. Every culture uses a particular set of resources to provide the food, clothes and other material goods needed

[1] F. J. Fisher, 'The sixteenth and seventeenth centuries: the dark ages in English economic history?' *Economica*, XXIV (1957).

by the population it serves. It has already been mentioned that any organic resources used are available at a particular rate of supply according to the conditions of their production, aided or unaided by man. The natural environment, if left to itself, tends to build up into what is called a 'climax community' of flora and fauna, such as the relatively stable natural forest cover which exists in many parts of the world. Within these natural communities of animal and plant species very little of the total natural organic production is in a form which man can use. Few of the animals will provide valuable sources of food or skins, and very little of the vegetation will be edible or able to provide either the fibres used in clothing or the necessary materials to meet other needs. The population density of people living just on the naturally occurring wild animals and plants would have to be very low – as it was among societies of hunters and gatherers. To support a larger population man is forced to follow a course of increasing intervention into the climax community of flora and fauna to divert a larger and larger part of the natural system's productivity into forms which humans can use. Human societies must find or create a large enough ecological niche for themselves in the organic food-chains of the biosphere. They must increasingly dominate and restructure their ecosystem to support rising population numbers. Much of the history of agricultural development is the history of attempts to increase the control and manipulation of the natural environment, and to use land for the specialized and increasingly intensive production of the crops and animals which particular societies depend on.

Even at this level of generality we can see the source of possible conflicts between increases in the supply of the means of subsistence and increases in the efficiency – or ease – with which subsistence can be gained. As the level of environmental exploitation increases, more and more of the production and processing of raw materials is dependent on the work of man rather on purely natural processes. At one time man could clothe himself from the skins of the animals he ate, later he had to grow or collect natural fibres which could be woven up into suitable material, and now, increasingly, he is having to make

artificial fibres from mineral resources from which he manu-
factures cloth. At each stage a greater quantity is available but
more and more of the processing has to be done by man. The
development of agriculture too contains numerous examples
of the cost of maintaining an artificially structured plant
and animal community in the face of natural tendencies
in other directions. We must look at this problem in more
detail.

Ester Boserup, in *The Conditions of Agricultural Growth*,[1] has
suggested that the predominant tendency in agricultural
development is towards methods which use land more intensively but frequently involve a decrease in the productivity of
labour. Increases in the amount of subsistence available are
increasingly hard to produce. The discussion which follows
summarizes Mrs Boserup's main points. The most primitive
forms of agriculture, using land very unintensively, seem to
provide societies with adequate subsistence while involving
them in remarkably little work. Slash-and-burn agriculture, as its
name suggests, involves clearing the forest cover from a plot of
land by fire, after first ring-barking the trees to kill them and
cutting off some of the branches. The productivity of labour in
this most primitive form of agriculture appears to be very high:
seed can be scattered directly among the ashes, or the tubers of
root crops can be planted using only digging sticks – no
ploughing is necessary. Burning destroys the seeds of many
potential weeds and the surrounding forest vegetation does not
include the grasses and other species which quickly invade
cleared ground: there is little or no need to do any weeding.
Nor is it necessary to spread fertilizer or grow rotation crops to
keep up soil fertility; a society with sufficient land can afford to
abandon plots after a few seasons as crop yields decline. The
regrowth of forest vegetation over two or sometimes three
decades restores soil fertility unaided by man so that the whole
process can be repeated. Figures quoted by Clark and Haswell
of the average number of hours worked per year by cultivators
in Sarawak, Borneo, Zambia and Ghana using a slash-and-burn

[1] (London, 1965).

system all lie between about 500 and 650 hours.[1] (Compare this with the 2000 hours worked by people in industrial societies doing a 40-hour week 50 weeks in a year.) Mrs Boserup's work tends to support figures such as these. An additional point she makes is that in societies where slash-and-burn methods are practised side by side with others, slash-and-burn agriculture is frequently referred to as the 'easy system'.[2] The relative freedom from long periods of arduous work explains the reluctance of many societies to adopt more intensive techniques with higher yields per acre.

As numbers grow and population density increases, societies are forced to shorten the fallow period and to use the land more intensively. By transposing Carneiro's equation for the carrying capacity of an area of land it is possible to express the length of the fallow period as a function of population size and a number of other variables:[3]

$$F = T\left(\frac{C}{PA}\right) - C$$

where F is the length of the fallow period in years
T is the total area of land available for cultivation
C is the number of years a plot of land is cultivated before being allowed to return to fallow
P is the number of people to be supported on the land
A is the average area of cultivated land needed to support a person for a year

As more labour is applied to a fixed amount of land the economist would also expect diminishing returns to labour in terms of the amount of work needed to gain an adequate subsistence. More intensive agriculture does seem to intensify the difficulties of cultivation. With a shorter fallow period there

[1] Colin Clark and Margaret Haswell, *The Economics of Subsistence Agriculture*, 4th ed. (London, 1970), p. 51, Table XI.
[2] Boserup, op. cit., p. 29.
[3] Robert L. Carneiro, 'Slash-and-burn agriculture', in A. F. C. Wallace (ed.), *Selected Papers of the Fifth International Congress of Anthropological and Ethnological Sciences* (Philadelphia, 1960), p. 230.

is not time for a regrowth of forest vegetation and the cultivators find themselves having to clear land of bush and rough scrub. Bush becomes the predominant vegetation in the area. The most important implication of this change is not the effect it has on the time required for clearing the land but its effect on the amount of weeding which is necessary. Because the ground is no longer shaded by forest, sunlight reaches the ground enabling the growth of grasses and other plants which provide a dense ground cover. The longer a particular plot is cultivated before it is allowed to revert to fallow the more weeding must be done. Boserup quotes sources which suggest that in some cases the amount of work involved in weeding may be as great as that involved in clearing a new piece of land.[1] But weeding is not the only additional problem. Under thin bush and scrub vegetation the exposed soil becomes much more compacted than the soft leafmould under forest cover. The hardness of the soil and the need to weed explains the introduction of the hoe during bush-fallowing. (It should be emphasized that the hoe is not primarily a refinement of the digging stick but a new tool to deal with a new situation.) Under a system of bush-fallowing the soil may well be less fertile than under forest fallow. A more rapid decline in yields from a particular plot may force people to clear new land more often, or alternatively it may involve them in doing additional work to improve fertility – hoeing in dead leaves and other vegetable matter collected in the surrounding bush is a common method.

There seem to be good reasons to accept Mrs Boserup's suggestion that labour productivity is lower under bush-fallowing than under forest-fallowing; but perhaps the most persuasive point is the fact that cultivators with plenty of land choose to wait until old plots are reafforested rather than bring them back into cultivation when only bush vegetation has had time to grow up. Mrs Boserup says that 'bush is never cleared as long as secondary forest is available'.[2]

In this rapid sketch of some of the more important aspects of agricultural development we must move on from bush-fallowing hoe cultures to plough cultures. Ploughing becomes

[1] Boserup, op. cit., p. 31.   [2] Ibid., p. 31.

necessary when population density has grown sufficiently to force the fallow period to be shortened until grass becomes the predominant vegetation. Grassland cannot be prepared for planting crops by burning. The turf survives fire and often grows with renewed vigour after it. The plough, like the hoe, is not introduced as a superior version of older tools to tackle familiar problems; it is introduced because grassland can only be prepared for sowing by ploughing – i.e. by the laborious procedure of cutting and turning over the turf. When the workload becomes as great as this and ploughing demands an amount of sheer physical power, man is forced to make use of draught animals as an additional source of power to his own limited reserves. If the fallow area is still larger than the cultivated area it is probable that there will be enough fallow grazing to provide adequate feed for the draught animals: under most conditions an animal needs a larger area of land for grazing than the amount it can plough. Where the fallow is inadequate the farmer finds himself sowing grass leys and hay-making to provide winter feed rather than relying on the natural growth of pasture. With such short fallow periods it is also likely that a considerable amount of additional work will have to be put into manuring and other techniques – such as liming and marling – to maintain soil fertility. Weeding can also become a severe problem, particularly with root crops and vegetables which do not hold their own as well as cereals against competition from weeds. But heavy as the workload is in this type of plough culture, the whole situation gets much worse as soon as the fallow and grass leys become inadequate to provide the grazing needed for draught animals. As population grows, forcing people to cultivate at any one time a higher proportion of the total land available to them, the consequent shortening of the fallow makes the problems of maintaining soil fertility and providing adequate animal fodder suddenly more acute. The situation is the same as that mentioned during the discussion of English agricultural development in the last chapter. As the balance between the amount of fallow grazing, the number of animals needed for ploughing and eating, and the supply of manure for maintaining the fertility of arable land is broken, each sector faces difficulties. The solution in Europe was to grow nitrogen-fixing rotation crops which improved soil fertility and also supplied much larger quantities of animal fodder. Though this increased the yield per acre quite dramatically, it did so only at an enormously increased labour cost. Fodder and rotation crops are essentially support crops for the ones consumed directly by human beings. Growing them presumably means doubling the work involved in producing the food crops.

The parts of the world with very high population densities which have developed intensive forms of irrigated cultivation have to face the same basic problem of the tendency for labour productivity to fall as the ratio of labour to land increased. A table of Mrs Boserup's showing the labour time needed to grow various crops on dry and irrigated systems in parts of India and China suggests that the amount of work per acre involved just in irrigating the land may sometimes be equal to that needed for all other tasks (preparing the ground, sowing, weeding, harvesting and threshing) combined under dry cultivation.[1] The total amount of work per crop acre may be two or three times as high in irrigated as in dry cultivation.

A proper numerical study of labour productivity in the course of longterm agricultural development would be almost impossible. Even if historical figures of the same society practising different forms of agriculture in different periods were available, it would be difficult to isolate the impact on labour productivity of the particular changes we are interested in. The cross-cultural comparisons which are available to us suffer even more from the influence of extraneous factors. One cannot compare societies which differ only in the intensiveness of their agricultural methods – there are always differences in climate, soil and crop varieties as well. But for what such comparisons are worth, Clark and Haswell have summarized a number of the better studies of labour productivity under different systems.[2] It appears, in almost every case, that the kind

[1] *The Conditions of Agricultural Growth*, p. 40.
[2] Clark and Haswell, op. cit., pp. 102–10.

of variations in the intensiveness of different forms of subsistence agriculture which occur within a single country are accompanied by severely diminishing returns to labour. The farms employing the highest ratio of labour to land have the lowest labour productivity. The figures for peasant agriculture in Yugoslavia are fairly typical. They show that areas cultivated with 1·67 men working per square kilometre produce the equivalent of 1·49 tons of grain per man-year, whereas with only 0·32 men per square kilometre the productivity per man moves up to 2·97 tons of grain.[1] Obviously the lower labour productivity is only tolerated because it is possible to support a larger population from a given area of agricultural land. In this case the yield goes up from 0·95 tons to 2·49 tons per square kilometre. These inter-farm comparisons for individual nations can be used to make cross-cultural comparisons, but the importance which can be attached to the results is obviously slight. However, because these figures are available and it is difficult to find more reliable assessments of the variations in agricultural methods which we are interested in, the data is reproduced in graphs *a* and *b* on page 98. Graph *a* appears to show cross-culturally that as the land is cultivated more and more intensively, labour productivity declines, but the curves for Nigerian cocoa, Nigerian food crops and the one for Gambia, all of which cover the same sort of range of labour input per hectare, should serve as a warning: they show the very important variations in labour productivity which are not explained by how intensively the land is used. Graph *b*, like graph *a*, shows diminishing labour productivity within individual nations; cross-culturally it provides no evidence of any upward or downward tendency in labour productivity as agriculture becomes more intensive. It should be pointed out however, that the productivity of agricultural labour shown in the two curves for Japan and the one for Taiwan are artificially raised by the use of machinery and other industrial inputs. (At this stage the discussion is not concerned with the impact of machinery on labour productivity. The figures shown for agriculture in other countries are not significantly affected by its

[1] Ibid., pp. 102 and 105.

use.) After allowances have been made for Japan and Taiwan,
we can conclude that the data available is at least consistent with

(*a*) *Labour productivity in agriculture*

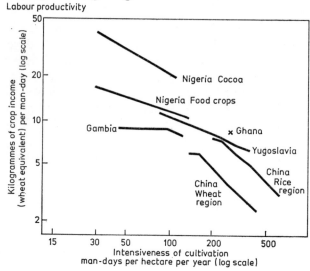

Source: Clark and Haswell, op. cit., p. 102.

(*b*) *Labour productivity in Asian agriculture*

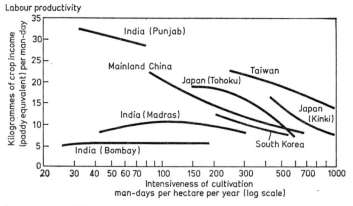

Source: adapted from Shigeru Ishikawa, *Economic Development in Asian Perspective* (Tokyo, 1967), pp. 230–1, Chart 3.3.

the hypothesis put forward here; it provides no evidence that the pre-industrial development of agricultural methods is set in motion primarily by a search for more efficient (in the sense of laboursaving) techniques. Instead, the development from the most primitive, extensive methods, to the most sophisticated, intensive ones, appears to fit the pattern suggested at the beginning of the last chapter. Development is primarily a matter of increasing the rate of environmental exploitation to support a growing population. Societies may try to maximize their efficiency but will become more or less efficient as they are subject to the technical problems of supporting a particular population size in a given environment. It is easy to see how graphs *a* and *b* fit into the framework outlined in conjunction with the diagram on p. 55 in the last chapter.

After discussing briefly some aspects of pre-industrial agricultural development it is now time to outline some of the implications of this approach for our interpretation of other aspects of economic development. The various stages of development which people have found – or thought they found – in the broad expanse of economic, technological, social or political history, are reflections of underlying ecological processes. Those associated with the Neolithic and industrial revolutions are of course the most fundamental. From time to time as population increases, societies grow out of their former ecological niche. Their aggregate subsistence demand for the particular resources which the cultural system is based on come to exceed the supply which the environment can sustain. The scarcity of basic resources encountered at this point forces the society to make some alteration in the way it gains its living from the environment. Sometimes a fairly minor alteration – such as importing the scarce raw material – may be enough to make ends meet once more. In other situations it will be necessary to develop ways of exploiting scarce resources more intensively – as happens during the process of agricultural development. In still other situations new resources will have to be substituted for old. The beginnings of agriculture were signalled by the breakdown of the ecological equilibrium established by hunting and gathering societies. As naturally occurring animal and plant populations became insufficient to meet man's needs, the artificial cultivation of crops had to be introduced for his continued support.

It seems that unlike other stages in the developmental process, the ground for the Neolithic revolution was almost literally prepared by environmental change. As the last Ice Age receded much of the European park-tundra was replaced by forest growth. If we accept Boserup's suggestion that crop production is easier in forested areas than in grassland, then this shift was favourable to the beginnings of agriculture, and probably unfavourable to hunting. (It is notable that present-day hunters and gatherers are largely confined to grasslands.) But there is evidence that hunting became more difficult. Perhaps because of the climatic changes or a tendency to overhunting or both, a considerable number of large game animals became extinct during this period.[1] The bones of animals killed for food show that man came to rely on smaller animals and food extraction had to be intensified.[2] There seems little doubt that average population densities were higher at the end of the last glaciation than during previous interglacials. Many marginal areas, previously uninhabited, were permanently colonized. For some groups the situation would have become critical as the climatic changes lowered the carrying capacity for hunters and gatherers, whether or not population densities were effectively stabilized. The beginnings of agriculture are still a controversial subject; however it is worth noting that the debate centres on rival ecological explanations which fit broadly within the present framework. Certainly neither the emergence nor the spread of agriculture can be explained simply in terms of new ideas and discovery. Modern evidence suggests that hunters and gatherers cannot avoid knowing a great deal

[1] P. S. Martin, 'Prehistoric overkill', in P. S. Martin and H. E. Wright (eds.), *Pleistocene Extinctions: the Search for a Cause* (New Haven, 1967).

[2] R. J. Braidwood and B. Howe, 'Southwestern Asia beyond the lands of the Mediterranean Littoral', in R. J. Braidwood and G. R. Willey (eds.), *Courses Towards Urban Life: Archeological Considerations of Some Cultural Alternatives* (Edinburgh, 1962).

about plant life and propagation, and the cultivation of what then amounted to little more than wild grasses is by no means a lucky break; nor is 3–4,000 years the time it takes for an idea to spread from the Middle East to Western Europe.

The industrial revolution was initially a matter of substituting mineral resources for landbased ones as population pressure on agricultural production increased.[1] Through the substitution of resources (such as coal for firewood) and changes in techniques (the replacement of animal transport by steam trains for instance), agricultural land was freed for the more specialized production of human foodstuffs. Most of the obervable technical and economic changes which contribute to development are however the secondary repercussions of comparatively few basic ecological changes. This is especially true of the process of industrialization; we must now move on to discuss the relationship between basic ecological changes and their secondary repercussions.

Part of the problem of understanding the course of economic development is a problem of understanding the order in which societies choose to exploit different resources. When a society moves into disequilibrium on its traditional resource-base, what factors condition its choice of substitute resources? The answer is quite simple: societies adopt the new resources and methods which come most easily to hand in the context of their established cultural system. The most primitive subsistence strategies are those which come most easily to the relatively ill-equipped hand, and each new strategy in the course of development is the next most easy in the context of the tools and technology of the existing culture. Ignoring technical problems, the most primitive societies with the lowest population densities have the widest choice of resources – more resources are capable of providing them with adequate subsistence. They choose to use the things in their environment which already approximate most nearly to the consumable state. Resources and materials such as wild animals and plants for

[1] See E. A. Wrigley, 'The supply of raw materials in the Industrial Revolution', *Economic History Review*, XV (1962), pp. 1–16; see also chapter 6 below.

food, with skins, bones, stone-flake tools, sinews and leather thongs for other purposes, involve the minimum amount of work and processing to prepare them for use. It is important to remember that – at least in their context – such choices may well indicate an optimum ecological strategy. During the course of economic development man has been forced over and over again to change the resources he depended on and the methods he used to exploit them. Slowly he has had to involve himself in more and more complicated processing and production techniques as he has changed from the more easily exploitable resources to the less easily exploitable. The example used earlier of the development of clothing materials from skins, to natural fibres, to artificial fibres is a case in point. At each stage clothing materials are more abundant but obviously involve more processing and working up into the finished product. There are two major consequences of this pattern. The first is the need for more and increasingly sophisticated tools to undertake the processing – i.e. for more capital equipment as economic development proceeds; and the second is a tendency which one might expect to find for the productive system to demand increasing amounts of labour time and power to produce the basic *per capita* subsistence. Although the increase in the amount of capital equipment used is a phenomenon we are all familiar with, the suggestion that the workload is increasing conflicts with our commonsense understanding of events. Clearly the amount of work people do cannot increase indefinitely; it is restricted by the number of hours in a day if not by more rigorous physiological constraints. But it is precisely this dilemma – the increasing workload imposed by the productive system and the limitations on the amount of work that people can do – which has stimulated man to bring additional sources of power to his aid and to develop laboursaving machinery and equipment. Leslie White, the American anthropologist, has tried to develop a theory that cultural development is the *product* of the increasing quantities of power – or energy – which man has harnessed.[1] Originally man had to rely just on his own labour power. With the help of fire, animal power, wind and water

[1] Leslie A. White, *The Science of Culture* (New York, 1949).

power and finally, in the 'Fuel Age', with the help of coal, oil and gas, harnessed by steam and the internal combustion engine, cultures were able to grow and blossom 'in all the arts – industrial, esthetic and intellectual'.[1] But in the context of the ecological approach we can see that these additional sources of power were not fortuitous discoveries which allowed the culture to blossom into new richness and splendour: instead they were a necessary response to an increasingly difficult subsistence situation. The introduction of draught animals which has already been mentioned provides a ready example. As the rate of environmental exploitation was increased during agricultural development, ploughing became a necessary part of the basic subsistence activity. The enormously increased amount of work involved and the need for greater physical power made it necessary to bring animal power to man's aid. Mechanical power was first introduced to facilitate the development of mining and bulk transport – both of which were stimulated by ecological factors. It is not difficult to see the potential which this framework has for explaining the application of increasing quantities of power to the productive process both before and after industrialization. However, this chapter is intended primarily to trace in the internal consistency of the ecological approach rather than try to substantiate it against the facts – that is the task of chapters 6 and 8 on English and American industrialization.

At this point it may be helpful to summarize – with the help of the diagram on p. 104 – the sequence of adaptive responses to ecological problems. The ecological disequilibrium which ushers in a resource scarcity may be dealt with in two different ways, or by a combination of both of them. The scarcity may cause a breakdown in local self-sufficiency and so lead to an attempt to fill the gap by importing materials. This would usually have to be supported by specialized production for export. Some examples of this response were included in the last chapter. The other form of response is to introduce new substitute resources or to develop ways of exploiting the scarce resource more intensively. In either case the result is likely to be

[1] Ibid., p. 372.

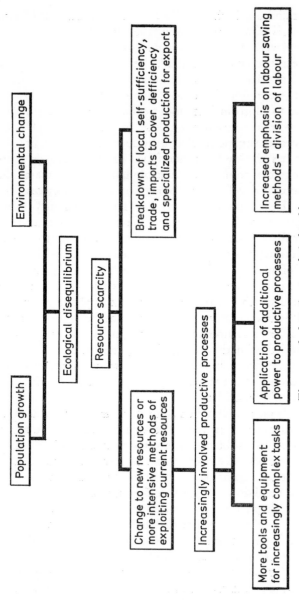

The course of adaptation to ecological problems

that the productive process becomes more complicated and difficult. If this was not so then the new resources and methods would have been used earlier – in preference to their predecessors. Man's historical shift from naturally occurring animal and plant resources, to agricultural resources, and then to mineral resources for more and more of his non-food requirements has clearly imposed increasing demands on the productive system. The problem of the increasing *complexity* of the tasks which the productive system has to perform has necessitated the dramatic development of new tools and productive equipment, while the increasing *workload* has only been absorbed by harnessing additional sources of power and by adopting laboursaving techniques including a greater division of labour. We can see here that the basic features of economic development are deducible from the assumptions underlying the ecological approach. As population grows and man is forced to exploit the environment more intensively, we have reasons to think that the productive system would have to develop to include trade, a greater division of labour, increasing quantities of capital equipment and additional sources of power. The empirical studies of development in chapters 6 and 8 will serve to show whether these features are in fact the product of the ecological forces suggested here.

Looking at economic development in its ecological setting effectively removes the idea of progress from the central position it has occupied in our view of the process. Instead of regarding development as a matter of 'progress' towards a 'better life' motivated by an incurable dissatisfaction with our present lot, we see that it is a process of solving a succession of problems which from time to time threaten the productive system and the sufficiency of our subsistence. In effect, human societies out of ecological equilibrium have to run to keep up; their development does not necessarily imply any longterm improvement in the quality of human life. This is not to say that technological change is incapable of yielding a net improvement. The negative effects of the changes in resources or methods which are forced on the productive system may be more than offset by the technical innovations designed to deal with them. But basically changes which are intended primarily to increase efficiency or the quality of human life are not the same as those associated with attempts to increase the level of environmental exploitation. All the evidence suggests that economic development is made up of elements belonging to the latter group of changes, and that efforts to increase efficiency take place in the context of the existing ecological survival strategy. The achievement of a basic survival strategy for a society of a given size of course takes precedence over matters of relative efficiency. Societies may be extremely interested in methods which will increase the efficiency of their basic mode of life, but yet show very little interest in the changes which we associate with economic development. The Siane, mentioned in the last chapter, are a case in point. They were very keen to have steel axes to replace their stone ones if they could get hold of them cheaply.[1] Steel axes reduced the labour required for subsistence activities considerably, but there was no land shortage and so no movement to introduce fundamental changes in their mode of life. There are numerous examples of societies which are keen to find improvements to their traditional way of life while resenting the pressures towards industrialization. During the course of economic development it seems likely that, with the intervention of technology, the level of economic efficiency may be regarded as subject to almost random variations. The amount of labour needed to gain a culturally determined level of subsistence may be permitted to rise until it approaches an upper limit beyond which further increases become intolerable. When this point is reached variations will tend to be quite small random upward or downward movements about the norm: ecological pressures will tend to add to the difficulties of production while any additions to working hours become progressively more intolerable. The task which the productive technology has to perform in resolving this dilemma therefore becomes increasingly rigorously defined. If the ecological situation continues to force changes which tend to increase the workload, then, in societies

[1] R. F. Salisbury, *From Stone to Steel* (Melbourne, 1962).

which already have full employment and a high *per capita* workload such as the advanced West, it becomes essential that technology should be designed to increase efficiency to save labour. The adequacy of subsistence would be threatened if it were not. We see then that in the special case where the supply of labour has become a limiting factor in the provision of subsistence that increases in efficiency will be a necessary condition of supporting a still larger population. Increases in efficiency in one area may just offset decreases elsewhere, with the overall level remaining unchanged.

So far we have only considered the human implications of development in terms of the changing workload – the quantity which fits most easily into the economist's concept of efficiency. But economic and technical changes have other implications with an important influence on people's willingness to accept them. In many societies people show a great reluctance to leave the land to become members of an industrial labour force. As E. H. Phelps Brown said,

> those who can stay on the land have seldom been willing, short of starvation, to leave it for employment as wage earners: the poorest peasants have been reluctant to commit themselves to work in the factory even though they can earn more there, and in Africa and Asia many of them still limit their commitment to a term of years. Wage earners who can get hold of land quit their employments – that was the experience of the colonists in America and Australia.[1]

Several of the examples of change in the last chapter showed the same reluctance to leave the land until forced by land shortage and economic necessity. Phelps Brown attributes the dislike of wage labour to a desire to preserve one's freedom and independence, but whatever its cause it is clear that it indicates a sacrifice people make to economic development. Some other implications of economic development are harder to identify. When dealing with subjective intangibles it is difficult to distinguish between reality and romanticism. However, it is better to make bad guesses than to ignore important issues. To mention a few

[1] E. H. Phelps Brown, *The Economics of Labour* (New Haven, 1962), p. 10.

of the most important possibilities: it seems likely that the division of labour carried to the extent which it is in industrial societies represents a reduction in the quality of life. As each person's work becomes highly specialized it is likely that it also lacks variation, becomes more repetitive and dull. Equally important is that it divides one person's experience from another's and acts to make people more isolated from each other. Each person's life activity covers a smaller part of the cultural totality; their views of, and indentification with, the whole society's social and productive activity is diminished and fragmented. Another feature of productive activity in developed nations is the alienation of people from the social purposes of their work. This seems to be partly the result of the division of labour, partly of people's exclusion from control of their work, and partly because in a market economy the market exchange value of the product, rather than its social utility, is seen as the purpose of productive activity. Interconnected with these issues, but perhaps most closely related to urbanization, is the break-up of small communities and 'face to face' societies. This is probably one of the most serious losses associated with industrialization. To the extent to which these factors are necessary features of economic development, they are as important as variations in the amount of work people have to do to our understanding of the choices societies make in the developmental process. If, instead of using the narrowly defined concept of economic efficiency, we examine the total impact of economic changes on society and individuals – not just variations in working hours but in these subjective matters as well – then we will get a better idea of what makes people hesitant to accept changes which would seem to bring with them the advantages of increased production. We can understand why people have shunned wage labour, the division of labour, factory work and urban society, in spite of the increased rewards, until their subsistence situation has forced them to value the increased material return more highly.

As man increases the rate of environmental exploitation he will frequently have to live with a productive system which imposes an increasing number of constraints on his life. But even if we do not accept that the quantitative material increases underlying economic development are necessarily accompanied by a qualitative deterioration in the conditions of human life, there is no reason to think that development is – of necessity – accompanied by any marked improvement. One of the advantages of reinterpreting economic development so that it is no longer synonymous with progress and improvement is that we no longer need to invoke ignorance as the explanation of the persistence of primitive modes of production in some societies. One's conceptual framework is freed from the need for such paternalistic attitudes.

The most basic change which underlies all others mentioned in this chapter is the concept of changing from one ecological niche to another, of substituting one resource-base for another. However, in addition to the implications of the changing resource base which we have discussed, resources clearly have an intimate link both with the prevailing technology and with the class structure.

The technology is designed to exploit the particular resources which the society uses. It must be able to extract them, manipulate them and turn them into the consumable objects which man needs. But in a self-sufficient society, the technology must also be produced from materials which that same technology can manipulate. The resources may almost be said to determine the technology. The 'organic' links between materials and technology are fundamental to understanding the detailed process of technical innovation: when the resource-base changes, so must the technology. Some of these links will be discussed in chapter 7.

Class divisions are linked to the resource-base because the ruling class derives its power and influence initially from its control of the scarce resources which a society depends on. In a peasant agricultural society the ruling class is the landowning aristocracy, but as the society grows out of that ecological niche and industries which process minerals and other resources become more important, a new ruling class emerges based on the ownership of the new resources and means of processing them. Power stems inevitably from control of people's access to their means of livelihood. In primitive societies where resources are not sufficiently scarce to control people's access to them effectively, widespread inequality lacks an important prop. In societies of hunters and gatherers or shifting agriculturalists, people always have the possibility of breaking away from the main community and setting up an independent group. Chiefs must gain their authority from other more complicated social sources; kinship systems and control of access to women are obviously among the factors which play an important role. It has been suggested that power structures in some African societies with relatively plentiful resources are based on control of the means of destruction rather than the means of production.[1] The bow and arrow is a democratic weapon because anyone can make themselves one; but weapons which can be monopolized may be used to maintain positions of authority.

Competition for subsistence resources obviously grows as the resources become scarcer. Communal arrangements are likely to break down in primitive societies, common land starts to disappear in peasant societies, and disputes over ownership and use become more frequent and intensified everywhere. Inequality is likely to increase as some members of a society are denied direct access to land altogether. These people become dependent on those who have land, thus giving those fortunate enough to be in the latter group new opportunities to strengthen their position – relatively and absolutely. These factors were obviously influential in the English enclosure movements.

The relationship between tightening class control and scarce resources throws a new light on the apparent wealth of the 'great' civilizations of the past. The splendour of their monuments and creations is more a reflection of the extent of class control over people's labour than of basic wealth. The societies which really were well off in terms of subsistence resources were unlikely to give rise to this type of production unless exploitation was maintained in some other way. But because of

[1] Jack Goody, *Technology, Tradition, and the State in Africa* (London, 1971), chapter 3.

the greater difficulty of maintaining class control where resources are plentiful, there is a tendency for the richness of a society's creations to be inversely correlated with its basic wealth.

Throughout this chapter – and indeed the rest of the book – relatively little attention has been paid to the possibilities of migration and importing as a response to scarce resources. The desire to explain development in the societies where it has taken place has meant that responses which tend to stave off the need for development have not been discussed as fully as if our aim was an exhaustive investigation of responses to the ecological problem. Failure to overcome ecological problems which implies a longterm toleration of serious and widespread poverty, as well as the amelioration of shortages through migration and imported materials, are fairly obvious factors which must be borne in mind throughout the analysis of development.

6 *The English industrial revolution*

Poverte is hateful good, and, as I gesse,
A ful greet bryngere out of bisynesse.
                    Chaucer, *The Wife of Bath's Tale*

The ecological roots of the English industrial revolution are not difficult to find. The initial stimulus to change came directly from resource shortages and other ecological effects of an economic system expanding to meet the needs of a population growing within a limited area. As the traditional resources became scarce new ones were substituted which usually involved more processing, used more productive labour and frequently resulted in what was regarded as an inferior product. As these initial changes made themselves felt in the economic system the pre-existing technical consistency was disturbed and various secondary changes set in motion.

The ecological background to the industrial revolution was an acute land shortage. In the centuries before industrialization the English population was dependent on the land for almost all its materials. The supply of food and drink depended on agricultural land, clothing came from the wool of sheep on English pasture, and large areas of land were needed for extensive forests: almost all domestic and industrial fuel was firewood, and timber was one of the most important construction materials for houses, ships, mills, farm implements etc. In addition, the transport system depended on horses and thus required large areas of land to be devoted to grazing and the production of feed. Even lighting used tallow candles which depended ultimately on the land supply. Land was bound to become in increasingly short supply as population increased.

We have already seen signs of the growing scarcity of agricultural land during the population rise of the sixteenth and
early seventeenth centuries.[1] The remaining areas of cultivable
waste had been brought under the plough and much marginal
land had been improved and reclaimed. Disputes over land-
use had become increasingly frequent and in many areas
villagers' rights to keep animals on the commons had had to
be subject to rigorous stints to preserve the grazing. The
growth of towns, trade and industry during the sixteenth and
early seventeenth centuries are futher signs of the pressure on
the land and the need to find additional sources of income as
traditional subsistence methods proved inadequate.

The relative stability of population from before the middle
of the seventeenth century to the mid-eighteenth century temporarily eased the pressure on the land. For a time prices ceased
to rise and real wages ceased their decline.[2] But when population started to increase again in the middle of the eighteenth
century, the pressure on the land was renewed and the adverse
movements in prices and real wages continued. It was – significantly – during the 1760s, at the beginning of the industrial
revolution, that Britain changed so dramatically from being a
net exporter of wheat to a net importer. (See the table on p.
114.)

The pressure which a land shortage puts on the agricultural
sector to increase the output per acre has already been discussed, as have some aspects of industrial development: we
have seen how new manufacturing activities may be taken up
as a way of supplementing incomes. In England however, the
industrial revolution was initially not so much a matter of
setting up new industries as of thorough-going technical innovation in established industries. The stimulus here came from
the limitations which the land shortage imposed on the supply
of industrial raw materials. As landbased resources became
scarce it became increasingly urgent to find substitutes for
them. The substitution of coal for wood is the most important
case.

[1] See chapter 4 above.   [2] See graphs *a*, *b*, and *c* on p. 71 above.

Trade in wheat and wheaten flour of Great Britain

Thousands of quarters

	Imports	Exports	Net
1700–4		434	−434
1705–9	2	614	−612
1710–14		608	−608
1715–19		480	−480
1720–4		751	−751
1725–9	115	409	−294
1730–4		1355	−1355
1735–9		1612	−1612
1740–4	13	1005	−992
1745–9		1902	−1902
1750–4		2701	−2701
1755–9	162	589	−427
1760–4		1958	−1958
1765–9	967	394	573
1770–4	374	116	258
1775–9	926	753	173
1780–4	1046	613	433
1785–9	483	682	−199
1790–4	1532	634	898
1795–9	2515	198	2317

Source: B. R. Mitchell and Phyllis Deane, *Abstract of British Historical Statistics* (Cambridge, 1962), p. 94.

English price indices (1451–1500 = 100)

	General	Firewood
1501–10	95	100
1511–20	101	106
1521–30	113	97
1531–40	118	106
1541–50	151	180
1551–60	215	265
1561–70	233	332
1571–82	257	327
1583–92	297	416
1593–1602	367	451
1603–12	389	567
1613–22	398	708
1623–32	437	1049
1633–42	451	1208
1643–52	513	759
1653–62	477	1026
1663–72	502	894
1673–82	539	1052
1683–92	494	1058
1693–1702	525	1058

Source: Figures reworked from Georg Wiebe, *Zur Geschichte de Preisrevolution des 16 und 17 Jahrhunderts* (Leipzig, 1895), pp. 375–6.

The shortage of firewood and timber for construction – the 'timber famine' – became acute during the population rise of the sixteenth and early seventeenth centuries. Wiebe's indices of the general price level and of prices of firewood are reproduced above. Although these figures are probably not always representative, they do indicate the general trend in price rises from the early sixteenth century to shortly before the middle of the seventeenth century. The index of firewood prices rises during the same period but much faster. By the 1630s wood had become about two and a half times as expensive in relation to other prices as it had been in the late fifteenth and early sixteenth century.

The quantities of timber imported grew but could do little to bring the price down. The 'timber famine' was a result of purely ecological forces. Population growth and the consequent extension of the economic system led to the conversion of woodland into arable land and a simultaneous expansion in the demand for wood. The growing scarcity placed both industrial and domestic consumers in serious difficulties. Attempts to conserve forests – and particularly supplies of timber for the navy – by legislation were frequent. So also were the comments of contemporaries. In 1631 Edmund Howes wrote

> within man's memory, it was held impossible to have any want of wood in England. But . . . such hath been the great expence of timber for navigation, with infinite increase of building houses, with great expence of wood to make household furniture, casks, and other vessels not to be numbered, and of carts, wagons and coaches, besides the extreme waste of wood in making iron, burning of bricks and tiles, that at this present, through the great consuming of wood as aforesaid, and the neglect of planting of woods, there is so great a scarcity of wood throughout the whole kingdom that not only the City of London, all haven-towns and in very many parts within the land, the inhabitants in general are constrained to make their fires of sea-coal or pit-coal, even in the chambers of honourable personages, and through necessity which is the mother of all arts, they have late years devised the making of iron, the making of all sorts of glass and burning of bricks with sea-coal or pit-coal.[1]

[1] Edmund Howes (ed.), Stow's *Annals* (London, 1631), p. 1025 (as quoted in W. H. G. Armytage, *A Social History of Engineering* (London, 1961)). The reference to the use of coal in making iron is probably a reference to the technique invented in 1614 for using coal to convert brittle cast iron into malleable bar iron, unless it is based on one of the many unsuccessful seventeenth-century experiments in smelting iron with coal.

This is just one example of the ecological pressures to substitute one raw material for another which lie behind the process of technological innovation throughout the industrial revolution. But before going on to other examples we must look at the implications of the substitution of coal for wood in more detail.

For many purposes coal could be substituted for firewood without serious technical problems. Where this was true the changeover happened quite quickly, either during the price rise or soon afterwards. Smiths and lime-burners had used coal from very early on and by the mid-seventeenth century it was also used in salt-boiling, dyeing, brewing and soap-boiling as well as in the preparation of alum, copperas, saltpetre and tallow candles.[1] Where substances were kept separate from the fuel in a vat or cauldron of some kind, it was quite easy to substitute a coal for a wood fire, but in processes such as metal-smelting, where the fuel was in contact with the raw material, or in drying processes where things were hung in the fumes above the fire, the fuel could have important chemical and other effects on the product. Bakers had to change the design of their ovens to avoid contaminating their bread with the fumes from the coal, brickmakers had to experiment with different kinds of coal till they found the less gaseous ones which did not fuse the bricks together, glassmakers used covered pots and the maltsters developed the use of coke to avoid the smoky gasses and tars given off by the raw coal. The reverberatory furnace, which threw the heat downwards over the metal, was introduced to allow lead and copper to be smelted with coal.

The only important industry which had not changed over to coal firing by the end of the seventeenth century was of course iron-smelting. All experiments in smelting with coal had proved unsuccessful and the output of the English iron industry was probably stationary or declining during the second half of the seventeenth century and the early eighteenth as a result. The growing demand had to be met by importing

[1] The best account of the substitution of coal for firewood is in J. U. Nef, *The Rise of the British Coal Industry* (London, 1932), volume 1.

iron mainly from Sweden. It was not until Abraham Derby borrowed the solution to the maltsters' and brewers' problems and used coke for iron-smelting at the end of the first decade of the eighteenth century that the iron industry could slowly begin to free itself from the constraints of inadequate supplies of raw materials.

Several points about the changeover from wood- to coal-burning should be emphasized. The innovations involved could not have appeared equally well at any other point in English history. They were a response to the particular problem of inadequate fuel supplies, and yielded improvements for a society facing that problem: the same innovations would not necessarily be beneficial to a society with a plentiful supply of wood. The main period of innovation and change could only have been the seventeenth century. The exact timing of specific innovations seems to have depended on the complexity of the problem – the tougher nuts took longer to crack. (Iron-smelting was a later innovation because it was complicated by the chemical interactions between the new fuel and trace elements which occurred in some of the ores.)

The shortage of firewood should not be seen merely as a stimulus to overcoming a kind of irrational technical inertia. The use of wood instead of coal in the preceding centuries represented a rational choice in a situation where wood was plentiful. If wood is available locally it is obviously much easier to use wood than coal. Using coal means paying very high transport costs or accepting severe limitations on loca-tion. Not only transport, but also differences in production and use suggest that wood may be the better choice. As soon as open-cast coal reserves have been used, deep mines have to be sunk making coal production considerably more difficult than felling trees for firewood. Although for some purposes wood had to be processed before use to turn it into charcoal, coal had to be put through a preliminary operation to turn it into coke for these industries as well as for others in which raw wood had previously been adequate. Harmful constituents of coal also posed problems for domestic consumers. The spread of coal as a domestic fuel during the late sixteenth and

E

early seventeenth centuries was paralleled by the spread of
chimneys as the smoke forced people to abandon the traditional
custom of having fires in the centre of the room with a hole
in the roof.[1] Significantly, legislation to control air pollution
from coal fires in towns has a long history. Wood fires were
preferred to coal fires as they still are, and the rich were able
to delay using coal longer than the poor. Likewise contemporary prejudices against cooking over coal fires could be
sustained longer by the rich than the poor.

As the demand for coal increased and production expanded to
meet it, open-cast coal deposits were soon used up and mines
had to be sunk deeper and deeper. The invention of the steam-
engine was a direct result of the new technical problems posed
by deep mines. In terms of the theoretical model used here, the
steam-engine was a response to the disturbance in the established technical consistency caused by an initial change in the
society's resource-base. The difficulties of ventilating the mines
and lifting the hewn coal up the shaft increased as workings
got deeper during the seventeenth century, but it was the
problem of drainage which led to the development of the
steam-engine. Clearly if a shaft is sunk below the level of the
water table it tends to fill with water. Mines on hillsides could
sometimes be drained by digging a special drainage shaft from
the bottom of the pit outwards to a point lower on the hillside
for the water to run out. In other areas it was possible to mine
close enough to a stream to have a waterpowered rag-and-
chain or bucket pump. Where water power was impossible a
horse-whim was used to drive the pumps. These systems were
all efficient enough while workings were fairly shallow, but
before the end of the seventeenth century depths up to 200 feet
were common in all fields and some reached nearer 400 feet.[2]
Numbers of Cornish copper mines had already been abandoned because of flooding, and now coal mines had also
reached depths at which existing methods of drainage became
impracticable. The method using a special drainage shaft was

[1] *The Rise of the British Coal Industry*, volume 1, p. 199.
[2] Ibid., volume 1, pp. 350–3.

obviously only practical while workings were still higher than the adjacent valley floor; beyond that depth pumping became necessary. On long lifts the rag-and-chain and bucket pumps ran into difficulties because too much of the available energy was used up in the mechanics of the pumping gear itself. The energy available from a mill wheel or a horse-whim may have been enough to lift an appreciable amount of water with fairly light equipment, but with the friction of the massive equipment needed for a long lift (the numbers of stuffed balls in a long rag-and-chain pump rubbing on the inside of the pipe, the greater weight of the longer chain as well as the friction of the clumsy wooden winding gear), little energy was left for lifting water after so much had been expended just on setting the equipment in motion. It became impractical to use these pumps on longer lifts. True, more power could be applied to a horse-whim by using more animals, but the equipment would have to be made correspondingly more massive and the inefficiency would still be very great. When long lifts were necessary it was more common to divide them into stages, building special chambers to operate pumps lower down.

Attempts to pump water from mines 'by fire' date back to 1631. Steam power was introduced not because it was potentially more powerful than a horse or a mill wheel, but because the power was delivered in a more appropriate form. The easiest and most direct application of steam power to pumping was to reduce the pressure above the column of water to be raised or to increase the pressure below it. The first practical steam pump – Thomas Savery's 'Miner's Friend' patented in 1698 – had no moving parts except for its valves. Steam from the boiler was piped into an oval-shaped container full of water, forcing the water up the outflow pipe. When the container was full of steam it was condensed with the help of cold water on the outside, and, with valves to prevent the return of the water just pumped out, the partial vacuum caused more water to flow in from a lower level. Two containers operated in this way alternately. It was the directness with which the expansion and contraction of steam could be applied to pumping that led to its introduction: it obviated the need for all the heavy mechanical equipment which on other pumps used for long lifts had wasted such a disproportionate amount of the available energy.

The potential application of steam power was not limited by the constraints on the supply of resources which limited other sources of power. The use of water power was limited by the number of streams with suitable sites for mills: new sites became scarce in many parts of the country during the seventeenth century. Animal power was dependent on the supply of land which could be devoted to growing fodder. As land became increasingly scarce, the relative cost of using animal power rose. In contrast, coal to fuel the steam engine was plentiful – especially at the pit head. The spread of steam power was ecologically favoured.

The design of pumping engines was of course modified. The steam no longer acted directly on the water, but operated a piston in a cylinder which was linked by a pivoted beam to drive another piston which did the pumping. Although this development reintroduced moving parts, it allowed heat to be converted more efficiently into work by separating the hot steam from the cold water which tended to condense it.

While enough sites were available, water wheels remained the easiest and most economical way of obtaining a rotary motion for powering mills. The use of the steam-engine was confined to a reciprocating pumping motion for almost a century. It was not until the late eighteenth century, when the new cotton mills began to add to the demand for rotary power and good mill sites were no longer available, that Boulton and Watt made the first steam-engine harnessed to produce a rotary motion. Before that time rotary steam power had not been an economic proposition. The problem of how to convert a reciprocating motion into a rotary one was not – as so often stated – a theoretical one: the crank had been known and used in other contexts since before the spinning wheel or treadle lathe. It is true that Boulton and Watt had to change their design because of a patent on this application of the crank, but the problem was quickly overcome by Watt's design for an alternative linkage.[1] Rotary steam power appeared as late as it did not because of the difficulties of invention, but because it was not needed earlier.

The initial introduction of steam power was then a response to new problems consequent on the growing use of coal. Its advantage lay in the fact that its power was delivered in a form which made it particularly suitable for pumping. If a mill wheel or a horse could be used to create pressure differences as easily, the steam-engine would not have been introduced when it was. The substitution at a later date of steam power for the rotary power of mills and horse-whims was a response to a growth in demand for rotary power at a time when the supply from traditional sources was relatively fixed. At neither stage was steam introduced to perform traditional tasks in preference to traditional methods. It was essentially part of an attempt to keep abreast of the growing difficulties of production encountered by an expanding society.

The development of transport was one of the central features of the English industrial revolution. As local populations ceased to be self-sufficient in the goods and commodities they had formerly produced themselves, they were forced to enter into increasingly important trading relationships. The expanding volume of trade put considerable strain on the established transport system. The growth of wheeled transport to carry this trade had imposed an increasing burden on the nation's roads, in particular on their surfaces. Packhorses, which had predominated before the widespread use of wheeled transport, do not rut the roads in the way that carts and wagons do, nor are they so hampered by uneven surfaces. Ruts are always a problem when wheeled transport uses unsurfaced roads and by the eighteenth century the situation had reached crisis proportions. An increasing volume of traffic was having to travel over roads reduced to worse conditions than ever before. Many roads became almost impassable because of the mud, and reports of coaches losing wheels or being overturned were

[1] Samuel Smiles, *Lives of the Engineers: Boulton and Watt* (London, 1904), pp. 260–2.

frequent. Arthur Young complained of 'barbarous' and 'execrable' conditions wherever he travelled, and described 'rocky lanes full of hugeous stones as big as one's horse, and abominable holes'. On one road he claims he passed three broken-down carts and measured ruts 4 feet deep 'floating with mud'.[1] Frequent attempts were made to protect road surfaces by legislation controlling maximum loads and minimum widths of wheel rims over which the load was to be spread.[2] But a more effective response to the problem came in the form of the turnpike trusts which appeared early in the eighteenth century and spread particularly rapidly from the mid-century onwards. With the creation of an institutional framework to pay for upkeep, the way was open for the surfacing innovations of Telford and McAdam later in the century.

The road surfacing problem was not the only difficulty that stimulated change in a transport system trying to serve an expanding society facing limited resources. Because coal supplies had – to use Wrigley's words – a 'scattered punctiform distribution' in contrast to the 'areal' distribution of wood, the growing use of coal created a demand for a national transport network capable of handling heavy bulk commodities.[3] The expanding trade in other bulk commodities – such as grain and metals – added to the demand for a bulk carrier, especially for supplying urban centres. Initially more rivers were made navigable and coastal shipping increased, but in 1757 and 1764 the first two canals were opened, one to link a Lancashire coalfield with the Mersey, and the other to link a neighbouring coalfield to Manchester. By the early nineteenth century the country had enough canals to provide a primary distribution network for bulk commodities.

Canals were of course an enormous improvement on wagons and packhorses for carrying commodities such as coal, but had

---

[1] As quoted in Samuel Smiles, *Lives of the Engineers: Metcalf and Telford* (London, 1904), pp. 80–2.

[2] W. T. Jackman, *The Development of Transportation in Modern England* (Cambridge, 1916), chapter 4.

[3] E. A. Wrigley, 'The supply of raw materials in the Industrial Revolution', *Economic History Review*, XV (1962), pp. 1–16.

they been built before it was necessary to transport these commodities they might well have proved unprofitable: indeed, canals built in the relatively unchanged rural areas did tend to be unprofitable. The basic rationale for these huge new works was the impossibility of maintaining an adequate standard of living for a growing eighteenth-century population within an economic framework of local self-sufficiency.

The other element in the ecological equation which affected the transport system was the all-pervasive land shortage. The cost of road transport used to vary with the price of horse feed.[1] Announcements in local papers such as the following were not uncommon:

> We the undersigned Magistrates acting for the West Riding of the County of York, have been applied to by the Carriers in the said Riding to make further Advance, upon Land Carriage, on Account of the very High Price of Hay and Corn, and it being our opinion that an Advance is reasonable and proper do hereby signify our Approbation ... to an ADVANCE of THREE-HALF PENCE per STONE on LAND CARRIAGE ... and do strongly recommend it to all persons to allow the same ...[2]

Estimates suggest that between four and eight acres of land under hay were needed to feed each horse.[3] Clearly as land became increasingly scarce and horse feed expensive, the incentive to economize on horses by building canals or using some other form of traction would also increase. Contemporaries were well aware of these benefits of canals and railways. An engineer writing in about 1800 on the proposed Grand Surrey Canal Navigation calculated that 'as one horse on an average consumes the produce of four acres of land, and there are 1,350,000 in this island that pay the horse-tax, of course there must be 5,400,000 acres of land occupied in providing provender for them. How desirable' – he remarks – 'any im-

---

[1] William I. Albert, *The Turnpike Road System in England 1663–1840* (Cambridge, 1972), chapter 8.

[2] *Leeds Intelligencer*, 20 January 1800, p. 3. As quoted by Albert, op. cit.

[3] Jackman, op. cit., p. 405.

provement that will lessen the keep of horses. . . .'[1] The Earl of Hardwick writing in favour of the Cambridge and London Junction Canal used a similar argument: 'If the canal should be the means of releasing 1000 horses from . . . employment, . . . 8000 acres of land . . . might be applied to more useful purposes, which would help to keep the labouring poor from suffering from want of bread.'[2]

The competition for food between people and horses could not be ignored, particularly during the Napoleonic Wars when restrictions on imports caused grain prices to rise to record levels. Undoubtedly one of the most important reasons for the commercial success of the canals was the high price of horse feed. Only when competition for land had forced the price of horse feed sufficiently high was it worth expending labour on the construction of canals which allowed larger loads to be drawn by fewer horses. The wartime prices must have added considerably to the 'mania' for canal promotions just before the turn of the century, and have led to the execution of many schemes which proved improvident when prices fell. Although the rapid expansion in the demand for transport did not permit a reduction in the overall number of horses in the country, more horses would have been needed had it not been for the canals.

Steam railways provided another way of substituting capital equipment – or indirect labour – for horses in the transport system. A report to the House of Commons on 'steam carriages' in 1833 contains the following calculation:

It has been said that in Great Britain there are above a million of horses engaged in various ways in the transport of passengers and goods, and that to support each horse requires as much land as would upon an average support eight men. If this quantity of animal power were displaced by steam-engines, and the means of transport drawn from the bowels of the earth, instead of being raised upon its surface, then, supposing the above calculation correct, as much land would become available for the support of human

[1] As quoted, *The Development of Transportation in Modern England*, p. 406n.
[2] Ibid.

beings as would suffice for an additional population of eight millions; ... The land which now supports horses for transport on turnpike roads would then support men, or produce corn for food, and the horses return to agricultural pursuits.[1]

Like the substitution of coal for firewood, the substitution of the steam locomotive for horses in the transport system represents a response to changes in relative prices caused by the land shortage. As land becomes increasingly scarce it is almost inevitable that at some point it will become worthwhile to manufacture a machine using a mineral fuel to replace horses using agricultural land. Again, the particularly high price of feed during the Napoleonic Wars made even the earliest and most inefficient locomotives economically viable in some situations. Rolt says it was these prices which 'forced (two Tyneside colliery owners) to consider more seriously the claims of an iron horse using fuel which they produced themselves'.[2] This is a particularly clear example of the way resource shortages can force a society to adopt more complicated productive procedures which may – at least initially – require additional work.

The steam locomotive and the railway track on which it runs are of course two separate innovations. The track is another response to the surfacing problem. In a number of collieries and other places where heavy goods had to be moved, rails and plateways were laid for horsedrawn trucks long before the introduction of steam locomotion. It was the weight of the engine with its cast-iron boiler that was responsible for the link between steam locomotion and the railway track.

Although both canals and steam railways yielded enormous economies in the use of horses, the numbers in the country were not reduced until the introduction of the bicycle and the

[1] N. W. Cundy, *Inland Transit*, Report of a Select Committee of the House of Commons on Steam Carriages, 2nd ed. (London, 1834), pp. 20–1.
[2] L. T. C. Rolt, *George and Robert Stephenson* (London, 1960), pp. 43–4.

car. The horse remained the most suitable form of personal short distance transport until the late nineteenth and early twentieth century. Only then was the economic climate right for the surrender of the obvious readymade advantages of the horse in favour of manufactured substitutes.

Once again it appears that a formidable group of innovations should not be regarded as the fruits of a society's search for progress, but as the outcome of a valiant struggle of a society with its back to the ecological wall. The development of transport during this period was a response to the development of the problems caused by two secular trends: the breakdown of local self-sufficiency, particularly in heavy commodities such as fuel and grain, and the growing pressure to economize on the use of agricultural land. As these problems became increasingly severe the society was forced to adopt solutions it would not otherwise have done. The problems became most acute – and the pace of innovation fastest – during the population growth and price rises of the second half of the eighteenth century and the first decade or so of the nineteenth; after that the measures adopted had begun to alleviate the situation.

An industry which underwent changes linked ultimately with the shortage of timber and the development of transport already discussed was the building industry. Until coal replaced firewood as the fuel for brick kilns in the seventeenth century, more wood was used to build a house in brick than to build it in timber.[1] Apart from a few exceptional areas, brick building before the seventeenth century was a departure from local styles which only the rich could afford – and few of them preferred it to stone. In some areas buildings used timber frames with in-filling of wattle and daub, clay or stone; in others they were made of local stone throughout. With the introduction of coal firing, brick production could be expanded without any increase in unit costs. After the Great Fire of 1666, legislation

[1] Nef, op. cit., volume 1, p. 196. For the consumption of coal and breeze in brickmaking see Edward Dobson, *A Rudimentary Treatise on the Manufacture of Bricks and Tiles* (London, 1850), part 1, pp. 91, 101; part 11, pp. 44, 96.

to guard against a repetition of the disaster, backed by changed economic conditions, secured the rebuilding of London in brick. As it became easier to transport coal to the brick kilns the relative advantages of building in brick increased. Timber houses ceased to be built and by the second half of the eighteenth century building in brick was general in many areas. Brickwork was usually regarded as inferior to stone and in the early nineteenth century it became fashionable – under Nash and others – to cover it over with stucco marked out to look like rectangular stone blocks. Not only did building with coal-fired bricks obviate the need for a timber framework, but the wooden lintels over windows and doors were replaced by the arched row of bricks arranged vertically which can be seen in cheaper housing from the nineteenth century onwards. On larger buildings, where longer spans were needed, this method was unsuitable and iron girders became increasingly common, Whole iron frames, particularly for industrial buildings, were used from quite early on in the nineteenth century. Concrete was introduced in the same period though reinforced concrete did not appear until towards the end of the century.

This process of substitution of materials followed the familiar pattern: scarcity drove it on in some areas while preferences or the availability of the older materials in others tended to hold it back. Clay was more easily obtained than quarried stone, particularly around many urban areas, but where stone could still be quarried easily people went on using it. Coal was more plentiful than firewood, and iron and concrete more plentiful than timber. With the introduction of artificial materials – including artificial stone in the later eighteenth century – supplied from extra-local sources, the complexity of the productive system and the demand for labour and transport were further increased.

The growth of the cotton industry, one of the dominant features of the industrial revolution in England, is a particularly good example of the process of materials substitution. The traditional clothing material was wool supplemented to some extent by linen and leather. The division of agricultural land between sheep pasture and arable land had long been a matter of contention. Conversion of arable to pasture had brought outcries against 'sheep (which) devour men' and had been a central issue in the earlier enclosure movement. The export of considerable quantities of woollen cloth no doubt made the crisis develop sooner than it would have done otherwise. Although cotton was – like wool – a landbased resource, the fact that it depended on the exploitation of land in India and America rather than in England meant that it could provide a way out of the domestic impasse. The manufacture of clothing could be expanded without threatening the production of food.

No longer having to pay woollen cloth prices inflated by the scarcity of land, the poorer domestic consumers substituted inferior – but cheaper – cotton cloth wherever possible. Describing the clothing of the working-class shortly before the middle of the nineteenth century Engels said:

> Linen and wool have practically disappeared from the wardrobes of both men and women, and have been replaced by cotton. Men's shirts are made of bleached or coloured cotton cloth. Women generally wear printed cottons; woollen petticoats are seldom seen on the washing-line. Men's trousers are generally made either of fustian or some other heavy cotton cloth. Overcoats and jackets are made from the same material. Fustian has become the traditional dress of working men, who are called 'fustian jackets'. Gentlemen, on the other hand, wear suits made from woollen cloth, and the term 'broadcloth' is used to designate the middle classes. . . . The working classes . . . very seldom wear woollen clothing of any kind. Their heavy cotton clothes, though thicker, stiffer and heavier than woollen cloth, do not keep out the cold and wet to anything like the same extent as woollens.[1]

This quotation shows not only the extent to which cotton was substituted for wool, but shows also a repetition of the pattern

[1] F. Engels, *The Condition of the Working Class in England* (Oxford, 1958), pp. 78–9.

by which scarcity forces the substitution of materials regarded, for many uses, as inferior to the traditional ones. The inferiority of cotton and the expense of importing it presumably explain why it did not begin to be used extensively until the renewed pressure of population growth during the second half of the eighteenth century. Cotton could have been used much more extensively earlier if people had desired it: it was not a material they were unfamiliar with. Raw cotton for stuffing and quilting and yarns for candlewicks had been imported for a very long time. Fustians had featured in European trade for several centuries before they were made in England and had been manufactured in Italy since medieval times.[1]

The methods and scale of the woollen industry had been precariously balanced to fit social, ecological and economic constraints. For those engaged in it, it was a source of additional family income. The spinners and weavers were often among the poorest in the community and took up their trade when their land holdings proved insufficient. The price and quantity of wool supplies were largely fixed by the land situation; markets were limited and, given the technology, highly competitive. Within this framework the comparatively inefficient machinery in use was maintained as a way of ensuring a sufficiently wide social distribution of the small rewards available. The introduction of new kinds of machinery was strenuously opposed because of the threat to employment in the industry. People resorted to machine-breaking and direct action against inventors and importers of new machinery.[2] Sometimes they were even successful in giving their opposition the force of law. From manufacture to marketing the industry was closely regulated by guilds and merchant companies.

The whole of this system was however at risk as soon as the relative prices of Indian cottons and English woollens moved sufficiently to give the advantage to the Indian goods. It seems likely that this situation would first have occurred some time

---

[1] A. P. Wadsworth and J. de. L. Mann, *The Cotton Trade and Industrial Lancashire 1600–1780* (Manchester, 1931), p. 17.
[2] Ibid., pp. 97–108.

during the population growth and price rises of the late sixteenth and early seventeenth centuries. By the late seventeenth century the Indian cottons imported by the East India Company were regarded as a substantial threat to the English woollen industry. But it was not competition in the domestic market – which could be protected – that brought the downfall of the old system, but competition in overseas markets where Indian cottons were potentially just as dangerous. However, instead of accepting a reduction of markets in face of competition from cotton, the English textile industry – supported by the appropriate duties, prohibitions and bounties – took advantage of the more plentiful raw material.

The political and economic handicaps imposed on the Indian cotton industry, and the possibility which plentiful cotton supplies provided for rapid expansion into overseas markets, meant that the introduction of new laboursaving machinery was less threatening than it had been when the possibilities of industrial growth were limited by constraints on the supplies of raw materials and on the size of the market. New machinery started to appear in the textile industry from the late seventeenth century onwards as arguments about unemployment could be increasingly easily countered by appeals to the need to compete abroad.[1] The classical innovations in textile machinery in the late eighteenth century should be seen in the context of almost a century of change in an industry which had never achieved a technology stabilized on purely economic grounds. Rapid expansion necessitated the use of spinning machines with larger numbers of spindles, hence demanding the application of additional sources of power. In the absence of suitable sites for water mills, the nineteenth-century factories made use of steam power. The woollen industry adopted similar methods and with the arrival of supplies of raw wool from Australia was able to expand output rapidly once more.

The development of the chemical industry during the industrial revolution and early nineteenth century may at first glance

[1] *The Cotton Trade and Industrial Lancashire*, pp. 102–3.

appear to present problems for the explanation of development put forward here. The modern chemical industry had its foundations in the manufacture of soda by the Leblanc process; it appears as a new industry rather than as a traditional one in which substitutes for scarce resources were introduced. But instead of the materials used in manufacture being subject to substitution as in the other industries discussed, the product of the early chemical industry was itself a substitute material for other industries.

The use of some form of alkali was important in the processing of a wide range of commodities including glass, soap, alum and saltpetre. When the industries making these commodities had used wood for fuel, alkali was readily available in the form of potash, but as coal-burning became general, supplies became scarce. Imports of potash eased the situation though demand continued to exceed supply.

Potash could of course be made by burning almost any vegetable matter and the fact that there could be a shortage at all is an indication of how serious the pressure was on agricultural land; the severity of the land shortage is doubly underlined when we see that supplies were augmented initially by burning seaweed instead of an agricultural product. The collection, drying and burning of large quantities of kelp along the seashore provides evidence of the ecological pressures behind development; as an attempt to exploit marine resources it is paralleled only by the efforts of the later nineteenth century to expand the fishing industry by importing tens of thousands of tons of Norwegian ice each year for preserving.[1] The sea was the only source of organic matter which did not add to the pressure on the land.

The kelping industry was introduced to England in about 1730 from Scotland where it had started a few decades earlier. It was an important source of alkali for a century before synthetic supplies of soda became available from the Leblanc process. Clow, the historian of the chemical industry, summarizing that industry's early development says 'as a subsidiary facet of the search for an alternative to wood we have the

[1] Charles L. Cutting, *Fish Saving* (London, 1955), p. 235.

search for a substitute for natural alkali'. After the discovery of the Leblanc process 'the industries using alkali became the focus of practically the whole chemical industry, and so remained for some fifty years.'[1] The establishment of a new industry was however a high price to pay to produce a substitute for what had previously been available free on the site in the form of wood-ash.

The Leblanc process involved manufacturers in the production of a number of other chemicals which proved useful elsewhere in the productive system. Sulphuric acid was needed to make soda but was also used to dissolve bones to make superphosphate fertilizer which helped to bring the much needed increases in agricultural yields. Noxious hydrogen chloride fumes, which had been allowed to escape from the factories of the soda manufacturers, were collected after legal action had been taken by local residents to prevent their release. The supplies of hydrochloric acid which resulted were used to make chlorine for bleaching.

The new bleach was particularly useful in papermaking. Under the impetus of the spread of literacy and the increased demand for paper for packaging, the papermaking industry had expanded up to the limits imposed by the available supplies of its raw materials. The scarcity of suitable rags had caused prices to rise sharply during the late eighteenth and early nineteenth centuries.[2] Imported rags began to supplement domestic supplies but the raw material problem remained acute. Experimenters who tried vegetable substitutes such as hay, straw, nettles and thistles met with little success. In this situation the first real advances came with the discovery of an effective bleach. Instead of being confined to white rags, bleaching meant that even the best white paper could be produced from dyed and printed rags.

The possibility of using a wider range of rags eased the raw materials problem for several decades, but it is worth noting that the effects of scarcity were only overcome at the additional

[1] A. and N. L. Clow, 'The chemical industry', in Charles Singer *et al.* (eds.), *A History of Technology*, volume IV, p. 235.
[2] D. C. Coleman, *The British Paper Industry* (Oxford, 1958), pp. 171–3.

cost of incorporating bleaching into the papermaking process. Bleaching was however only a temporary solution. Experiments with substitutes soon continued and during the middle of the nineteenth century some paper was made from cotton waste, hay and straw, as well as rags. It was not until the 1880s that the technique for making paper from wood pulp was discovered. This discovery of course marks the beginning of the relative decline of the industry in England in favour of timber-rich areas such as the Baltic countries and North America.

One more case of substitution worth mentioning before we move on to discuss some of the general implications of this pattern of development is the substitution of gas lighting for tallow candles.

The possibility of lighting by gas was demonstrated publicly shortly before the end of the eighteenth century. The demonstration was intended as a matter of scientific curiosity rather than as a commercial venture, and it seems that gas lighting was bound to have remained a curiosity while the gas was obtained from wood rather than coal. Tallow candles which were the traditional form of lighting were obviously dependent on the land supply. As prices rose, increasing quantities of tallow, vegetable oil and whale oil were imported to supplement domestic supplies, but the problem was not solved. Gas lighting, in its initial stages early in the nineteenth century, was used almost exclusively in factories; the long hours worked in cotton mills, the high price of imported animal and vegetable oils, and the extraction of gas from coal all helped to make gas lighting a commercial success. The importance of relative price movements in the substitution of coal gas for tallow was emphasized in a paper of William Murdock's, read to the Royal Society in 1808, in which he compared the costs of the two forms of lighting in a cotton mill which underwent one of the earliest conversions.[1] Outside the factory gas light-

[1] William Murdock, 'An account of the application of the gas from coal to economical purposes', read before the Royal Society by Sir Joseph Banks in 1808. As quoted by A. and N. L. Clow, *The Chemical Revolution* (London, 1952), p. 432.

ing spread more slowly. The fumes from the impure gas were so unpleasant that people preferred to go on using the older oils, and when they did use gas they sometimes went as far as mounting the lights outside the window to avoid the fumes. In 1838 Britain still needed to import over £1 million worth of vegetable and whale oil.

We have seen how English society was forced to change its established technology by a shortage of the resources which the technology was designed to exploit. Every change discussed in this chapter was either a direct response to a particular resource shortage or was a response to changes caused by resource shortages elsewhere in the economy. These initial changes were made under duress. They were notably not introduced when the traditional economic system was functioning in ecological equilibrium – when the choice could be made freely – but were instead adapted when scarcity threatened the continuation of the established system. The reasons why the technological innovations underlying the industrial revolution were not adopted earlier are clear. Just as pre-industrial agricultural development involved the expenditure of increasing quantities of labour to gain an adequate subsistence, so did the new technology. Not only was the product produced by the new technology often regarded as inferior, but the productive processes became more complex and frequently involved more labour. The innovations were only improvements in the context of the crisis situation into which they were introduced; they would not have been regarded as beneficial in the equilibrium conditions of several centuries earlier. Improvements – for instance in the system for transporting heavy goods – would have been merely wasteful in an economic system that had not developed the initial inefficiency of having to transport such goods. That the new technology, methods and materials were introduced because they were profitable is not at issue. However, it would be foolish to assume that they would always have been profitable: inevitably their profitability rested on the particular ecological context. All economic relationships take place within an ecological context, and given a set of these

relationships it is hardly more than a truism to say that innovations are introduced because of their profitability; the real
problem with which we are concerned is to see how these relationships change historically to make one set of choices
rational in one period and another in the next.

That an increasingly complex productive system was being
foisted on to a society while its original choice of resources
was disallowed explains why the workload during the industrial revolution was so great. The extraordinarily long
hours worked by men and increasing numbers of women and
children are well known. The arduous factory routine contrasted sharply with the much shorter hours and seasonal
work associated with some earlier periods of English history
and with many underdeveloped countries today. Such long
hours of work were a reflection, on one side, of the increased
difficulties of production, and on the other, of the individual's
response to poverty. Growing poverty and rising prices during
the second half of the eighteenth century were, in turn, the
direct results of population pressure and scarcity.

As the workload increased during the industrial revolution
period, the productive system became unmanageable without
the introduction of laboursaving equipment. Laboursaving
innovations are of course almost always desirable, but they are
rarely essential. The amount of work necessary to gain subsistence can – if all else fails – be allowed to increase until it
begins to approach the maximum people are capable of doing.
Beyond this the system is no longer viable. Undoubtedly this
point was reached for a significant proportion of the English
population during the industrial revolution: the workload rose
to the limits of human endurance. Although this situation was
caused by social inequality as well as by the technical and
ecological factors under consideration, it is clear that there
had been a longterm increase in the *per capita* workload
necessary to gain subsistence as population expanded. It was
this situation which made it essential to introduce laboursaving
machinery. For obvious reasons it was essential for self-em-
ployed people working maximum hours; it was also essential
from an employer's point of view because he could not pay

less than a minimum subsistence wage for an employee and his dependents and still maintain his labour force: he had to find ways of keeping labour productivity above the level needed to produce bare subsistence on maximum hours. (The Speenhamland system of poor relief introduced during this period is a testament to the severity of this problem – particularly during the high wheat prices of the Napoleonic Wars. While it was applied, it allowed for the payment of a supplement to wages where the economic wage was below subsistence level.)

The maximum possible workload per individual cannot of course be accurately defined, but it is safe to assume that the toleration of additional hours decreases as the workload increases. As the amount of labour needed to gain subsistence increases, the labour supply becomes the effective constraint on the supply of subsistence and so demands the transformation of the technology to economize on labour.

Many of the important innovations involving changes in the resource-base came, as we have seen, long before the classical industrial revolution period of the late eighteenth century. Industrial expansion was made possible by earlier changes in the resource-base. The introduction of new resources owes more to the pressure created by the population rise which ceased in the early seventeenth century than it does to the rise which started in the mid-eighteenth century. Liberated from the constraints of the land supply, industrial expansion was almost an inevitable consequence of the next population rise. When the section of the economy established on the more plentiful resources became large enough to absorb a significant rate of population growth, the pressure to delay marriages and limit family size was diminished, and the preconditions for industrialization had appeared. (If the part of the economy with sufficient resources to expand is only say 10 per cent of the whole, then it would have to expand at a rate of 20 per cent per annum to absorb an overall population growth of 2 per cent per annum.) No doubt the privations of the Napoleonic Wars accelerated the spread of techniques using new resources. As well as increasing the demand for some commodities still further, the wars also hampered the import of materials which had partly offset the effects of scarcity. The first response to resource shortages is often to import additional supplies. Among the materials we have discussed, Britain had imported timber, iron, raw wool, grain, tallow, rags for paper and potash, to name only a few. The war intensified the longterm crisis, but the innovations which were the keys to continued survival had appeared much earlier.

7 Innovation and technical consistency

We have seen how ecological pressures consequent on a growing population can usher in fundamental changes in a society's resource-base and technology. But after the initial ecological changes have been completed, technical change continues for a while. This chapter attempts to explain why it should continue and what are the boundaries of further change.

The typical developmental pattern seems to be that an ecological disturbance is followed by a spate of technical change which gradually tails off until stability is regained. Although this makes intuitive sense when it is viewed as a process of adjustment to the new resource-base, it is less clear what is happening in more analytical terms. After all, even where subsistence is adequate it seems fair to assume that there would still be a desire to increase the efficiency of the productive system – to reduce the amount of work required if not to increase output. We have explained why the desire to increase output varies, but we cannot assume that the desire to increase the efficiency with which a given output is produced is also an important variable. Why should there have been periods of technological stability waiting to be disturbed by new ecological pressures? The explanation for the waxing and waning of technical change seems to lie in variations in the practical constraints and opportunities for technical change.

It is clear that actual technical progress is a lot more restricted than the abstracted indices of economic efficiency may appear to be. Technical innovations cannot be introduced haphazardly. Although no one would expect a society with a technology based largely on wood to be able to produce motor cars, the severity of the constraints which innovations have to meet is often underestimated. Even with the advanced engineering abilities of the industrial countries in the late nineteenth century, the ignition problem in internal combustion engines was serious. The sparking plug and the diesel engine were developed almost simultaneously as alternative solutions to the problem, but the former required considerable electrical apparatus, and the latter required the production of pistons and cylinders capable of producing very high compression over a wide range of temperatures. Examples such as this show the need to introduce technical innovations in a strict order; one element may be impracticable unless others have been introduced beforehand. Often it may only be possible to introduce technical changes in single file; this clearly imposes limitations on both the range and speed of change.

These problems serve to indicate the importance of the technical self-consistency and cohesiveness of the productive system. The different parts of the productive technology relate to each other as the parts of an organic system. Any proposed innovation must fit into a context in which both means and ends are already established. New tools and equipment are only practical possibilities if their manufacture lies within the productive capabilities of the existing technology (except of course for the limited supplies which can be imported), and are only desirable for the contribution they make to the established productive task. The problem of the innovator is to find improved ways of bringing existing means to bear on existing tasks. This problem situation provides the context in which changes in economic efficiency take place.

The basic problem situation that the productive technology has to deal with is defined by the ecological situation. As we have seen, this is the source of the more or less severe constraints on the choice of methods and materials. In the context of an established resource-base, the transformation tasks which the technology must achieve are already spelt out. Within any ecological situation there may be some choice of resources, but once the culture and technology has *de facto* made these choices, much of the problem situation is defined. The technology may exploit additional resources – such as the various metals – to help it achieve the basic productive tasks, but for most of the time the basic productive means and ends will be far from fluid. On the level of the individual elements of the productive technology, as opposed to the productive systems as a whole, the restraining context in which each has to operate is of course defined primarily by the rest of the productive technology. The interrelations within the technology provide the constraints on its component parts.

Opportunities for successful innovation are greatest when there is a shift in the problem situation confronting the established technology. Instead of searching for further improvements within a static framework of productive capabilities and tasks, the innovator is provided with an altered conjunction of new productive opportunities with which to tackle a new range of problems. The bulk of technical change throughout economic development has been derived from successive problem shifts. The creation of new ecological problems has led to a repeated regeneration of opportunities for innovation. Modern economies, instead of doing the same productive tasks as primitive societies more efficiently than they did, are concerned with a completely different range of tasks and activities. One of the most striking features of longterm economic development is how little overall increase in efficiency there has been in producing subsistence and maintaining the necessary life-support systems. Ecological pressures change the optimum choice of materials and techniques. They make it beneficial to exploit new materials and develop new techniques. Priorities change and new productive problems are substituted for old. The needs and choice spectrum which formed the context of the established technology is suddenly altered.

Where there are no ecologically stimulated problem shifts, the possibilities of technological development are limited. With an unchanging set of tasks and productive possibilities the potential range of innovations is fixed. The technology – for instance – of an agricultural society, will be designed to assist with tasks such as clearing the ground, planting and harvesting. The society may have the means at its disposal for shaping wood, and so may be able to exploit this material to its maximum potential to bear on these agricultural tasks. There is however no reason why such a society should always contain within it the means to produce a more advanced technology to achieve the same tasks. But more crucially, even if a sophisticated metal-working technology was available, it is more than likely that it would not be justified by the advantages of using reapers instead of scythes, or seed drills instead of sowing broadcast. A similar situation exists in relation to the transport needs of many societies. Animal transport and human portage may look very inefficient, but the demand for transport may not be sufficient to justify the production or upkeep of mechanical aids. We saw that even in eighteenth-century England canals proved unprofitable in areas where transport needs had not developed sufficiently to generate enough traffic for them. We can see from examples such as these that the creation of a sufficiently difficult ecological situation may be a necessary preliminary to the development of some technologies. Only when the workload becomes great enough will expensive solutions be justified. We may guess that even among the Siane of New Guinea mentioned in chapter 5, the advantages of European steel axes over their own stone ones would not have been great enough to justify domestic production had supplies from trade dried up.[1] An advanced technology applied to the small range of comparatively simple tasks facing a primitive society would surely be an inefficient and top-heavy arrangement. Much of the developmental problem could be posed in terms of whether or not the ecological difficulties of producing food, clothing, shelter and so on were great enough to form an economic foundation for a complex technology.

Without a shift in the problem situation new opportunities for innovation will become increasingly scarce. As time goes on most of the profitable possibilities will have been taken up. Once this situation is reached, it becomes extremely unlikely

[1] See p. 106 above.

that any new process of change will be initiated by the discovery of more efficient ways of performing traditional tasks in an unchanged economic environment. Further development will have to await the breakdown of ecological equilibrium. Thus there emerges the possibility of a society which has achieved a high degree of technical stability consistent with the desire to maximize economic efficiency.

We know that new opportunities for innovation will be exploited for the benefits they bring in increased economic efficiency, but this tells us very little about the course of technical change which follows an ecological problem shift. Initially, renewed innovation is stimulated by the creation of new demands on the technology. The first technical responses then disseminate a series of derived demands throughout the rest of the productive system, breaking the prevailing technical consistency asunder. Each new demand acts as an 'inducement mechanism', stretching the existing technology to develop in new directions. Steam power was first used in response to the pumping problem in mines as coal production was expanded, and was later used to help meet the growing demand for transport. The early engines had to be designed so that they could be built in an alien technological context. So severe were the productive constraints that it was only just possible to produce a workable engine of any kind. Newcomen's engine, which used leather packing and water to make a seal between the piston and the cylinder, was extremely inefficient. When Smeaton saw Watt's improved design he believed that 'neither tools nor workmen existed that could manufacture so complex a machine with sufficient precision'.[1] Smeaton had been involved earlier in the development of better cylinder-boring machines, and his judgement proved correct to the extent that Watt's engine was only built with the help of a modified version of a new machine for boring cannon. The stimulus which the steam-engine gave to the development of mechanical engineering is clear. It was a practical innovation because it came just

[1] T. K. Derry and T. I. Williams, *A Short History of Technology* (Oxford, 1960), p. 322.

within the society's productive potential, but it was also instrumental in spreading change because it made new demands on the existing technology. Many of the key developments in the machine-tool industry have been traced by Nathan Rosenberg to the stimulus provided by a succession of new productive tasks.[1] Textile machinery, railways, arms production, sewing machines, bicycles and automobiles gradually pushed the machine-tool industry to greater heights of sophistication. Standardized screw threads, hard cutting steels, the theory of gear cutting, turning, milling and boring, ballbearings and lubrication were gradually added to the mechanical engineering repertoire. A particularly important element in this context was the need for power-driven tools. The working of metals involves the application of much more power than for instance the working of wood. A wood-working lathe can be treadle-driven, a metal-working one cannot. Generally, the use of more minerals and heavy commodities in the productive system, the increased scale of operations, and the broad shift towards the more plentiful but less amenable materials necessitated the application of increasing quantities of power. The ecological limitations on the use of more animal power for transport or more water power for industrial purposes were evidenced in the last chapter. Just as animal power began to be used when ploughing became necessary, so mechanical sources of power had to be developed to meet this new situation.

So far we have dealt more with what might appear to be the practicalities of technical change than with the economics which decide between alternative practicalities. To understand the dynamics through which gains in economic efficiency are achieved, it is helpful to view the productive system as a pattern of trade-off relationships working through a network of technical interrelations. Thus wherever there are moving parts in a machine, a trade-off relationship is created between the cost of friction in terms of wear and tear and power loss and the cost of improvements in bearings and lubrication.

[1] Nathan Rosenberg, 'Technological change in the machine tool industry, 1840–1910', *Journal of Economic History*, XXIII (1963), pp. 414–43.

A society's methods of production and technology create a network of such relationships which spell out the economics of production. Over each of these relationships development will continue until costs of further improvements equal the benefits derived from them. The cost of heat loss from processes which require the maintenance of high temperatures

Reductions in fuel consumption of steam-engines resulting from increases in thermal efficiency

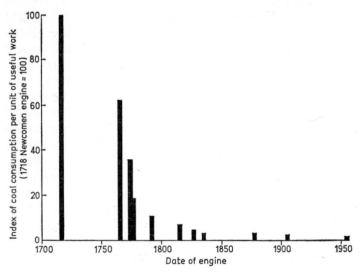

Source: The Science Museum, *Synopsis of historical events: mechanical and electrical engineering* (London, 1960).

will be balanced against the cost of techniques of insulation. One of the dominant influences on the development of the steam-engine came from the trade-off between fuel-saving and the costs of the increasingly sophisticated engineering necessary to increase its thermal efficiency. The graph shows how the evolution of mechanical engineering abilities and design improvements allowed the thermal efficiency of steam-engines to be raised and the fuel costs lowered. Within a stable price structure, we can see that developments in this direction would cease where economic efficiency was maximized.

In many fields such as this, the tendency for development to slow down is strongly reinforced by diminishing returns to further improvement. In the case of the steam-engine, the remaining possibilities of fuel-saving were inevitably reduced as thermal efficiency was increased. A doubling of efficiency this century would obviously have saved much less fuel than – say – a 10 per cent increase during the eighteenth century; it would also have been much harder to achieve. Similar cases of diminishing returns are very common. In the example of the trade-off between heat loss and better insulation, heat losses will tend to become insignificant as insulation improves. The same relationship holds in the development of insulation for refrigeration.

Another contribution to the establishment of a stable self-consistent technology comes from the attainment of research objectives. Thus, the colourfastness of dyes will cease to be the subject of development as colourfastness is progressively achieved, and the strength of glues will not be increased after they have become as strong as the materials they are designed to stick together.

Viewing some of the detailed aspects of technological development in terms of trade-off relationships illustrates how dependent the direction of development is on the ecological context. Although the productive technology creates its own internal price structures, they must tie up eventually with the external ecological situation and its implied price structure. Clearly any degree of stability or balance achieved in a particular trade-off relationship is dependent on the price structure in which it operates. If the steam-engine's fuel had been more expensive, more effort would have been devoted to increasing the efficiency of engines. As the ecological situation changes, altering the relative prices of materials and the urgency of people's needs, it is clear that the stable consistency established in any society's technology will no longer represent the optimum set of choices. Technical change will be rekindled to a greater or lesser extent depending on the scale of the problem shift.

*   *   *

The process of technical change, ironing out technical problems, exploiting new productive opportunities, and developing a more integrated productive technology is the positive element in economic development. It is the main source of any real progress which may be achieved during any of the various stages of development. The ostensibly negative role is played by the successive ecological problem shifts. The initially damaging changes forced on society by ecological pressures are at least partly countered by new technological development. Wherever possible the best of the old productive methods will of course be retained. To these will be added the fruits of new technological developments. During those periods of development when the general level of efficiency improves, we must conclude that the productive system's built-in potential for innovation was more than enough to counter the latest set of ecological difficulties. Rosenberg believes that technical change usually does more than overcome the difficulty which stimulated it – typically it 'overshoots the mark'.[1]

Although this last statement may be true in relation to the increasing efficiency of specific productive methods during industrialization, it would be dangerous to make inferences from this concerning human progress more generally. Perhaps only when technical change continues in the absence of ecological changes of any kind is it safe to assume real progress is taking place. In such a situation one can at least be confident that the changes are voluntary and are not merely offsetting mounting ecological difficulties. The continued development of industrial societies is obviously a mixed phenomenon. Population growth and resource shortages have caused a continuous problem shift, but there has also been an important development of the technical possibilities opened up much earlier. We shall return to the question of progress in chapter 9.

[1] Nathan Rosenberg, 'The direction of technological change: inducement mechanisms and focusing devices', *Economic Development and Cultural Change*, XVIII (1969), p. 8.

8 *American economic development*

> The wilderness masters the colonist. It finds him a European
> in dress, industries, tools, modes of travel, and thought. It
> takes him from the railroad car and puts him in the birch
> canoe. It strips off the garments of civilization and arrays him
> in the hunting shirt and moccasin. It puts him in the log cabin of
> the Cherokee and the Iroquois and runs the Indian Palisade
> around him. Before long he has gone to planting Indian corn
> and ploughing with a sharp stick. . . .[1]

There are few countries where the basic resource situation
could look more different from England's than America's did
during her early development. On a small densely populated
island, the British population had long been aware of the
limits which the environment imposed on the expansion of the
economic system. In contrast America, with its vast reserves
of unsettled land and unknown resources, was regarded as
providing an unlimited supply of all the natural resources
people needed. In fact, in the mercantilist view of the mother
country, the main purpose of colonization was to ensure
supplies of raw materials which were becoming scarce in the
domestic economy.

The difference in resource endowment means that American
development provides a special challenge for a theory of development which locates resource shortages at the centre of
the developmental process. It will be particularly striking if
the relationships described in earlier chapters, in such different
societies, hold true through all the apparent anomalies of
American development.

Frederick J. Turner, *The Frontier in American History* (New York, 1921),
p. 4.

The concept of ecological equilibrium is fundamental to any understanding of American development. The methods which various communities used in different periods and regions to wrest a livelihood from their environment were often short-term strategies. Areas would boom and then die as virgin resources were exploited and worked out. The methods and rate of exploitation often placed a strict time-limit on the survival of different types of economies. On the other side of the ecological equation, population growth and the increasing density of settlement made any longterm equilibrium impossible. People were continually forced to adopt more intensive methods in order to maintain their standard of living. Malthus used the rate of population growth in the American states in the late eighteenth century as an indication of the potential of population to expand given an unlimited supply of land: 'In the northern States of America ... the population has been found to double itself ... in less than 25 years.'[1]

It is tempting to suggest a pattern of sequential development by which successive economic frontiers moved across the country reflecting different stages in man's development, each stage corresponding to the exploitation of a different resource. Turner wrote of a series of 'frontiers' – 'the procession of civilization, marching single file ... the Indian, the fur-trader and hunter, the cattle-raiser, the pioneer farmer – and the frontier has passed by'.[2] Although this kind of schema has its uses and gives due weight to frontier activities such as the fur trade, we must concern ourselves more with what went on after these frontiers had passed. One could preserve the framework by adding 'frontiers' of intensive farming and industry behind the others, but its usefulness declines as the economic interactions become more complicated. From our point of view it is worth mentioning because it suggests the general ecological pattern of sequential resource exploitation.

The appearance of resource shortages and poverty in

[1] T. R. Malthus, *An Essay on the Principle of Population* (London, 1888 edition), p. 3.
[2] Turner, op. cit., p. 12.

eighteenth-century New England seems unlikely on the face of it. There are reasons, however, to think that many early New England settlements followed a pattern of development reminiscent of the village communities mentioned in chapter 4. Under the pressure of population growth, land holdings were subdivided, and within a few generations there were signs of a land shortage and a concomitant appearance of increasing numbers of landless poor. Lockridge found that in many New England settlements the average size of land holdings had shrunk to one-third or less of the original grant a century and a half earlier.[1] Under population growth sometimes as high as 5 per cent per annum, population density increased and average land holdings declined from 150 acres or so to somewhere around 50 acres. Additional evidence of a growing land shortage comes from the doubling or tripling of land values during the century 1660–1760, and from the increasing cultivation of marginal land.[2] By the mid-eighteenth century we are told that 'the wandering poor had become part of the landscape' in older settled areas of New England.[3] But even as early as 1721 it was possible for someone living in Massachusetts to say '. . . many of our Old Towns are too full of Inhabitants for Husbandry; many of them living upon small shares of land, and generally all are Husbandmen; . . . And also many of our people are slow in Marrying for want of Settlements. . . .'[4] In a study of a Connecticut town called Kent, Grant says that 'economic opportunity, which appeared exceptionally bright . . . from 1740 to 1777, was darkened after the Revolution by the pressure of population (swollen by the high birth rate) against a limited supply of land'.[5] Grant traces the division of land holdings over three generations and concludes 'There was insufficient land for the third generation.

[1] Kenneth Lockridge, 'Land, population and the evolution of New England society, 1630–1790', *Past and Present*, XXXIX (1968), pp. 64–8.
[2] Ibid., p. 69.   [3] Ibid., p. 73.
[4] 'Amicus Patriae', *A word of Comfort to a Melancholy Country* (Boston, 1721); reprinted in *Colonial Currency Reprints*, volume 2 (Boston, 1921), p. 189.
[5] Charles S. Grant, *Democracy in the Connecticut Frontier Town of Kent* (New York, 1961), p. 170.

F

Some stayed and remained in a poorer status than that of their fathers and much poorer than that of their grandfathers. Others left at the rate of about fifty a year.'[1] That New England as a whole became an area of emigration from about 1790 suggests that this pattern may not have been confined to Kent. With large families and partible inheritance, land holdings quickly approached the minimum practical size (Grant's work suggests between 40 and 89 acres) and primogeniture, which forced younger siblings to emigrate, became more common.[2] During the revolutionary period Kent developed 'a growing class of propertyless men'. 'By 1796 not only had the percentage of poor climbed from its long-term plateau . . . but for the first time there emerged a significant number of men destined to remain poor. In 1796 there were twenty-two permanent proletarians in Kent, comprising 11 per cent of the adult male population.'[3]

Pressure for economic expansion and change and for the early development of an industrial labour force is also indicated by the existence of poverty in the larger towns. It is clear from the timing of legislation and the administration of relief that poverty became a problem in several areas in the late eighteenth or early nineteenth centuries. In New York for example, a £10,000 almshouse was opened in 1797, and in 1808 the state legislature voted almost $500,000 for poor relief.[4] By 1817, 15,000 people – or one-seventh of the city's population – were in receipt of public or private charity during the year.[5] New Jersey acted earlier, introducing a comprehensive poor law in 1774.

It seems likely that some of this poverty was the result of the initial difficulties in settling immigrants from Europe, but contemporaries tended to see it as a longterm problem and

---

[1] *Democracy in the Connecticut Frontier Town of Kent*, p. 100.

[2] Ibid., pp. 36–7; Philip J. Greven, *Four Generations: Population, Land and Family in Colonial Andover, Massachusetts* (Ithaca, 1970), pp. 131–2, 230.

[3] Grant, op. cit., p. 97.

[4] John Duffy, *A History of Public Health in New York City, 1625–1866* (New York, 1968), p. 261.

[5] Ibid., p. 261.

to show the same prejudices towards it as their European counterparts did, passing it off as the result of excessive drinking, immorality and vice. Certainly it would be a mistake to think that a city like New York did not suffer from most of the problems associated with poverty which were chronic in European cities. By the beginning of the nineteenth century New York had its slums, squalor, brothels and child labour, and people were able to debate whether it was better or worse than European cities.

Initially the rural economy of New England was almost entirely self-sufficient. The role of the market and the division of labour was extremely limited. Each family tended to provide not only all its own food, firewood and building materials, but most also made their own clothes and shoes using leather, skins, flax and wool. Activities such as iron-smelting and flour-milling were among the few which were at all specialized; elsewhere unspecialized production was an 'inefficiency' people could afford. European tradesmen who emigrated to America tended to give up their trade and become farmers; there were frequent complaints about indentured servants, brought over at great expense, who left their masters as soon as the period of their indenture had expired. While the land supply was adequate, life in small settlements of self-sufficient subsistence-farmers was preferred to employment in manufacturing, whether rural or urban. The development of manufacturing waited on the appearance of scarcity and the breakdown of local self-sufficiency. We have seen this preference expressed in the behaviour of other societies and its significance was well known to the American colonists: writing early in the eighteenth century 'Amicus Patriae' said

> to pretend to Manufactures, without a great Overplus (to our Husbandry) in our Number of People, is but to talk of Chymaeras. . . . But when our Country is fill'd with People; . . . we can afford some Towns fully stock'd with Artificers, Combers, and Weavers, etc. . . . then we may do something to Purpose in Manufactures, but not before. This seems plain, from the Examples of Old Countries, where being

over-crowded with inhabitants, they are fain to Beg, Steal or Fight for their living, or work for six-pence or a Groat a Day, great Numbers of them.[1]

The self-sufficiency of farming families, or of rural communities with few market transactions, cannot be easily breached by outside influences. Their lack of dependence on the external economy means that change cannot – so to speak – be 'imported'. Self-sufficient economies are likely to remain inviolable until forced to change by the internal pressures associated with ecological disequilibrium. The poverty which began to assume significant proportions in the older settled areas in the late eighteenth century is an early sign that the worsening land to population ratio was creating the conditions 'Amicus Patriae' had been looking forward to. But the growing disequilibrium between population and resources had other facets. The large size of the original land grants had encouraged the development of less intensive methods of land-use than those practised in Europe: in conventional terms there had been a regression in agricultural techniques. Manuring and crop rotations were only rarely practised and yields declined as the land became less fertile. By the late eighteenth century the impoverishment of the soil seems to have been a problem in many of the older areas. Ellis says of eastern New York that the original humus soil had produced over 20 bushels of wheat per acre.[2] By 1813 he says yields had declined to 12 or 13 bushels and by 1845 they were often as low as 8 or 9 bushels per acre. The New England wheat crop had been in difficulties during much of the eighteenth century. Wheat growing had gradually been forced into new areas as the older areas suffered progressively from declining soil fertility and crop diseases such as rust and blast.[3] Lockridge found at least one reference to 'worn land' in the inventories of New England estates as

[1] 'Amicus Patriae', op. cit., pp. 189–90.
[2] David M. Ellis, *Landlords and Farmers in the Hudson–Mohawk Region, 1790–1850* (Ithaca, 1946), pp. 186–8.
[3] Percy W. Bidwell and John I. Falconer, *History of Agriculture in the Northern United States, 1620–1860* (Washington, 1925), pp. 92–3.

early as 1700.[1] Usually people changed to growing Indian corn after the soil had been spoiled for wheat, but their self-sufficiency was often seriously compromised. In neither New England nor in eastern New York State was production able to keep up with increasing consumption. Both areas became dependent on grain-stuffs imported from other areas.

Grain was not the only basic commodity in which the more densely populated areas lost their self-sufficiency. Timber scarcity in America was never a matter of an absolute shortage – wood was always available somewhere; the problem was one of increasing transport costs as it became necessary to go further and further afield for supplies. By the late eighteenth century the population's demand for agricultural land had led to dangerous incursions on the amount of woodland available in some parts of New England. The townships established since the beginning of the eighteenth century seem to have had about 25 acres of woodland left per adult man by the end of the century.[2] In the older townships the incursions had gone further and they were left with only about half that amount. In a few areas local supplies of timber were nearing exhaustion much earlier. For instance, in 1670 a law of Plymouth, New Hampshire, said that several towns 'are already much straightened for building timber'.[3] By the post-revolutionary period some of the inhabitants of Cape Cod had taken to burning peat, and local timber shortages had begun to appear at a few points in the interior.[4] As local timber supplies were exhausted and wood had to be transported over increasing distances, coal began to gain an advantage. Blacksmiths with good access to the Pennsylvania coalfields began using coal instead of wood from the first decade of the nineteenth century.[5] By 1820 a number of New England forges had also made the changeover.

---

[1] Lockridge, op. cit., p. 73.   [2] Ibid., p. 69.
[3] Victor S. Clark, *History of Manufacturers in the United States* (Washington, 1916), volume 1, p. 75.
[4] Louis B. Schmidt and Earle D. Ross (eds.), *Readings in the Economic History of American Agriculture* (New York, 1925), p. 183; Clark, op. cit., p. 75.
[5] Clark, op. cit., p. 331.

The first rolling mill and wire-drawers began using anthracite in about 1812 and many others followed suit within a decade. There are records during the 1820s of a Boston glassworks which began using coal, and of a number of calico printers and dyers who also adopted the new fuel.[1] Coal also began to replace wood as a domestic fuel in the cities of the eastern seaboard. By 1826 coal and anthracite accounted for very nearly a quarter of the domestic fuel used in Philadelphia.[2] The iron industry, which had been scattered throughout almost every state in the early nineteenth century, began to use mineral fuel in the late 1830s. By 1854 almost as much pig iron was made with anthracite as with charcoal.[3] But the dynamics of the changeover were not as simple in America as in England. The English iron industry was forced to make the change in the eighteenth century whether it liked it or not. The American timber supply held out for long enough to give an element of choice between fuels for a number of decades. In addition to the relative prices of the fuels, the choice was also influenced by changes in the type of iron demanded and the development of smelting techniques. Charcoal smelting was more suitable for the production of the general purpose bar iron supplied to blacksmiths for agricultural uses. But as the industrial demand for pig and other types of iron grew, the balance shifted further in favour of mineral fuels.[4] At first the Pennsylvanian supplies of anthracite – 'natural coke' – were used in preference to coking bituminous coal. Coke did not have to be used until techniques of coke smelting had improved and sulphur-free supplies had been discovered.[5] However, where demand was

---

[1] *History of Manufacturers in the United States*, p. 332.

[2] Sam H. Schurr and Bruce C. Netschert, *Energy in the American Economy 1850–1975* (Baltimore, 1960), p. 50n.

[3] Peter Temin, *Iron and Steel in Nineteenth-Century America* (Cambridge, Mass., 1964), p. 52.

[4] L. C. Hunter, 'The influence of the market upon technique in the iron industry in western Pennsylvania up to 1860', *Journal of Economic and Business History*, I (1929), pp. 241–81.

[5] Peter Temin, 'A new look at Hunter's hypothesis about the ante-bellum iron industry', *American Economic Review*, Papers and Proceedings (1964), pp. 344–51.

right and timber was still plentiful, charcoal smelting continued on a large scale as late as the third quarter of the nineteenth century and, in some instances, into the beginning of the present century. For raising steam on riverboats, railway engines and steam-engines used in manufacturing, the change-over to coal came at widely differing times. In the east, where the timber scarcity occurred sooner and coal was more plentiful, the changeover was under way by the late 1820s. By about 1830 most of Philadelphia's steam-engines were burning coal, and in 1861 the Pennsylvania Railroad withdrew its last wood-burning freight engine.[1] The western riverboats and railway engines continued to burn wood well into the late nineteenth century.

The Americans knew of the basic techniques which would allow them to substitute coal for wood in most industrial and domestic uses long before they used them. The general argument that an inferior fuel and technology was used because of lack of knowledge or inventiveness is not available to the student of American history. The change of fuels can only be explained by reference to the altered supply conditions. The belief that wood was inferior and that coal and the technology that went with it represented progress – in any meaningful sense – must be dropped.

The growth of river navigation, turnpikes, canals and railways – in fact of the whole transport system during the first half of the nineteenth century – is a measure of the rapidity with which local resources became inadequate to meet the needs of the expanding eastern population. The principal commodities carried were just those in which we have already seen scarcities developing. In order to survive, the east depended on the development of a transport system capable of bringing from the interior vast quantities of the basic commodities in which it was deficient. The traffic down the Erie Canal in 1825 – the first year it was open – was made up largely of over $32\frac{1}{2}$ million square feet of boards and planks, 656,000 cubic feet of

[1] Clark, op. cit., p. 332; John F. Stover, *American Railroads* (Chicago, 1961), p. 162.

timber, 221,000 barrels of flour and 704,000 bushels of grain.[1]
In 1827 an estimated 40 million feet of timber were shipped
down the Susquehanna.[2] The Chesapeake and Delaware Canal
in 1835 carried over 18 million square feet of boards and
planks, 130,000 bushels of grain and 15,000 barrels of flour.[3]
The figures for coal carried in that year are not available but
it was certainly the fastest growing of the major cargoes. By
the mid-century coal had become the most important commodity shipped on the tidewater canals of the east coast, and
by 1856 it accounted for 42 per cent of the total tonnage carried
by the Pennsylvania Railroad.[4] There were of course many
other minor commodities which had to be transported, but it
was the demand for these bulk commodities which necessitated
the development of canals and railways. There had always
been some trade in salt and iron for tools but, as in England,
the major innovations in transport were a response to the
breakdown of local self-sufficiency in wood – especially firewood – and grain. It was unthinkable that such vast quantities
of these commodities could be carried by the traditional means.

Apart from stimulating the development of trade and transport facilities, the breakdown in local self-sufficiency had other
effects. By the late eighteenth and early nineteenth century the
agriculture of New England had become poorer than that in
any other region of the country. Many of the earliest settled
areas experienced falls in population from about 1790 onwards, and by 1820 there was a general outflow from the rural
areas of northern New England. Some regions had had to
become importers of foodstuffs as early as the second half of
the eighteenth century, but the aggregate population of the
region continued to grow. Wheat growers continued to be
hampered by all the old difficulties as well as by two new kinds
of parasite. By the 1820s and 1830s, many farmers whose land

---

[1] Caroline E. MacGill, *History of Transportation in the United States before
1860* (Washington, 1917), pp. 192–3.
[2] George R. Taylor, *The Transportation Revolution 1815–60* (New York,
1951), p. 171.
[3] MacGill, op. cit., p. 220.
[4] Taylor, op. cit., p. 170.

had become too poor to support economic crops were changing to sheep farming – particularly in the hill farming areas.[1]

More and more New England families found their land area too small and unproductive to maintain their self-sufficiency. They had to buy goods produced elsewhere and they had to earn the money to do so. At one time the domestic handicrafts practised in New England settlements had been devoted almost entirely to supplying each household's own needs. In the early eighteenth century clothing needs could be satisfied fairly easily; the relatively plentiful supplies of leather, buckskin and bearskin reduced the need for spinning and weaving natural fibres. Bridenbaugh says in his work on colonial craftsmen that 'Countrymen almost universally wore breeches made of home-tanned leather'.[2] However, as successive scarcities set in, flax and then cotton became more important raw materials. But it was not until the need for additional sources of income became sufficiently pressing that domestic production turned towards the market. A domestic industry organized along the lines of the European putting-out system grew up, employing the poorer farm women. Raw materials were supplied, and the products marketed, by an agent who paid the women on a commission basis. By 1830 or 1840 the domestic production of shoes, straw hats and bonnets, men's clothing, and several other products, was undertaken primarily for the market.[3] The economic situation of people with an even smaller stake in the land than these domestic workers made them more amenable to industrial labour in the mills. The strongest economic pressures are necessary before people are willing to sacrifice their independence and accept terms of factory employment profitable to an employer. This point is borne out by the remarks of an employer talking from his experience in textile mills in Massachusetts during the early nineteenth century. He said that the people who applied for work in the mills were 'poor families, and generally those

[1] Paul W. Gates, *The Farmers' Age, Agriculture 1815–1860* (New York, 1960), p. 27.
[2] Carl Bridenbaugh, *The Colonial Craftsman* (New York, 1950), p. 35.
[3] Bidwell and Falconer, op. cit., p. 253.

having the greatest number of children, those who have lived in retired situations on small and poor farms, or in hired houses ... These families are often very ignorant and too often vicious.'[1] But the mills still had difficulty in getting all the labour they wanted. To attract more workers they sent recruiting agents round the rural areas who, to be successful, had often to paint a very misleading picture of life in the mills. Records show that in 1845 most of the girls employed in the famous Lowell mills in Massachusetts came from the hill farms in northern New England, but few seem to have been sufficiently attracted by the realities of factory life to stay for more than a couple of years.[2] It is interesting that amidst the controversy that surrounded the work of these agents, one of their number should have needed to assert that the girls his firm employed 'are not paupers'.[3] All in all it is not difficult to see the importance of the economic background in providing for the development of the 'free' contractual wage labour which eliminated the need for indentured and slave labour.

The 'shake out' of the growing rural population into industry seems to have been rapid. Apparently by 1840,

> it would have been difficult to find 50 out of 479 townships in southern New England which did not have at least one manufacturing village clustered around a cotton or woollen mill, an iron furnace, a chair factory, or a carriage shop, or some other representative ... of manufacturing which had grown up in a haphazard fashion in every part of the three states.[4]

The similarities and differences between the early use of steam power in England and America are interesting. The first use of

---

[1] George S. White, *Memoir of Samuel Slater* (Philadelphia, 1836), as quoted in Caroline F. Ware, *The Early New England Cotton Manufacture* (Boston and New York, 1931), p. 200.

[2] Harold F. Wilson, *The Hill Country of Northern New England* (New York, 1936), p. 67.

[3] Ware, op. cit., p. 217.

[4] Percy W. Bidwell, 'The agricultural revolution in New England', *American Historical Review*, XXVI (1921), p. 686.

steam power in America was for pumping out mines just as in England, and there seems little need to go into this further. But among the earliest American uses, steam was employed to drive riverboats – a development not paralleled in England. Like the problem of pumping out mines, the problem of powering large boats on American rivers imposed new demands on the technology which could not be solved by traditional means. The application of steam to American river transport was a response to a new situation which England had not had to face; it should not be seen as an unsolicited improvement in the way a traditional task was performed. The rivers which played an important part in the American transport network were on a scale unlike anything found in the British Isles. For a waterway to be utilized efficiently by barges pulled from a towpath by a horse, there must be a reasonable depth of water close to the bank, the bank must be sufficiently tamed to have a towpath free of forest and silted marshes, the boats must not be too large and the river must not be so wide that it cannot be properly used from the towpath. Many American rivers could hardly have been less suitable for horsedrawn barges. The Mississippi for instance was littered with mud banks and shallows which meant steering to keep well into the main stream. Thousands of miles of important rivers ran through virgin territory where towpaths were virtually impossible. As the east's deficit in various bulk commodities grew it gave rise to a vast egress from other regions. In several instances the catchment areas of the large rivers were many times the size of the British Isles and generated a flow of goods more closely matched by European coastal than inland trade. The great width of the rivers allowed the development of flatbottomed boats capable of carrying hundreds of tons of cargo. These features combined to make horse traction impracticable. Nor was sail a realistic alternative – tacking up a winding river with a large flatbottomed shallow draught boat would have been too difficult. Because of these problems many of the boats which were used before steam was introduced had to be sold as timber after making one downstream trip; it was not worth making the 'tedious upstream transit propelled by poles, sweeps, and ropes'.[1] An observer who saw the introduction of steam on the western rivers has described the difficulties of taking barges upstream before steam power was used:

> The barge is of the size of an Atlantic schooner . . . and carried from fifty to an hundred tons. It required from twenty-five to thirty hands to work it up stream. . . . it was worked up stream by the operation called 'warping', – a most laborious, slow and difficult mode of ascent, and in which six or eight miles a day was good progress. It consisted in having two yawls the one in advance of the other, carrying out a warp of some hundred yards in length, making it fast on a tree, and then drawing the barge up to that tree by the warp. When that warp was coiled, the yawl in advance had another laid, and so on alternately. From ninety to an hundred days was a tolerable passage from New Orleans to Cincinnati. One only need read the journal of a barge on such an ascent, to comprehend the full value of the invention of steam boats.[2]

Steamboats obviously provided the easiest solution to the new navigational problem which the Americans faced. The problem too seems bound to have arisen in that environmental context as soon as population growth and the prevailing methods of resource exploitation turned the east into a deficit area no longer ecologically viable on its own.

Steam-engines came to be used in American mills and factories in much the same circumstances as they had been in England. But according to the conventional view, in which steam power is regarded as more efficient than water power, it appears anomalous that the Americans should have been so slow to use steam in their mills when the technology they

[1] John W. Oliver, *History of American Technology* (New York, 1956), p. 192.

[2] Timothy Flint, *The History and Geography of the Mississippi Valley* (Cincinnati, 1832); excerpt reprinted in Ernest L. Bogart and Charles M. Thompson, *Readings in the Economic History of the United States* (New York, 1916), p. 379.

needed was already available across the Atlantic. However, if we assume that water power was preferable to steam, then we should not expect steam-engines to be used to drive mills until good sites for water mills were no longer available. This pattern of development which took place in England earlier was repeated in the United States. Clark says that 'By 1830 the smaller streams of New England were utilized to nearly their full capacity, and the distribution of water-using industries resembled that in England before the introduction of steam'.[1] He gives several examples: apparently the Woonsocket river in Rhode Island drove 25 mills which were strung along its banks within a mile of each other, and the Singletary River had 7 mills within a mile and a half.[2] The greater economic efficiency of generating power from water rather than from steam is indicated by figures which show that in 1839 the annual cost per horsepower generated from the former was many times less than that from the latter.[3] Presumably this explains why it was possible to sell water rights at Lowell on the Merrimac for as much as $200 per horsepower.[4] But when no more water power was available manufacturers had to use steam in spite of its cost. Thus, at Lowell again, we read that 'By 1835 over 2,500 horsepower was in use, and (that) about ten years later steam engines were introduced to carry additional machinery'.[5] Steam power was introduced as an inferior substitute when supplies of water became inadequate to meet the society's growing needs. Once more, it cannot be argued that development was held up by problems of invention: the Americans chose not to use existing technology. The strength of the thesis that development is not chosen in preference to traditional methods but is a response to ecological pressures seems to be confirmed.

The discussion of the rapid development of the eastern United States and its repercussions on other regions would seem to prepare the way for a few remarks on American industrialization generally, but first it is important to discuss some aspects

[1] Clark, op. cit., p. 404.   [2] Ibid., p. 404n.
[3] Ibid., p. 410.   [4] Ibid., p. 405.   [5] Ibid., p. 405.

of the pattern of agricultural development as it spread across the rest of the continent.

The early colonial farmers took time to adapt their methods to suit conditions where land was plentiful. Naturally enough they thought they had to clear the forest and remove stumps from the ground to make the kind of fields they were familiar with instead of adopting the hoe-culture of the aborigines. They would often choose readymade clearings not realizing they were frequently the remains of fields abandoned by the Indians because of declining soil fertility. As a New Englander, Jared Eliot, pointed out, the first settlers'

> unacquaintedness with the Country, led them to make choice of the worst Land for their Improvement, and the most expensive and chargeable Methods of Cultivation: They tho't themselves obliged to stubb all staddle, and cut down or lop all great Trees; in which they expended much Cost and Time, to the prejudice of the Crop and impoverishing the Land. [1]

Although in many areas people did adopt something like the extensive Indian methods which entailed periodic shifts to more fertile land, tightly knit communities – such as the Pennsylvania Dutch – did not allow a regression in techniques. They maintained their geographical stability by practising rotations and using enough manure to keep up soil fertility. Such communities provide an interesting example of the importance of social factors in the maintenance of ecological equilibrium. In most parts of New England agricultural regression did not go very far. Although they did not always use equilibrium techniques and so became poorer as soil fertility declined, only comparatively small areas of land ever had to be completely abandoned. When the amount of land available per head was large, very little work was necessary to keep soil fertility high enough to feed a farmer and his family. Where rotations were used in the later seventeenth and eighteenth centuries they often resembled the medieval three-course system,

[1] Jared Eliot, *Essays upon Field-Husbandry in New England* (Boston, 1760), p. 1.

and fallow fields were usually left to grass over without being sown. Little or no manure appears to have been used in most places. There was no need to dig the soil deeply and many farmers managed with hoes; what ploughs there were did not turn more than the top few inches of the earth. But in other parts of the country the process of substituting land for labour seems to have gone much further than it did in New England. Again and again we find that the land is being cultivated without any attempt to maintain soil fertility; when yields decline, new land is cleared and the old abandoned. For instance in Virginia and Maryland, according to one historian, tobacco planters found that

> A superior tobacco could be produced only on fresh land, and after the second crop – usually the best – the quality and quantity began to decline. The planter seldom counted on more than three or four crops from his land before it was abandoned to corn and wheat and then to pine, sedge, and sorrell growths which usually characterize 'sour lands'. . . . the terms 'tobacco lands' and 'new lands' soon became synonymous. A constant clearing of the forest was carried on and a constant abandonment of 'old fields' followed at the other end.[1]

Techniques were reminiscent of the slash-and-burn agriculture discussed in earlier chapters. The forest cover was cleared by cutting down the smaller trees, ring-barking the larger ones and burning as much as possible. Stumps were left in the ground and hand tools used for cultivation. But perhaps the most important point was the widespread preference for clearing new land rather than doing the work necessary to maintain the fertility of the old. Such behaviour would seem to support the argument that primitive forms of agriculture have a higher labour productivity than more intensive ones. As Thomas Jefferson said when answering Arthur Young who was puzzled as to how American farmers could produce so much wheat while using so little manure, 'manure does not enter

[1] Avery O. Craven, *Soil Exhaustion as a Factor in the Agricultural History of Virginia and Maryland, 1606–1860* (Urbana, 1926), p. 32.

into this because we can buy an acre of new land cheaper than we can manure an old one.'[1]

Things would have been all right if the land had been allowed to revert to forest after an initial period of cropping. But instead of being left to recuperate naturally – as it would have been in other parts of the world where similar techniques have been used – the soil was used for a succession of crops until useless for any of them. As the tobacco growers moved on to new lands, the wheat growers moved in behind them. The older parts of the country experienced the results of declining yields before others; in parts of Virginia and Maryland for instance, Gray says 'Poverty, deterioration, and despairing inertia spread over the face of the country like a pall. Many of the counties showed a decrease in population for several decades following the census of 1790.'[2] By 1850 much of this area was a waste of 'old fields and abandoned lands covered with underbrush and young cedars'.

The prospect of areas booming and then dying as the virgin resources – soil, timber and minerals – were exploited and destroyed is common in American history. The kind of devastation that followed in the wake of the tobacco planters happened in other agricultural areas – perhaps the best known is the South's Old Cotton Belt. Gray describes the whole cycle:

> The first three decades after the introduction of cotton was a period of financial prosperity and rapid development in upper South Carolina and middle Georgia, but by 1820 the uplands first devoted to cotton were gullied and bare of verdure, or covered with a thin growth of broom and sedge; and the evil spread progressively over the areas later occupied.[3]

One of the important differences between the ecology of resource exploitation in America and the situation in more

[1] *Soil Exhaustion*, p. 34.
[2] Lewis C. Gray, *History of Agriculture in the Southern United States to 1860* (Washington, 1933), p. 909.
[3] Ibid., p. 910.

densely populated parts of the world, is that when things got bad in America people could migrate to new areas. They did not have to find a solution to their problems within the area: places could be left to die. Much of the impetus to westward expansion came from this source. People were continuously moving further west in search of fresh land and virgin stands of timber as they 'mined' out the resources of the older regions. Places where the soil was unsuited to agriculture would die as soon as the timber had been cut and sold to eastern markets. This is what happened in what came to be known as the 'Cut-over Region' of northern Minnesota, Wisconsin and Michigan. In the words of a government report, 'No thought was given either to perpetuating the (timber) resource for later generations or to promoting the lasting prosperity of the region itself.'[1] Trees were felled at an almost incredible speed: in the winter of 1880-1 it is estimated that approaching three-quarters of a million acres of forest were cleared in Michigan alone, and of that state's original stand of some 380,000 million board feet of saw timber about 180,000 million were apparently burned and wasted.[2] When the area was cleared, timber companies and land agencies sold the land for farming, but much of it turned out to have thin leached soils, poorly drained and stony. The region became one of rural poverty and decaying isolated settlements with most of the land going unused after many would-be farmers had been forced to abandon the struggle.

The ecological parameters which spelt out the pattern of American economic development are not difficult to discern. There seem to be three main elements: first was the rapidity of population growth – weak social constraints and immigration combined to give rates of increase which were often twice as high as any recorded in England; second was the extraordinary rate at which the stocks of virgin resources were exploited, wasted and destroyed, forcing continuous westward expansion; third was the failure to develop methods of re-

[1] William N. Sparhawk and Warren D. Brush, 'The economic aspects of forest destruction in northern Michigan', US Department of Agriculture, *Technical Bulletin*, XCII, p. 6.
[2] Ibid., pp. 7, 9.

newing and conserving resources – that is equilibrium methods which could halt deteriorating environmental productivity. American economic development sprang from the lack of equilibrium between these ecological parameters. The fact that the degree of disequilibrium was greater in America than in England explains why development was so much more rapid in the former. The degree of disequilibrium and the problems it created were often extremely severe. We have already mentioned some examples of soil destruction. In some instances the damage was done by exhausting the soil of crop nutrients, in others agricultural methods exposed the soil to natural erosion. Virginia, Maryland and North Carolina were among the worst affected states early on. In 1817 it was estimated that the amount of land abandoned in North Carolina was equal to, if not greater than, the amount of land in cultivation.[1] Some four generations later, in 1938, a presidential committee reported that

> An expanse of Southern farm land as large as South Carolina has been gullied and washed away; at least 22 million acres of once fertile land has been ruined beyond repair. Another area the size of Oklahoma and Alabama combined has been seriously damaged by erosion. In addition, the sterile sand and gravel washed off the land has covered over a fertile valley acreage equal in size to Maryland.[2]

In areas with resources to spare, the lack of social constraints on population growth was tolerable, but in others it led to a Malthusian situation with extreme poverty and malnutrition. In the 1930s the southern Appalachians and the Old Cotton Belt were among the poorest regions and yet had rates of natural population growth far above the national average.[3] Only largescale migration prevented the pressure on the economic system rising higher than it did.

*   *   *

[1] Gates, op. cit., p. 7.
[2] Thomas D. Clark and Albert D. Kirwan, *The South Since Appomattox* (New York, 1967), p. 101.
[3] Carter Goodrich *et al.*, *Migration and Economic Opportunity* (Philadelphia, 1936), pp. 56, 61, 130–2.

In the populous east – and particularly in the expanding urban industrial north-east – the soil was not allowed to deteriorate into unproductive waste. Land near the population centres was too valuable to be entirely neglected, and soon it was scarce enough to be subject to the demands of more intensive cultivation. Instead of moving further afield where land was more plentiful, farmers found that the growing markets for agricultural produce made it worthwhile to undertake the extra work involved in gaining higher yields. The revolution in agricultural techniques began early in the nineteenth century. Like other aspects of development which we have discussed, agricultural innovations were not introduced in America as soon as they had been discovered in Europe, but waited until the ecological situation required them. Sometimes the introduction of particularly laborious new techniques was resisted longer than was economically sensible. Economic calculus indicates that it was not worthwhile introducing new techniques where the land still retained its natural fertility, or where it did not have the advantage of proximity to the markets to discourage a simple migration to greener pastures. The agricultural revolution took root in the east when the problems of declining soil fertility and inadequate yields reached crisis proportions. Growing subsistence problems in the traditional rural economy precipitated the development both of manufacturing and of agriculture. The association of agricultural and industrial revolutions observed in so many parts of the world occurs because both are a response to the development of poverty. Thus in eastern New York State around the mid-nineteenth century when almost every county suffered from 'serious soil exhaustion', agricultural improvements were spreading and the proportion of the population occupied in manufacturing was increasing. New England reached the same situation a few decades earlier. During the first half of the nineteenth century the use of gypsum, lime, manure and rotation crops appeared in all the north-east and middle Atlantic states. More intensive farming also entailed deeper ploughing and the use of more draught animals than were necessary for the shallow cultivation which had been sufficient earlier.

The general course of American agricultural development follows a predictable pattern if we accept that it was basically a process of adopting more onerous intensive techniques as the land to population ratio became less favourable. Both the initial regression in techniques which continued in many areas until methods resembled the Indian slash-and-burn extensive agriculture, and the preference for clearing new forest land rather than maintaining the fertility of the old, are features we would expect where land was so plentiful. The choice of forested land rather than clearings, and later rather than the prairies, also has a familiar ring. Though the tendency of settlers to skirt the prairies has traditionally been explained in terms of the shortage of timber on the grassland, the problem of ploughing the grassland is known to have been important. As mentioned in chapter 5, grassland cannot be cleared for sowing by burning, but must be ploughed. The hoes, cultivators and shallow ploughs which could be used elsewhere were of little use in breaking the prairie sod. Largescale settlement of the prairies was impracticable before the development of heavy steel ploughs – the 'prairie breakers' – pulled by six to twelve oxen. The need for such implements must have raised the cost of cultivation considerably.

There is some direct evidence of the ease with which subsistence could be gained before the development of more intensive agricultural techniques. Though people producing crops for market may have chosen to work long hours it was not always necessary. Congressman Porter speaking of the newly settled areas of his constituency in western New York State in 1810, said

> Such is the fertility of their land that one-half their time spent in labour is sufficient to produce every article which their farms are capable of yielding, in sufficient quantities for their own consumption, and there is nothing to incite them to produce more. They are, therefore, naturally led to spend the other part of their time in idleness and dissipation.[1]

[1] As quoted in G. S. Callender, 'The early transportation and banking enterprises of the states', *Quarterly Journal of Economics*, XVII (1902), p. 123.

If the hours worked by soldiers is any guide to social norms, evidence from early Virginia suggests that the workload may have been remarkably light. Of the routine of men working in the fields under the command of Captain John Smith, who became president of Virginia, we are told that '4 houres each day was spent in worke, the rest in pastimes and merry exercise'.[1] New military rules drawn up a few years later for Virginia, although generally extremely strict and often providing for barbaric punishments for offenders, only advised about six hours' work a day.[2] At least it seems likely that people did not have to work such exceptionally long hours as they did in some later periods. The additional work involved in manuring and liming the land and in growing rotation crops must have been very considerable, and when it comes to factory work the hours were often inhuman. Long hours of work and the employment of young children spread from one part of the country to another with the development of manufacturing. It started to be a problem early in the nineteenth century in some of the older manufacturing towns and cities of the northeast, and continued in the southern states into the present century with adults working eleven or twelve hours a day, and children as young as ten sometimes even working night shifts.[3]

England's discovery of the solutions to a wide range of resource shortages before America ever faced them meant that America could innovate and substitute new resources for old before shortages had become really acute. The important inventions and discoveries which provided for the transition from an agricultural to an industrial resource-base were made – as we have seen – long before the English industrial revolution. The American economy could then proceed much more smoothly from one resource-base to another. Problems did not

[1] John Smith, *Works 1608–1631*, edited by Edward Arber (Birmingham, 1884), p. 149.
[2] William Strachey (ed.), *For the Colony of Virginea, Lawes Divine, Morall and Martiall* (London, 1612), pp. 61–2.
[3] C. Vann Woodward, *Origins of the New South 1877–1913* (Baton Rouge, 1966), pp. 416–17.

have to become sufficiently acute to stimulate invention. Another factor which made the American transition smoother
than the English is that a growing resources shortage in any
part of America meant only that supplies had to be brought
from more distant places. Scarcity meant increased transport
costs: supply was not as inelastic as in England. Substitution
took place at different times in different regions as supply lines
lengthened. For instance, the changeover from woodburning
steamboats and railway engines to coalburning ones gradually
shifted across the country according to the location and costs of
the two fuels. Substitution came first in the east. Boats on the
Hudson turned to burning coal in the late 1830s and 1840s.
As wood became scarcer on the western rivers, coal-burning
spread further down the Ohio from the upper reaches in west
Pennsylvania where supplies were cheap. Between the mid-
century and the civil war, coal-burning became well established even on the lower Mississippi, but on rivers such as the
Missouri, where coal was distant and wood was still plentiful,
wood remained the predominant fuel for at least another
twenty or thirty years.[1] The changeover on the railways followed a similar course. The iron industry too made the substitution at different times from place to place; even as late as
1917 some 376,000 tons of pig iron were smelted with charcoal.[2]

Though severe resource crises were rare, the growing dependence of the American economy on mineral resources is
clear; indeed this has been called the most striking feature of
US economic growth during the half century following the
civil war.[3] The iron industry expanded to meet the growing
need for all forms of transport equipment, but particularly for
rails, for more sophisticated agricultural equipment (including
deep ploughs, associated with more intensive cultivation) and

[1] Louis C. Hunter, *Steamboats on the Western Rivers* (Cambridge, Mass.,
1949), pp. 269–70.
[2] Harvey S. Perloff *et al.*, *Regions, Resources, and Economic Growth* (Baltimore, 1960), p. 210n.
[3] Louis C. Hunter, 'Products of the earth, 1866–1918', in Harold F.
Williamson, *The Growth of the American Economy* (Englewood Cliffs,
N.J., 1951), p. 454.

the widespread use of steam-engines. One of the few resources which did undergo its first important commercial development in America during this period was oil, and significantly it owes its early development to a more than usually acute resource shortage. The rapid expansion in the demand for lighting and lubricants could not easily be met from traditional sources. In 1857 the *Scientific American* reported that 'The whale oils which have hitherto been much relied on in this country to furnish light, are yearly becoming more scarce, and may in time almost entirely fail, while the rapid increase in machinery demands a large proportion of the purest of these oils for lubricating'.[1] Attempts to find other sources of lubricants and illuminants, which included distilling fractions of coal, ended in 1859 when an oil drilling in west Pennsylvania proved successful. As soon as mineral oil was included in the nation's resource-base its other potential uses were quickly developed. At a time when most areas were already dependent on fuel which had to be transported long distances, the need to transport fuel oil did not put it at a disadvantage. By about 1880 three-quarters of the crude oil produced was being used as fuel oil for raising steam and heating buildings.[2]

Other minerals which became important in the period after the civil war included phosphates and sulphur primarily for fertilizers, salt for soda and other alkalis, as well as building materials such as sand, gravel and lime for cement.

In conclusion we can say that even in the anomalous circumstances in which American development took place, the population showed many of the same preferences that we have seen in other societies. When they could, they chose to clothe themselves in furs and leather rather than woven cloth; they used wood rather than coal, water power rather than steam, primitive extensive agricultural methods rather than the more intensive European ones they were familiar with. They went on using the older established methods and resources long after

---

[1] *Scientific American*, XII (27 June 1857), as quoted in Hunter (1951), op. cit., p. 466n.
[2] Hunter (1951), op. cit., p. 467.

they need have done, when they were fully aware of the alternatives. We have seen that the growing use of coal followed the appearance of regional timber scarcities which meant felling forests further and further afield, that steam power was not introduced into mills until additional water power was no longer available, and that people did not adopt intensive agricultural methods until forced by ecological pressures. Self-sufficient communities were forced to change their way of life by the appearance of local resource shortages and by the development of individual poverty. Urbanization and industrialization became significant with the emergence of a sizeable group of people who were unable to produce their own subsistence independently. The development of transport and distribution networks owed its origins to the breakdown of self-sufficiency in basic bulk commodities and to the increasing centralization of manufacturing production. With the forced adoption of more difficult modes of production and less amenable resources, industry and agriculture required increasing quantities of labour and power. People worked longer hours and traditional sources of power were doubled up or supplemented by new sources whether in agriculture, in transport, in mills or in metal manufacture. Variations in the incidence of poverty or in working hours suggest that we should be wary of assuming any simple pattern of improvement with the arrival of successive features of economic development. It is not merely a romantic comparison between the quality of life in one of the stable eighteenth-century New England communities and life in modern American cities which casts doubt on the ideology of economic progress. But without the most uncontroversial evidence of progress it is difficult to explain development unless it is traced to the ecological effects of a burgeoning population, the lack of equilibrium techniques and the technical interactions derived from these elements.

9 Industrial societies: production and consumption

We have seen how the early stages of industrialization were instituted to deal with a set of problems confronting the established economic system. Change was impelled by the shortage of landbased resources and by the increasingly acute subsistence needs of the population. But industrial development did not cease once subsistence needs had been catered for on a new and reasonably secure footing. Industrial societies have reached higher standards of comfort than were common earlier and enjoy a range of completely new consumer goods. Whereas people in many pre-industrial societies preferred to do only the amount of work necessary to secure their subsistence and then to maximize their leisure time, people in industrial societies have been willing to go on working to secure more than the minimum. Pre-industrial societies tend to show what economists call a 'leisure preference'. They use an increase in their real wages to increase their leisure time: in effect subsistence can be earned in a shorter time. This was the pattern in England before the industrial revolution, but things seem to have changed at some point during the second half of the eighteenth century.[1] Perhaps partly influenced by rising prices, people began to use any rise in earnings to increase their consumption rather than their leisure time. Even today, the dominant desire is for higher consumption rather than increased leisure. Whenever the basic working week is shortened people prefer to work additional hours overtime, increasing their earnings rather than their leisure.[2]

[1] A. W. Coats, 'Changing attitudes to labour in the mid 18th century', *Economic History Review*, XI (1958), pp. 35–51.
[2] See p. 187 below.

The difference between the pre-industrial leisure preference and the industrial consumption – or work – preference cannot be explained simply in terms of the differing productive potentialities of the two societies. Although modern consumer goods such as television sets and telephones were, for reasons of technical consistency, obviously beyond the reach of pre-industrial agricultural societies, many peasant populations could very well have used some of their leisure time to improve their housing, clothing, household goods and often their diet as well. The difference in behaviour is to some extent a genuine reflection of differing attitudes to consumption.

The urgency of consumption provides some indication of the subjective experience of need. We know however that in terms of man's genetic make-up, industrial man is born with the same basic needs as his agricultural predecessors. Whatever those needs are they will not have changed and so cannot be used to explain the apparent new urgency for consumption at increasingly high levels. To understand the modern growth of consumer demand, the directions it has taken and people's willingness to work for it, we must look at the changing context of life in industrial societies.

Before discussing specific aspects of changing lifestyles it may be helpful to sketch in the broad framework in which the discussion is set. The industrial revolution we have seen was a response to the increasing problems encountered in providing subsistence through the established economic system. As new methods were implemented and industrial production grew, the old subsistence problems were gradually solved, or were at least greatly alleviated. But the development of industrial production imposed a completely new way of life on the population and placed them in a drastically altered physical and social environment. The insanitary conditions of nineteenth-century towns, the overcrowding, the high death rate, and the break-up of rural culture and social life are well known. On balance it seems likely that society had to pay for increased production of basic subsistence items by undergoing a worsening of cultural, social and environmental conditions during at least part of the nineteenth century. People only accepted the rigours of early urban industrial life in the hope of improving their subsistence situation. We have seen the sort of pressures which drove people off the land and out of domestic industry to join the ranks of the urban workers. This may have been the easiest way of providing for a growing population, but although increasing numbers gained the bare necessities of life, they suffered from severe cultural, social and environmental deprivation. They came near to living on bread alone.

The changing context of life led to a kind of accumulating debt – or poverty – in one aspect of existence after another. Society exchanged poverty in one sphere for poverty in others which seemed less vital. Problems of transport, urban sanitation, entertainment, education and social activity became increasingly pressing. It is to the development of problems such as these that we owe much of the modern urgency of consumption. New needs sprung from the changing lifestyle and environment in two ways: the old methods of satisfying many human needs were destroyed or rendered obsolete, and new problems demanding new solutions arose out of the new pattern of living. Society has relied heavily on the economic system to right this situation. Man has had to be encapsuled increasingly in his own creations to make his urban industrial lifestyle workable.

Many of the goods and services enjoyed by modern industrial societies would also have been appreciated by populations in pre-industrial societies. The argument is not that these goods would not have been desired by pre-industrial populations; it is merely that they were not things which people would have been prepared to work for. Only the development of particular needs has made the possession of these goods sufficiently important to work for. There were undoubtedly many aspects of the pre-industrial way of life which were especially satisfactory, and it was only after the disruption of this way of life that people experienced some particularly pressing needs outside the sphere of traditional subsistence. Without the enormous increases in incomes and consumption which continued industrial development has produced, we would surely have been worse off than our agricultural predecessors. In human terms the real standard of living in the early and mid-nineteenth century was abysmal. Incomes had to increase sufficiently to offset the losses before real progress was possible.

We must now look at some specific examples of the ways in which increases in consumption are related to particular new needs. This is a difficult subject to arrange at all systematically: most needs are satisfied by a number of different goods and each good contributes to the satisfaction of several different needs; there is no simple one-to-one relationship.

Modern systems of waste and sewage disposal are obviously a response to the problems of urban sanitation which became particularly pressing in the early stages of industrialization. Outside 'privies', soak-aways, cesspools, sewage discharged directly into streams, and wells and pumps for fresh water are adequate arrangements for small communities and rural areas. They become dangerously inadequate in large densely populated urban settlements. Streets and streams become open sewers and underground water sources become seriously polluted. In densely populated areas sewage is almost certain to overburden natural drainage systems and organic purification processes: sewers have to be laid and filtration plants built. Likewise, fresh water must be supplied through non-porous pipes from pure or purified sources. The development of modern methods was clearly a response to the problems created by largescale urban development. The filthy conditions which appeared in many of the larger cities before effective action was taken are well known, and even today a great many people in the rural areas of industrial countries manage quite adequately using older methods such as cesspools.

Refuse disposal also requires special attention in urban areas. The urban dweller usually has more refuse and less opportunity to dispose of it than people in agricultural societies did. The extremely complicated distribution system required to support urban life leads, almost inevitably, to a growing use of disposable tins, glass bottles, paper and plastic packaging materials. The small amount of waste generated by pre-industrial agricultural societies is likely to be organic matter which can either be used to advantage on the land or can be burnt on domestic fires. In towns, where most people have neither gardens nor solid fuel fires, public refuse-disposal services are necessary. Once again we find that people in the rural areas of industrial societies still have less need of these modern services. Many rural households separate out vegetable waste for garden compost, and others use some of the waste paper for lighting fires. This leaves them with only the modern surplus of tins, bottles, plastics and surplus paper.

The need for larger quantities of packaging materials is linked to the wider problem of preserving perishable goods as supply lines get longer and distribution systems become more complex. Much of our food is now tinned, dried, frozen, vacuum-packed or has artificial preservatives added. In pre-industrial societies it was only necessary to smoke, dry or salt some foods for winter, but modern preserving methods are now essential all the year round for such basic items as foreign meat, fruit and vegetables. The same methods have made a much wider range of foods available and most kinds of fruit and vegetables can now be bought out of season, but historically the development of preserving techniques was not a response to the desire to reap these benefits. Indeed, from the point of view of the consumer these changes are not an entirely unmixed blessing: few people are now able to enjoy really fresh food from their own plot of land, frozen food is a second best and to partake of the variety available in the shops it is impractical not to have a refrigerator. Although refrigerators have become part of our basic cultural equipment, and new houses and flats no longer contain space for a larder, by 1971 over 30 per cent of all households in the United Kingdom were still without refrigerators.[1]

The type of work which the population of an industrial society must perform has several fairly obvious effects on their needs as consumers. People have to adapt themselves physically, mentally and environmentally to meet the demands which their

[1] UK Central Statistical Office, *Social Trends*, III (1972), Table 55, p. 103.

work imposes on them. Education is perhaps the most important consumer good serving this purpose. Not only do most
jobs now require a formal and specialized training – even most
of those classed as 'manual work' – but a basic level of education
and literacy has long been necessary for everyone just to cope
with the complexity of everyday urban industrial life. The
coming of compulsory education, first primary and then
secondary, and the current growth of higher education were
not purely fortuitous events; they are so closely linked
with the demands which economic development has made
on the population that several economists have suggested
that this 'investment in human capital' is the basis of development.

The demands of work and the journey to work account for
a large part of the consumers' use of transport. People in
industrial societies live much further from their work than the
peasant did from his land. In 1963 very nearly half the American
working population had to do a round trip of twelve miles or
more to get to work and back each day.[1] Only 3 per cent walked
to work.[2] In England and Wales in 1963–4, about half the
mileage clocked up in cars run by private households was
accounted for by journeys to and from work, or travelling in
the course of employment.[3] Figures are not available for the
corresponding use of public transport, but one would guess
that a rather higher proportion is used for the journey to and
from work. Some idea of the proportion of consumer expenditure involved may be gained from the 1971 figure of 12·5 per
cent of total consumer expenditure for the purchase and
running of cars and for other forms of transport.[4]

The clock plays a much more important part in industrial
societies than in pre-industrial ones. Most people rely on an
alarm clock to wake them in time for work. Once at work many

---

[1] US Department of Commerce, *1963 Census of Transportation*, volume I,
p. 64, Table 2.
[2] Ibid., p. 64, Table 3.
[3] UK Ministry of Transport, *Private Motoring in England and Wales* (1969),
p. 35, Table 3.3.
[4] UK Central Statistical Office, *Social Trends*, III (1972), Table 54, p. 102.

workers have to clock in and out. Even outside working hours people's activities have to be co-ordinated in time not just for catching buses and trains, but for a host of other arrangements which have become part of everyday life. Industrialization has obviously created a need for watches and clocks. People cannot function effectively in their environment without them.

Clocking in and out at work is a symbol of the routine of industrial employment. The increased division of labour and growing mechanization has meant that many people function primarily as appendages to machines, while others are forced to lead entirely sedentary working lives. The daily and seasonal variations in the type and intensity of agricultural work have no part in industrial employment. The routine is protected from seasonal variations in daylight hours by electric lighting, and repetitive machines control the pace. In this situation regular holidays become a physical and psychological necessity. Although in agricultural societies the year has periods of intense activity, in many it also has slack periods of perhaps several months' duration when there is little work to be done. These natural breaks and the variations in work mean that people are less in need of formal holidays. In Britain during 1971, 67 per cent of all full-time workers got a minimum of three weeks formal holiday, but 28 per cent had only two weeks.[1] In an industrial society holidays are also an opportunity to get away from the urban environment and spend a few days in the countryside or beside the sea. British residents took 40·4 million holidays away from home in 1971 (that is holidays of four or more nights away from home), of which 6·4 million were spent abroad.[2] These figures cover a population of some 54 million, and if allowance is made for people who had more than one holiday, it suggests that perhaps as many as 15 or 16 million people did not have a holiday away from home at all.

Having mentioned a few examples of the kind of way people's needs – and so consumer demand – can be affected by

[1] Ibid., p. 78, Table 26.   [2] Ibid., p. 81, Table 30.

the coming of urban life and industrial employment, it will be instructive to go on to discuss some of the effects of the break-up of settled rural communities. Community life could of course develop in urban areas; in those places where the population has remained settled for any length of time, it has. Because good community relations take so long to develop, a reasonably stationary population is a prerequisite. Although some people get to know each other faster than others, the general importance of a settled population is both well documented and rather obvious.[1] Enormous variations in the level of community interaction – or neighbourliness – are possible. On the one hand there are people in areas which have been settled for several generations who feel that on their street they are 'one big family' and there is often some literal truth in it, while on the other, there are new estates where perhaps only the minority have anything to do with their neighbours at all, and where people are lonely and feel that the area is unfriendly or even actively hostile.[2] Though it would be impossible to measure any longterm trends in the level of community development at all accurately, it is undoubtedly a most important sociological variable. The best overall clue is perhaps the population's geographical mobility. The 1966 Sample Census migration tables showed that some 10 per cent of the population of England and Wales had moved house during the previous year, and that 31 per cent had moved at least once during the previous five years.[3] In the USA 19 per cent of the population moved house in the year ending March 1969, and 50 per cent moved during the five years 1955–60.[4] These averages must hide great variations between groups within the population, but few people would argue that rural, pre-industrial societies could produce figures anything like them.

[1] See for instance Michael Young and Peter Willmott, *Family and Kinship in East London* (London, 1957), chapter 7.

[2] Hannah Gavron, *The Captive Wife* (London, 1968 edition), p. 99.

[3] UK General Register Office, *Sample Census 1966*, Migration Summary Tables part 1 (London 1968), p. 2, Table 1A; p. 24, Table 1B.

[4] US Bureau of the Census, 'Mobility of the population of the US', *Current Population Reports* (1969), p. 7, Table 1. US Department of Commerce, *Statistical Abstract of the U.S. 1969* (1969), p. 34, Table 39.

The names on tombstones in a country churchyard often show how normal it was for the same family to live in the same village, for generation after generation. That many manorial tenants enjoyed hereditary rights to land and housing is another indication of the stability of rural society. Apart from periods of rapid population growth or decline there was little reason or opportunity to move. The figures of mobility in industrial Britain and America must be taken as an indication of a much lower level of social interaction, community and neighbourliness. Mobile people cannot get to know their neighbours or even their relatives as well as if they had lived in close proximity to them all their lives.

The breakdown of the local community – of the 'neighhood' as a social reality – created a need both for new forms of entertainment to replace the disappearing social activities and traditions, and for transport and communications systems to allow contact between geographically separated friends and relatives. A government survey showed that in 1965–6 women in Britain spent only 9 per cent of their leisure time in specifically social activities; men spent only 3 per cent or, if the time they spent at the pub is added in, 6 per cent.[1] For how long this has been the state of affairs it is difficult to say, but it is clear that the response to it in terms of organized and commercial entertainment developed more rapidly during the second than the first half of the nineteenth century. Music halls, competitive factory brass bands, football clubs and various other spectator and participatory sports became important in the later period. During the first half of the nineteenth century, after rural cultural life and festivals had been rendered obsolete by urbanization, there seems to have been a depressing lack of any mass – or working-class – culture. Cockfighting seems to have been one of the few activities which survived even the onset of industrialization. In the twentieth century however, the cinema, radio, popular music, record players and, most important of all, television have taken over. Television now fills much more of people's leisure time than anything else; over 90 per cent of

[1] UK Central Statistical Office, *Social Trends*, III (1972), p. 80, Table 29.

G

households in the UK have a set, and in 1965–6 men and women spent 23 per cent of their leisure time watching it.[1] This compares with the next most important activity – for men, gardening (12 per cent of their leisure time) and for women, 'crafts and hobbies', mainly knitting (17 per cent). Evidence tending to confirm the suggestion that economic provision for entertainment becomes more important after the breakdown of good social relationships within a community comes from a study of Bethnal Green and 'Greenleigh'.[2] In Bethnal Green, where community life was highly developed, 32 per cent of households had television in 1955, but in the new estate at 'Greenleigh', where there was very little social interaction, 65 per cent of households had a set – although most of the 'Greenleigh' people were rehoused from Bethnal Green.

The form and content of much modern entertainment and of the mass media also indicate that they have grown to fill a specifically social vacuum. The 'human interest' element appears as the modern equivalent of gossip in the popular press, the romantic short stories in the weeklies, the films and paperback novels which aim to make their audiences feel part of a human drama, the radio and television 'personalities' who create the illusion of a personal relationship with their audiences, the social cravings expressed in 'pop' songs and perhaps, in a displaced sexual form, in pornography. The passive reception of manufactured images, fiction and fantasy, substitute increasingly for a disappearing social reality.

The mass media of course fulfil other functions than that of catering for directly social desires. Now that people are dependent on national and international political and economic events, news conveyed by word of mouth is no longer adequate. The provision of news media has become a necessity. Another less welcome function of the media is the establishment of social norms and attitudes. Where there is a high level of social interaction within a community, the community itself will provide behavioural norms for its members. The necessary social approval, disapproval, rewards and sanctions can be generated within the community. But in modern industrial

[1] *Social Trends*, p. 80, Table 29.   [2] Young and Willmott, op. cit., p. 143.

society the media play an increasingly important role as the reference point from which people develop their individual behaviour and attitudes. The popular press is full of explicit and implicit moral judgements, while editorials and discussions between experts indicate the norms on wider political and social events.

A high level of geographical mobility means that friends and families are likely to be widely scattered. In their study of Bethnal Green, Young and Willmott gave some figures showing how the frequency with which married women visited their mothers varied according to how far away their mothers lived. (See table below.) Although the sample excluded those

Contacts between married women in Bethnal Green and their mothers, according to the distance between their homes[1]

(Sample: 133 married women with mothers alive and not in same dwelling.)

Mother's home	Number of married women	Number of women who saw their mother in twenty-four hours before survey interview
Same street or block of flats	23	23
Elsewhere in Bethnal Green	49	33
Adjacent borough	25	4
Elsewhere	36	3

women who were actually living with their mothers, 54 per cent of the rest had mothers living in the same borough; of these, two-thirds had seen them in the twenty-four hours before the survey. Of the 46 per cent with mothers living in other boroughs, only 10 per cent had seen them in the last twenty-four hours. Men saw their parents less often than the women

[1] Ibid., p. 48.

did, but generally family contacts – including contacts between brothers and sisters – were very important in Bethnal Green. From our point of view, these figures show both how important the extended family tends to be where people can still live close to each other, and also how decisive distance can be in severing these relationships. Modern transport and communications can, of course, help reintegrate separated friends and families, but most people in Bethnal Green were not well enough off to make much use of them. In a sense the table gives an indication of the latent demand for a 'perfect' transport and communications system incurring neither time nor cost. As the spatial separation of friends and families increases this 'latent demand' increases. We have already seen how work and the distance to work contribute to the private consumer's need for transport: the social need adds another important new element to the demand for transport. People who cannot afford transport or a telephone are forced to rely much more than others on the resources of the isolated nuclear family. Better-off people who live apart from family and friends are able to drive to see them at weekends. Hannah Gavron emphasizes the role which the telephone plays in keeping middle-class families in touch over long distances and quotes one housewife who said she rang her ageing parents every day.[1] The potential social demand in a fragmented society is also indicated by the advertising slogans: 'Your phone gets you closer to someone' and British Rail's 'See a friend this weekend'.

The examples we have been through give some indication of the ways in which the real needs of individual consumers may change and expand as a result of industrial development and urbanization. Although people are considerably better off now than they were in earlier periods of industrialization, feelings of need or deprivation are still genuine enough – given the context – for a large part of the populations even of the more advanced industrial countries. In the United Kingdom in 1971, 62 per cent of all households were without a telephone, amidst declining public transport 49 per cent were without the use of a car, 31 per cent had no refrigerator, 9 per cent did not have

[1] Hannah Gavron, op. cit., pp. 101, 103.

television and many were without a wrist watch.[1] The 1966 sample census shows that 18 per cent of the population of England and Wales lived in houses without inside lavatories.[2] Incomes are lower than is often imagined. In 1970 about 10 million people in the UK lived below, at, or very little above the supplementary benefits level, and *average* consumer expenditure per head of the total population was less than £11 per week.[3] Relative poverty apart, it is not surprising that industrial development has produced a range of new consumer goods to meet the new needs. Although these goods go some way towards solving the problems thrown up by our changing lifestyle, there seems little reason for thinking that solutions can always be found faster than new problems are generated.

From what has been said, it appears that industrialization requires a more extravagant lifestyle than the modes of production that preceded it. The problems it creates and the needs it sets up make increased consumption a necessity if people are to lead reasonably satisfactory lives. The continuous expansion of gross national product which this requires should perhaps be regarded more as a reflection of the rising real cost of living than an indication of increasing welfare.

In the most recent period of industrial development, ecological problems and the forces of technical consistency have continued to stimulate change. Oil products have provided an important group of new materials. Plastics and polythenes have been used as substitutes for wood in a variety of ways: polythene sheet is replacing cellophane and paper (both made from wood pulp) for bags and wrappings as well as for a number of other uses, and heavier plastics are being substituted for wood in mouldings where rigidity and heat resistance are unnecessary.

---

[1] UK Central Statistical Office, *Social Trends*, III (1972), Table 55, p. 103.
[2] UK General Register Office, *Sample Census 1966*, Housing Tables, p. 127, Table 11.
[3] Nicholas Bosanquet, 'Banding poverty', *New Society* (2 March 1972), p. 448. UK Central Statistical Office, *Monthly Digest of Statistics* (January 1972), Tables 5 and 10. On poverty see also Child Poverty Action Group, *Poverty* (winter 1971).

In many areas where plastics are unsuitable, metals are increasingly used to replace wood. Examples range from draining boards and window frames to coachwork of all kinds. Fibreglass is coming to fill many of the intermediary roles between metals and plastics where until recently plywood was the typical material. The stimulus given to these substitutions by the increasing scarcity and high price of wood is well known. The laborious way in which waste wood is now reconstituted to make hardboard and chipboard shows the severity of the timber shortage. After seeing the disappearance of wood as a fuel in the early stages of industrial development we are now seeing its eclipse as a common constructional material.

There are many other examples of the continuing ecological pressures to substitute minerals for landbased resources. Artificial fibres made from oil are rapidly replacing natural landbased fibres in clothing. The demand for rubber is supplied increasingly from synthetic sources, detergents have largely replaced soaps made from vegetable oils, and more recently a porous plastic material has been introduced as a substitute for leather, especially for shoe uppers.*

As a result of these and earlier changes the productive task facing industrial societies has become enormous. The dramatic expansion of basic needs, many of which can only be satisfied by highly sophisticated products, and the growing demand for the less amenable resources and raw materials have together created production problems unimaginable in any previous society. Each person in an industrial society is dependent on what amounts to a vast life-support system in which he plays only a minute part. Where the members of a family could once

---

* It often seems surprising that such a wide range of materials can be produced from oil. Oils are hydrocarbons – a major group of materials which spring from the propensity of carbon atoms to link together in long chains. Almost all living matter is based on the same property of carbon atoms. The very large number of these materials is a function of the possible variations in the length of the chain and in the combinations of other elements along it. Silicon is the only other element with similar properties, but the number of possibilities it has is smaller and its potential as a source of new materials much more limited.

clothe themselves in woollens and leather using their own raw materials, we are now dependent for clothing on oil wells, oil tankers, refineries, the chemical industry, textile-machinery manufacturers, and the metal and power industries needed to back them up. The same goes for our food, heating, transport and almost every other item we consume. The productive system depends increasingly on worldwide distribution networks, it is forced to undertake more fundamental and radical transformation processes and the technology it needs becomes ever more sophisticated.

We must now examine how the ever-increasing difficulties of production have been met – how society has managed to perform such a vastly expanded productive task.

First it must be noted that contrary to the popular impression, hours of work have not decreased over the last half century or so – despite the massive introduction of labour-saving machinery. Although innovations in the nineteenth century did make it possible to reduce the length of the working week from the peak reached during the industrial revolution, there has been no significant change in hours since at least the 1920s. As the 'basic' working week has shortened, people have worked an increasing number of hours overtime instead of having more leisure. Thus the actual weekly hours worked per adult male operative in the UK was about 46 in the mid-1920s, 48 in the mid-1930s, about $46\frac{1}{2}$ in the late 1940s, $48\frac{1}{2}$ in the 1950s, and around $47\frac{1}{2}$ in the mid-1960s.[1] Not only have hours of work shown little change, but the proportion of the population working (the 'activity rate') has at best stayed level since accurate records began. Figures for the American economy suggest that the activity rate has risen at least since 1890. Excluding children under sixteen, the proportion of the population working in that year was 56 per cent, in 1947 it was 59 per cent, and in 1967 it was 61 per cent.[2] We know little of the activity rates in the early nineteenth century, but it seems

[1] B. C. Roberts and J. H. Smith (eds.), *Manpower Policy and Employment Trends* (London, 1966), p. 112.

[2] Lloyd G. Reynolds, *Labor Economics and Labor Relations* (Englewood Cliffs, 1970), p. 30.

likely that the total productive workload required per head of
the population has not decreased for a very long time, certainly
not in the last fifty years when it may actually have risen. (In
the period since the 1920s, Japan and Canada are probably
almost the only industrial countries to show a significant decline
in the *per capita* workload once activity rates are taken into
account.)

As the productive task has grown, the pressure to raise the
level of efficiency with which labour is used has increased.
People in marginal jobs such as domestic service have been
drawn into the mainstream of production and have been
replaced by domestic machinery. Part of the increase in the
activity rate has of course been the result of the spread of
domestic machinery allowing more housewives to go out to
work. But no conceivable changes in the amount of work the
population did would be enough to meet the demands of the
productive system. Every aspect of man's productive powers
has had to be augmented, both in quality and in quantity.
Human labour is now able to supply only an insignificant
proportion of the physical power needed. Mechanical sources
of motive power have come to the rescue on an enormous
scale, consuming vast quantities of energy resources. Coal, oil
or nuclear power are used directly or converted for distribution
as electrical energy. In the British economy, the productive
system uses much more electricity than all private consumers
combined.[1] Power-driven machinery has become essential
because of the nature of the tasks it has to perform. The
transportation needs of industry and commerce obviously
cannot be met without a highly mechanized transport system.
By far the greater part of all road, rail and other transport
services are used by industry and commerce rather than by
private consumers.[2] Where man does not lack the power he
lacks the speed needed to perform the enormous number of
simple repetitive operations generated within the productive
system; machines speeding up manual operations have been

[1] UK Central Statistical Office, *Input–Output Tables for the United Kingdom
1963* (1970), p. 55.
[2] Ibid., p. 55.

introduced throughout production. All but a small fraction of the output of the mechanical and electrical engineering industries is used in industry.[1] Man, unaided, is not equipped to perform many of the complex and dangerous productive processes which have become necessary, however much labour he uses. In these areas the development of highly specialized tools and equipment has been essential. Lastly, the sheer complexity of the productive system and the necessity for advanced planning and research have led to the need to supplement even the powers of the human mind: the volume of calculations generated with the aid of mushrooming new statistical techniques has fostered the development of high-speed computers. Simultaneously the use of desk calculating machines continues to grow throughout industry and commerce.

Such a quantity of tools, equipment and power is needed for use in the productive process that most industries now sell most of their output to other producers. The needs of the private consumer are only very indirectly the reason for production. Apart from what amounts to the output of little more than the subsistence industries, the demand for goods is dominated by producers. Inessential consumer goods look like the 'spin-offs' or chance byproducts of a complex technology developed to produce subsistence items rather than goods developed expressly for consumers in their own right.

There can be little argument with the claim that the productive task is increasing. When the amount of labour used is not decreasing, the amount of energy used in production is increasing, and semi-automated laboursaving machinery becomes more and more common, there can be no other explanation. The need to supply the increases in *per capita* consumption already discussed, and the demands of a growing population must account for some expansion of the productive task; but the difficulties of increasing – or in some cases maintaining – output are also growing.

It is not immediately obvious how decisions taken by separate individuals and manufacturers in the name of progress, which are intended to increase efficiency and decrease the

[1] Ibid., p. 55.

workload, could be consistent with a longterm increase in the workload. How can decreases in efficiency get past a price system which is meant to equate cost-reducing behaviour with increasing efficiency? To answer this question it will be helpful to divide monetary costs, rather too simplistically, into two parts. The major part is the cost of the direct and indirect labour incurred in the productive processes. It is a measure of the productive workload in terms of the capital equipment, tools and labour needed to produce an item. As we are interested in the workload to be borne by society this social element will be called the 'real' cost. The other element in cost results purely from scarcity, and serves to allocate scarce resources between alternative uses. When any item is scarce in relation to the demand for it, its price is likely to go up. Such a price rise does not mean that the object took more work or equipment to produce; it is simply the result of scarcity. Any item may have a scarcity element in its price, but with a few such as land where almost none of the cost is attributable to production, there is very little else. We can now see how the scarcity of any commodity could lead to the substitution of materials which increase the total workload while being cheaper in terms of monetary cost. The original material has a low real cost, but as its scarcity cost increases it becomes more expensive than another commodity with a higher real cost. The increase in real costs may be anything up to the full amount of the scarcity cost of the material being replaced.

In some respects the scarcity price of a commodity is a measure of the growth of the workload in the economy: it shows the amount of extra real cost people can and do incur to avoid the high scarcity price. Thus people are prepared to pay the extra real costs of transport from their suburban homes to the city centre each day to avoid paying the high scarcity prices and rents of land and housing in the city centre. The same high land prices make organizations willing to pay the higher real building costs of building upwards to save land rather than outwards. When a commodity becomes scarce and its price goes up suppliers will also be willing to go to greater lengths – in terms of real costs – to get supplies: traders will import

from more distant places, farmers will be willing to use more
fertilizer and poorer land, mining firms will find it profitable to
extract lower-grade ores and timber merchants will reconstitute
sawdust and offcuts to make chipboard.

Another way in which the workload may be increased is
through the social costs of people's actions. Thus before the
Clean Air Act of 1956 it was estimated that the cost of polluted
air in terms of extra cleaning, the damage to buildings, and
other losses was about £250 million a year at 1954 prices, or
about £5 per head.[1] But the prevention of dark smoke has also
incurred costs. People have had to change over to smokeless
fuels, and factory boilers and chimneys have had to be fitted
with devices to prevent the emission of dark smoke.

Increasing traffic congestion adds to the cost of labour and
fuel used in the transport of goods. The alternative to congestion – keeping an increasing volume of traffic flowing
freely – means introducing more one-way schemes which
increase the distance travelled, more traffic signals, parking
meters, traffic wardens and so on.

Increasing real costs often appear in the form of new products
designed to deal with new problems. Parking meters are
an example, others include waste-disposal systems and many
of the consumer goods discussed earlier, as well as a whole
host of equipment and services used within the productive
system.

In the same way as the role of government administration
and the amount of law constantly expands to cope with new
problems, so does the productive system. Like the progress
of medicine, which has improved the general health of the
population and eliminated many of the earlier causes of death
only to find other diseases on the increase, so industrial
development has satisfied many needs only to find new ones
appearing.

Before leaving the problem of the expanding workload, it is
worth noting that it has a paradoxical implication for the
amount of human labour which may be required in the future.

---

[1] UK 1954, Command paper 9322, *Report of the Committee on Air Pollution*,
  p. 45.

As the total productive workload is increased, and a growing proportion of it has to be undertaken by machinery, man's contribution becomes less and less significant. It may remain high in absolute terms, but as a proportion of the whole, man's physical energy, manipulative ability and brain power is of decreasing importance. As this trend continues, it will become easier and easier to eliminate human labour altogether. The means of replacing the remaining uses of human muscle power, brain power and manipulative ability are constantly being expanded. In pre-industrial societies it was inconceivable that human labour could have been eliminated because there was nothing to replace it with; but in industrial societies, although hours of work may not be declining, the ability to reduce them is growing.

The possibility of a higher standard of living and of a society freed from work may well be eclipsed by future problems. Once again the problems which pose the most fundamental threat are ecological. The non-renewable mineral resources we are using are bound to run out at some time, and ecologists warn that it will be sooner rather than later. But now that the scale of productive operations has become so enormous and so much of it no longer centres on organic processes, environmental pollution has also become a major hazard. One of the more recent and alarming estimates of the rate of resource depletion was contained in a document produced by a group of ecologists entitled 'A blueprint for survival'. On future supplies of oil and natural gas it said:

> At present rates of consumption, known reserves of natural gas will be exhausted within 35 years, and of petroleum within 70 years. If these rates continue to grow exponentially, as they have done since 1960, then natural gas will be exhausted within 14 years, and petroleum within 20.[1]

Of the reserves of sixteen of the most important metals it said:

[1] 'A blueprint for survival', *The Ecologist*, II (January 1972), p. 42.

at present rates of consumption all known reserves of these metals will be exhausted within 100 years, with the exception of six (aluminium, cobalt, chromium, iron, magnesium and nickel). However, if these rates of consumption continue to increase exponentially at the rate they have done since 1960, then all known reserves will be exhausted within 50 years with the exception of only two (chromium and iron) – and they will last for only another 40 years![1]

The discovery of new reserves, rising scarcity prices, recycling and the invention of methods of exploiting poorer quality deposits will throw these estimates out, but essentially the point remains. Future resource shortages will inevitably involve vast changes in the productive system and greatly increase the complexity of its task. There have already been experiments with synthetic foods and suggestions for using enormous quantities of nuclear energy to extract traces of valuable minerals dissolved in sea water. These possibilities clearly lie within the established tradition of economic development; no doubt they will appear as major technical advances increasing the efficiency of the productive system and the quality of human life.

The problem of finding substitutes and adapting to resource shortages may well prove insurmountable if the supplies of too many materials fail in a short space of time. The faster these resources are used, the closer together will be their expiry dates. Though it is impossible to prevent non-renewable resources running out at some time, slower consumption will allow a longer period for adaption. This provides the best chance of avoiding another period of upheaval and human suffering to match that of the industrial revolution. Restraint on the growth of population and production seem to be an ecological necessity.

In this chapter we have seen that the changes which go on around us are part of a dynamic process initially set in motion

[1] Ibid., p. 41.

by the need for ecological adjustment. Basic changes in the resource-base and productive methods produced secondary, higher-level problems, but the underlying direction of development was still determined by ecological factors. Our lifestyle and environment had to be accommodated to an industrial mode of production as a matter of necessity. Only a privileged minority have ever been able to devote a significant part of their expenditure towards an open-ended pursuit of the 'good life'. Most people's expenditure continues to be motivated and directed primarily within the channels we have discussed. In Mishan's words, 'as the carpet of "increased choice" is being unrolled before us by the foot, it is simultaneously being rolled up behind us by the yard.'[1] The continued urgency of consumption and the low priority given to leisure must be taken as indications of the increasing 'real' cost of living in an industrial society. Industrial development creates problems as well as solving them, and in some periods it may be in danger of creating more than it solves. Although at the moment the standard of living in most industrial societies is genuinely quite high, it would be dangerous to regard this as an inevitable consequence of industrialization. Historically, industrial development has not been a process of uninterrupted progress, and it is not difficult to imagine the coexistence of the industrial mode of production with widespread poverty in countries such as India. As a support system industrial production does not have an unlimited yield.

For the older industrial nations there must be serious doubts about the wisdom of continued economic growth *per se*. Present and future ecological problems and the demands of social welfare make it clear that we should be much more discriminating about the forms which development takes. The experience of none of the industrial countries suggests that further development will of itself eliminate poverty, reduce slums or cope with any of our social problems. Production in a market economy is influenced more by the expenditure of the rich than by the needs of the poor. The improvements which have been made in these areas have resulted from actions and

[1] E. J. Mishan, *The Costs of Economic Growth* (London, 1969), p. 119.

policies designed specifically to redirect productive resources towards the needs of the poor. But even leaving special poverty aside, increases in gross national product cannot be regarded as sound evidence of a general increase in social welfare. A rising GNP may just as well be taken as evidence of the increasing needs and problems which make higher consumption necessary. That GNP can be increased by undesirable events cannot be denied: car crashes increase garage incomes, increased traffic and aircraft noise adds to the demand for soundproofing materials, increased urban sprawl adds to the demand for transport from people wanting to see the countryside and increased social isolation boosts the sales of television sets. But whether or not the growing quantity of goods people want is regarded as a reflection of the increasing real cost of living, it is clear that much current production is essentially a flow required to make up for the wear and tear on the stock of goods in use. Boulding recommended a change from the concept of a flow economy to a stock economy for ecological reasons.[1] He suggested that the production of clothes, for instance, should be regarded as an activity undertaken to service the stock of clothes in use, and so as a quantity it would be desirable to minimize. Though it is in the interests of business to maximize this flow and minimize the durability of products, maximizing the flow could only make sense in an economy concerned predominantly with food and fuel – where use involves destruction. In an industrial economy concerned increasingly with consumer durables, the standing stock of goods in use is the important welfare factor and production is primarily a measure of how quickly goods wear out.

Although economic development inevitably has dramatic implications for human welfare, the increasing workload and the various interpretations which can be given to rising *per capita* consumption warn against any simple statement of the relationship. Industrial development, like agricultural development before it, is rooted in responses to increasingly formidable ecological problems, but at each step development provides

[1] Kenneth E. Boulding, 'Environment and economics', in William W Murdoch (ed.), *Environment* (Stamford, Conn., 1971), p. 359.

man with increasingly formidable powers to tackle the problems. In this process of mutual escalation, the balance of advantage in terms of man's welfare continues to sway uncertainly back and forth.

10 *Explanations of underdevelopment*

For those who regard the blessings of economic development as unmixed, the existence of so many underdeveloped societies must seem particularly enigmatic. Usually the theoretical problem of underdevelopment is posed by the belief that man has lived in great poverty through most of his history and yet persevered with highly inefficient technology. But the ecological approach to development modifies our view of both the poverty and the inefficiency, and reveals that many societies have remained underdeveloped because of strategic factors which have acted to maintain a stable equilibrium in which basic human needs are satisfied. Using this approach we have less need of the conventional explanations of underdevelopment than do those who fail to recognize the fundamental importance of the break with ecological equilibrium and the reappearance of subsistence problems. However, it must be recognized that development is not always forthcoming even when it is desired. There are factors which stand in the way of development. This is a problematic situation even within the ecological framework; later in this chapter the concept of technical consistency is used to elucidate it. But first we may take advantage of the freedom which our lack of need for the conventional theories of under-development gives us to criticize them.

For anyone trying to explain why pre-industrial societies do not abandon their ways and use more efficient methods there is an obvious tendency to impugn either the institutional structures of stable societies or the mental characteristics of their populations. It is often said that peasants do not make economic decisions rationally, and social institutions are

H

frequently criticized for not providing individuals with incentives to innovate. The cultural arrogance with which industrial societies have viewed their own achievements has led almost inevitably to a bigoted interpretation of pre-industrial societies. Suggestions of economic irrationality have been taken seriously enough to elicit a number of studies designed to test the hypothesis.[1] For what they are worth, they indicate that peasant societies do allocate resources rationally, weighing up the pros and cons of any recommended changes carefully; but one suspects that these conclusions are underpinned by the difficulty of defining irrational behaviour. If we do not buy things from the shop we know to be cheapest we presumably have some reason for not doing so which makes the decision rational – the shop may be inconveniently far away for instance. In a sense, an irrational action is one for which there is no possible rationalizing reason or cause. If someone in another society makes different decisions from our own it probably indicates that he has a different hierarchy of values and priorities, not that his behaviour is irrational or mistaken. If a man prefers increased leisure to higher consumption it is difficult to see the merit in persuading him otherwise.

The role of capitalist institutions with their built-in incentives and 'individualism' – emphasized by W. A. Lewis and given pride of place by Schumpeter – looks an important factor in development because of the apparent historical conjunction between the development of capitalism and industrialization.[2] But inequality and exploitative relationships were a long-established product of the scarcity of the means of independent production, and were intensified (for instance by enclosures) as

---

[1] See for example W. D. Hopper, 'Allocative efficiency in a traditional Indian agriculture', *Journal of Farm Economics*, XLVII (1965), pp. 611–24; R. D. Sanwal, 'Agricultural extension in a Kumaonese village', *Journal of Development Studies*, I (1964), pp. 384–98; T. W. Schultz, *Transforming Traditional Agriculture* (New Haven, 1964), chapter 3; Delane E. Welsch, 'Response to economic incentive by Abakaliki rice farmers in eastern Nigeria', *Journal of Farm Economics*, XLVII (1965), pp. 900–14.

[2] W. A. Lewis, *The Theory of Economic Growth* (London, 1955); J. A. Schumpeter, *The Theory of Economic Development* (Cambridge, Mass., 1951).

pre-industrial scarcities became more severe.[1] Capitalism was merely the same system of class relationships adjusted to fit new means of production. Far from aiding change, the market system and class ownership of the means of production served to isolate production from the poverty which constituted the need for change. The poor, who objectively had the most interest in change, were not only completely divorced from control of production, but were placed in a situation which frequently made them actually opposed to the introduction of improved techniques which threatened their employment. An institutional system which alienates the employed majority of the population from improvements in productive techniques is surely cutting itself off from a valuable source of innovation. In the more egalitarian primitive and peasant societies, where the community maintains direct control of production communally or individually, the productive system is inevitably sensitive to their decisions and needs: laboursaving methods can be welcomed unreservedly for their benefits rather than opposed as threats to employment. It is a wonder that major economic development – as opposed to the accumulation of wealth – ever took place within a rigidly class society; historically it must be the exception rather than the rule. The benefits which a ruling class gains from the poor and its desire to maintain its privileged position are among the reasons why ruling classes have typically acted as a conservative force preventing change in spite of poverty. The numerous attempts to emphasize the particular aspects of capitalist institutions which favour change must be seen as an attempt to make a basically *post hoc propter hoc* argument sound more plausible. The truth of the matter is that scarcity is both a precondition for exploitative relationships and the motive for development, and a state of plenty favours stability and egalitarian community life – hence Marx's primitive communism and future communism based on industrial plenty. It is the underlying ecological situation which is or is

[1] For evidence of relationship in colonial America between growing land scarcity and inequality see Kenneth Lockridge, 'Land, population and the evolution of New England society, 1630–1790', *Past and Present*, XXXIX (1968), p. 72.

not 'innovatory'. Social institutions can only prevent or allow adequate responses. Capitalism was simply the result of people being allowed to cash in on the new opportunities.

Education is often regarded as a panacea for the problems of underdevelopment just as it is for almost every other ill. Although it does not of itself bring forth new technology, education and training are obviously among the necessary adjuncts to the introduction of a technology requiring skilled operators. In this role it appears as an element in the developmental process rather than as an independent cause of change. Education is also valued for its ideological power. It serves in effect to extricate people mentally from the ideas, expectations and values of their own culture, and implants a new set from a more developed culture. Among a community of traditional farmers and fishermen on the Lower Volta in Ghana, we are told that 'The unquestioned acceptance of the traditional standard of living is a fundamental impediment to economic growth'.[1] The problem seems to be that these people have no land shortage and manage to gain an adequate subsistence working an average of only 4·1 hours a day for 174 days in the year. Social values apparently discouraged ostentatious displays of wealth, and opportunities for increasing production were not used.

If education increases people's belief in science and their willingness to accept expert advice it should also further development by easing the work of agricultural extension officers and the like. A great many studies stress the empirical approach of peasant farmers who insist on practical demonstrations of new techniques or visit neighbouring farms to see them in action rather than take expert advice on trust.

Some of the emphasis on education is no doubt misplaced. Once again misconceptions about the problem of underdevelopment are at the bottom of it. In part, education is seen as a way of making people 'rational', but the emphasis also reflects a belief that it is easy for educated men to find practical

[1] Rowena M. Lawson, 'Innovation and growth in traditional agriculture of the Lower Volta, Ghana', *Journal of Development Studies*, IV (1967), p. 143.

improvements in pre-industrial methods. We shall see later that this belief can usually be sustained only by ignoring many of the contextual constraints in which any improvement would have to operate.

Economic theories of underdevelopment tend to lie within a recognizable tradition. Most of them spring from the basic doctrine that all production results from combining the 'factors of production'. As land, labour, capital and entrepreneurship receive respectively rent, wages, interest and profit, the doctrine has its uses in the analysis of the social distribution of income from production, but it has bedevilled the analysis of production itself. Production is a technical process whereas payments demanded from production depend on particular social institutions, concepts of ownership etc. One is a matter of the laws governing natural processes, the other of rules governing social processes. Too often the latter masquerade as the former. If it was believed that all chemical reactions in productive processes required a payment to the gods or their earthly representatives, presumably the economists would discover a new 'factor of production' and decide they had never recognized the true importance of chemical reactions in production. Similarly, for social reasons land would not have been considered a 'factor of production' before it was scarce enough for people to demand payment for its use. But whatever the limitations of the concept of 'factors of production', many economists have continued to use them as if they were a silhouette of the actual physical techniques of production rather than the shadows of social institutions. Once it was accepted that all production results from combining factors of production then it seemed a safe assumption that any deficiency in total production must be caused by a shortage of one or other factor of production. Capital was selected as the factor most plausibly in short supply. Not only was it the only factor which looked scarce in underdeveloped as compared to developed countries, but it also appeared to increase during industrialization. More important however was the convenient possibility of attributing increases in physical productivity to the progressive substitution of capital for labour.

The belief that economic development entails using increasing quantities of capital lies at the basis of a vast bulk of economic literature. Capital-shortage theories of underdevelopment dominate the field. What relationship these theories have to practical reality is however not an easy question to answer. There is no reason to think that more capital is not invested because of lack of savings. The existence of great poverty does not mean that there are not also rich people with money to spare. The mark of many underdeveloped countries is that savings are used unproductively on ostentatious living. Present-day underdeveloped countries are able to afford armaments and wars when necessary, just as wars and country mansions have always been part of European history. It has been estimated that the English industrial revolution was financed up until the end of the first quarter of the nineteenth century simply by using existing savings more productively.[1] Enclosures, canals, turnpikes, the Napoleonic Wars, the transformation of the iron industry and much of the textile industry, and the early railway building were achieved without additional saving. The unproductive use of savings suggests – as argued later – that a society has an established technical consistency which does not provide profitable opportunities for new investment.

Historical increases in output during US economic development indicate that only a small proportion can theoretically be 'accounted for' by increases in the amount of capital or other factors used. The most important element in growth has been the increase in the productivity of factors. (This is of course a form of change which is masked by a 'factors of production' approach. That most increases in production have in fact come from innovations which allow less of each factor to be used shows how misleading the economists' traditional tools have been.) R. M. Solow estimated that in America between 1909 and 1949 output per man-hour approximately doubled, and 'about one-eighth of the increase is traceable to increased capital per man-hour, and the remaining seven-eighths to technical

[1] Phyllis Deane and W. A. Cole, *British Economic Growth 1688–1959* (Cambridge, 1964), pp. 304 and 308.

change'.[1] Similarly, Abramovitz estimated that in the seventy-five-year period between 1869–78 and 1944–53 the American input of labour and capital per head (only) increased by some 14 per cent. He concluded that to account for a quadrupling of net national product per head the productivity of a representative unit of all factors must have increased some 250 per cent.[2]

These studies show the expected dominance of technological and other qualitative changes in development. We have seen that economic growth is a process of qualitative change which appears as a response to a situation in which it is no longer possible to make quantitative extensions to the established economic system. Much formal development theory has failed to come to grips with technical change and is forced to assume a constant relationship between various factor inputs and production. The simplest example is Rostow's assumption of a constant capital to output ratio. If the ratio assumed constant is that three units of capital equipment produce one unit of output a year, and it is desired to increase national product (net of investment) by say 4 per cent per year, then, according to the theory, the growth will be achieved by raising the rate of capital investment to 12 per cent per year of net national product. The ratio is assumed constant whether or not the labour force is growing equally fast, regardless of whether there is room for further extension of the economy or whether economic development necessitates qualitative change.

Keynesian theory, and most of the growth models which spring from it, also fail to distinguish between quantitative extension and qualitative change. This may have been relatively unimportant from the point of view of the short-term analysis Keynes was interested in, but for growth theory concerned primarily with changes in *per capita* income it is an essential distinction. Once again the problem arises from the use of

---

[1] R. M. Solow, 'Technical change and the aggregate production function', *Review of Economics and Statistics*, XXXIX (1957), pp. 312–20. Solow's figures are for real, private, non-farm GNP.

[2] Moses Abramovitz, 'Resources and output trends in the United States since 1870', *American Economic Review*, Papers and Proceedings, XLVI (1956).

socially defined factors of production to analyse technical processes. The relationships between the monetary aggregates to which the discussion is confined are truisms at one level, and constantly falsified by the flow of productive innovations at others. Everyone knows both that innovations are likely to be factor-saving and that they are the central feature of development. Yet models continue to be constructed which imply that development is nothing more than a growing circular flow of funds which can be set in motion by a little monetary 'pump priming' or by turning on the 'monetary tap' – depending on the plumbing. Many models, perhaps particularly those which have grown out of the original Harrod-Domar formula, are merely exercises in equations which generate an annual growth in the value of the symbol representing GNP. Their basic trick is to assume that an element which determines this year's growth is some function of the amount of growth last year; thus, given an initial push, the thing will keep going. So little do they have to do with the real dynamic forces in society that most of these models are just as likely to be set off in reverse by an initial chance fall in income as they are to go forward from a rise. Their dependence on a basis of short-term cyclical analysis is only too apparent.

Although by far the most important increases in production have come from increasing factor productivity, there has obviously been some increase in the ratio of capital to labour. Each workman now needs more tools and equipment to work with than he used to. The ecological approach to development explains this trend quite simply: it is the result of having to use less amenable raw materials and of other changes which increase the complexity and difficulty of the productive task. Industrial production could not be carried on adequately by hand. Traditionally economists have tried to explain the increasing ratio of capital to labour by saying that capital was cheaper than labour. For those who believed industrialization was a process of substituting one factor for another, the cause was then reasonably clear: see for instance T. S. Ashton's guarded statement that the single most important factor leading up to the English industrial revolution was the lowering of the interest rate over the previous half century.[1] But the link between the interest rate and the use of capital goods is not as simple as that. A firm of – say – shipbuilders which won a contract to build a tanker could presumably borrow money during the construction period to pay for capital equipment or wages equally well. The decisive consideration is which of two methods of doing something is the most efficient: one using more labour and less tools and equipment or one combining the proportions the other way round. As tools and equipment are also made by labour the question is whether the total costs of labour are lowest using more indirect or direct labour. If equipment has to be purchased with borrowed capital then the interest rate represents a small surcharge on the price of indirect labour, but it could be argued that there is an equivalent opportunity cost on funds used for the payment of wages. The belief that a shortage of labour causes an increase in the use of capital equipment is of course erroneous except in so far as it is anyway more efficient to do so. At best it can be argued that a shortage of labour encourages a more efficient use of labour – in whatever direction that may indicate. If we look at the distribution of the available labour force between capital-goods and consumer-goods industries, the use of more capital goods will not help increase production unless it decreases the need for labour in consumer-goods production by more than it increases it in capital-goods production. Of course if the relative prices of labour in capital – and consumer – goods production changed this would affect the choice of techniques, but any secular trend of this kind which there may have been would be a decidedly marginal factor. The important factor determining the choice of methods and technology is always a matter of the relative efficiency of the alternatives in terms of labour – direct and indirect. Other factors are marginal in the long run, and only dangerously extended and tortuous arguments can rope them in to explain the increasing use of capital equipment.[2] If it is

[1] T. S. Ashton, *The Industrial Revolution 1760–1830* (London, 1948), p. 11.
[2] See for example H. J. Habakkuk, *American and British Technology in the 19th Century* (Cambridge, 1962). As well as the arguments above, it is worth noting that in terms of the ability to produce subsistence, labour

thought that the increased use of capital equipment has brought real increases in social productivity, then there is no need to try to attribute it to purely institutional factors such as the interest rate and relative prices of labour. Laboursaving innovations appeared for no more baffling reason than that they were laboursaving. But now that we have removed the marginal institutional factors from their pre-eminent position they cannot be used to explain why laboursaving capital goods did not appear before (and that was their chief function). However, the changes which precipitated the industrial revolution were not economic ones making capital plentiful and labour scarce; the important changes as we have seen were in the task which the productive system had to undertake. It was the changes in the nature of this task which demanded new methods and more capital equipment. More tools became necessary as the productive task became more formidable.

We may now return briefly to the view that development may be hindered by a shortage of capital. Financial capital represents power to command productive resources, to buy things and to employ labour. The fact that someone has saved over the years, been left capital, or has managed to get a loan is no guarantee that the economic system has productive resources to spare. The political power exercised by capital through the market could as far as that goes be controlled through other institutional channels. It is important to recognize that capital accumulation is merely an institutional means of gaining a type of economic power: it is not an essential preliminary to exercising this power. The real – as opposed to the institutional – question is when the exercise of this power to further development will prove beneficial. The most common argument is that in poor countries productive resources for making capital goods cannot be spared from the already minimal production for the population's current consumption. But one might equally well say that a poor country could less well afford to continue with

---

was scarcer *per capita* in England than America. The relationship between population and environment was the key to the difference between American and British technology.

inefficient techniques if others were available. If there is already unemployed labour or labour with very low productivity in the economy, it would be beneficial to employ it to improve the country's capital equipment. Where there is already full employment the situation appears more complicated. But if the use of more capital equipment in the production of consumer goods really increases efficiency, then shifting some workers from production of consumer goods to capital goods should enable the production of consumer goods to be increased. No one would introduce spinning wheels to replace distaffs unless the combined labour, including the labour of those making the spinning wheels, could spin more yarn that way than if everyone spun with distaffs. The only possible difficulty arises where the capital equipment has a long pay-off period. The labour spent building a road or railway may take several years to pay for itself. But the problem of maintaining sufficient consumer goods production during the construction period would only be serious if projects such as these amounted to a significant proportion of national income. Even then a flow of much shorter-term improvements would ease the situation. (The arguments in this paragraph do not apply to shortages of capital in the form of foreign exchange which is of course governed by different rules.)

It is often said that one of the limitations on the permissible rate of new investment is the threat of inflation. However, the appearance of inflationary price rises in developing economies is not necessarily an indication that this limiting rate has been reached. Inflation often occurs in economies with high unemployment where Keynesian theory would least predict it. Where natural resources are limited, population growth and pressure to expand the economic system can cause prices to rise. The English price revolution of the sixteenth and early seventeenth centuries (see graph *b*, p. 71) is believed to have been caused by population pressure on the economic system. Prices of agricultural commodities rose fastest because supplies could not usually be increased without an increase in real costs. The bottleneck in industrial goods was not so formidable and innovations to increase supplies prevented prices rising quite as fast. In those countries where prices are rising because scarcities and diminishing returns are forcing up real costs, increased investment and innovation may be the best way of countering them. It must have been the rapid rate of innovation which prevented British prices rising for so much of the nineteenth century. Although general inflationary or deflationary price movements may often have purely monetary causes, they sometimes serve as useful indications of the dynamic movements in the real economy. Relative price movements are however a more reliable tool. They show the developing scarcity of different materials and the pressure to find substitutes. The advantages and disadvantages of different technologies and the benefits of innovation will also be reflected in relative price movements.

After this brief criticism of some of the more common views of underdevelopment we are left with a few basically common-sense propositions. There is no reason to think that people in underdeveloped societies are any more or less rational than those in industrial societies: productive resources in under-developed societies seem to be allocated efficiently within the given economic framework. It is tempting to adopt T. W. Schultz's characterization of underdeveloped societies as 'poor but efficient'.[1] But although in Western eyes all pre-industrial societies may look poor, it is clear that the societies which live within a well-maintained ecological equilibrium may not experience any of the subjective reality of poverty. The populations of such societies may not regard economic development as particularly advantageous: from their standpoint it may seem to entail sacrificing leisure and some of the other advantages of their way of life to obtain unnecessary increases in production. On the other hand, societies which are out of equilibrium and do experience poverty are likely to regard development as desirable. Most of these manage to achieve rates of change which compare favourably with those recorded during the historical development of the industrial nations. We must now

[1] Schultz, op. cit.

turn our attention to the remainder which do not. Obstacles to desired development are of several different kinds. A shortage of capital may sometimes be a hindrance, but this must be much rarer than is commonly imagined. More often the problem results from a division within the society over the desirability of development. A powerful ruling class, which benefits from the *status quo*, may try to prevent change by staving it off with economic and social legislation. But where these difficulties either do not exist or have already been tackled, change may still not be forthcoming. Here, it will be argued, the main problem which stands in the way of development is simply that of finding innovations which are beneficial within the given economic and technological context.

It was suggested in chapter 7 that a society with a stable population, on an adequate and enduring ecological base, will develop a technology which is self-consistent and integrated within that context. To recap, the technology will tend to stabilize as most of the advantageous opportunities for innovation available within that context are used up. After several generations of relative stability it is unlikely that there would be many very obvious improvements available which rational people had not taken up. While the society's needs and environment remain unchanged, we should not expect to find them. (For the moment this does not cover the introduction of imported technology which could not be produced locally.) In this situation there is nothing to be gained from new investment. The rate at which capital is ploughed back will settle down to what is needed to maintain the existing stock of capital equipment. People will invest the amount in traditional equipment which is justified in ordinary terms of profit and loss: they do not buy another bullock cart or keep an additional plough team because it would not be economically beneficial.

With a growth of population and a break with ecological equilibrium the experience of poverty makes people alter their choice of technique in order to increase production. Given that the existing technology is a well-integrated system, the problem is to find practical ways of increasing production which do not disrupt the system so much as to offset the benefits of the new methods. We know that considered in isolation, modern science has solutions to problems such as how to increase rice yields, or any of the others which pre-industrial countries may face. This does not mean that the technology and materials needed are within reach of pre-industrial societies, nor does it mean that the solution could coexist with other productive activities. Attempts to get some Indian villagers in Uttar Pradesh to use the higher yielding Japanese method of paddy cultivation were unsuccessful partly because the change meant upsetting the rest of their cropping pattern.[1] Although rice yields were higher under the new method it decreased the efficiency of the system as a whole. An improved variety of seed also brought difficulties because – unlike the ordinary seed – it produced straw and husks unsuitable for winter feed for cattle. Generally, problems of internal consistency tend to increase as farming gets more intensive. Each farm becomes a highly integrated unit with draught animals providing essential power and manure and requiring grass fallow and winter feed in return. The ratio of arable land to land under fallow and feed crops has to be practical both from the point of view of rotations and soil fertility, and from the point of view of how much land an animal can plough compared with how much it needs for grazing.

Often modern technical solutions to problems are not justified by the scale of the problem in underdeveloped countries. Human portage and animal transport may look inefficient, but the amount of transport needed in under-developed countries may not justify either the production or ownership of motor vehicles. On Indian farms in a district of Mysore state it was reported that the few people who had been persuaded to buy tractors only had work for them on their own farms about 40 days in the year.[2] By hiring them out to other farmers and doing transport jobs they managed to keep them employed for an average of 130 days in the year, but that still

[1] Sanwal, op. cit.
[2] K. K. Sarkar and M. Prahladachar, 'Mechanization as a technological change', *Indian Journal of Agricultural Economics*, XXI (1966), p. 181.

left them totally idle for the equivalent of seven or eight months a year. The lack of demand for tractor services was of course primarily a reflection of prevailing agricultural methods. We are told that it would have taken 'a major adjustment in farm practices and cropping pattern' to reap the full benefits of mechanization.[1] A report on agricultural change in Haiti suggests that the need to plough with draught animals was often not great enough to justify keeping them, but where they were already used to drive sugar mills ploughing spread without encouragement.[2]

Where methods of production have evolved sufficiently to justify the introduction of a new technology, and the innovation will not harmfully disrupt the rest of the system, it still remains to be seen whether the new equipment comes within the society's productive potential. Modern technology cannot be produced easily in underdeveloped countries, but imports are necessarily limited. The problem of finding solutions which lie within the productive potential of a society's established technology is one of the most important obstacles to development. A World Bank report on the problems of establishing automotive industries in underdeveloped countries contained the following paragraph:

> Automotive manufacturers (in underdeveloped countries) experience a great difficulty in obtaining an adequate supply of required components and parts. Quality has been deficient on such items as electrical equipment (spark plugs, starters, ignition coils, distributors and various instruments). Difficulty has also been experienced with forgings and casting (especially aluminium castings and iron engine blocks), chrome-plated items (grill work and bumpers) and various plastics and vinyls (in some cases reverting to paper-covered wires proved more practical and cheaper). Most body manufacturers have had to import sheet steel . . . because the local product had substantial ductility when used in the

[1] Ibid., p. 181.
[2] C. J. Erasmus, 'Agricultural changes in Haiti', *Human Organization* (winter 1962), pp. 20-6.

heavy-duty stamping presses, and consequently a high rejection rate.[1]

A case history of a large American company making diesel engines which set up an Indian subsidiary shows similar problems.[2] It appears that there was no difficulty with capital supplies; the parent company was willing to spend where it seemed profitable – but problems which can only be described as problems of technical consistency were enormous. The mass of technical specifications and standards which the engines required ran into ten large volumes and included 439 basic materials specifications. It was originally planned that 90 per cent of supplies should be Indian, but after a year of production domestic supplies accounted for only 15 per cent of the total and after another year they had risen to around 20 per cent. Sample parts purchased from suppliers had a rejection rate of around 50 per cent, and selected supplies for production between 10 and 20 per cent. Gaskets were too hard, cylinder liners were not hard enough, piston rings were too soft or too brittle, rubber oil seals leaked at different temperatures and so on. Some fairly minor design changes were made to meet local conditions: pressed-steel sumps were replaced by sandcasted ones and other parts previously made from aluminium were made from iron to facilitate sandcasting. Baranson, the author of this case study, concluded: 'Contrary to widely held beliefs among development economists about capital deficiencies, the evidence seems to indicate that the basic difficulties lie in limitations imposed by the scale of local markets and overall deficiencies in supplier capabilities.'[3]

Many of the difficulties were of course made more severe because the manufacturers were trying to produce a complicated object designed in a different technological environment. In the earlier quotation it seems surprising, in view of the problems they created, that the chrome-plated grills and bumpers should

---

[1] Jack Baranson, *Automotive Industries in Developing Countries*, World Bank Staff Occasional Papers, VIII (Baltimore, 1969).

[2] Jack Baranson, *Manufacturing Problems in India: the Cummins Diesel Experience* (New York, 1967).   [3] Ibid., p. XI.

have been retained, and it would almost certainly have been possible to redesign body panels in simpler shapes which could have been stamped out of the local steel sheet – after all current car-body designs have evolved with the technology from less complex shapes. Another writer who studied thirteen US corporations with plants in six underdeveloped countries makes the same point:

> Many American companies assumed that their product must meet the same specification in the foreign countries as in the United States, and hence rigidly adhered to domestic specifications. This made it unnecessarily difficult in some instances for vendors abroad to meet specifications.[1]

The problem would remain however even if products were completely redesigned. The minimum technical specification for a workable internal combustion engine – especially a diesel engine – would be beyond the capabilities of many societies.* We have only to remember by what a hair's breadth the steam-engine designers in eighteenth-century England brought their invention within the society's productive potential.[2]

Developments in the qualitative range of a society's productive potential come from making new demands which stretch the existing technology. Each extension in the qualitative range is likely to provide possibilities for applying new methods in other areas. The technical links between one sector and another are fundamentally important in this respect. Technical change in one industry means that new demands will be placed on suppliers and new technical opportunities will be available to the productive system as a whole. Technical change spreads through these technical links. Initially an

[1] Wickham Skinner, *American Industry in Developing Economies* (New York, 1968), p. 136.
* Since this chapter was written, General Motors and Ford have announced plans for cheap cars specially designed for underdeveloped countries. The building of the simplified body shapes and all assembly work will be done in underdeveloped countries using imported engines and gearboxes etc. (*The Guardian*, 19 May 1972).
[2] See chapter 7 above.

industry may be driven to change its methods by ecological pressures, as happened with the English iron industry. After breaking the established technical consistency it may then act as a powerful stimulus bringing change to other sectors. In England the iron industry added impetus to the development of coalmining which in turn led to the development of pumping techniques and canal transport. On the supply side the appearance of cheap iron was a precondition for the development of railways and a largescale mechanical engineering industry. A single sector may play a disproportionate part as an initiator of change throughout the productive system. At first sight this seems similar to Rostow's theory of a 'leading sector', but Rostow was primarily concerned with the monetary impact of a leading sector.[1] In the English industrial revolution he singled out the cotton industry because of its role in generating incomes. But of all industries, cotton was one of the most lacking in backward and forward technical linkages with the rest of the domestic economy. All raw materials were imported and most of the product exported. Without the possibility of innovation elsewhere in the economic system the increased incomes generated by the cotton industry could not have brought further additions to the total social product; they would merely have been choked off in inflationary price rises. The question which must be asked about innovation in any single sector is what possibilities does it provide for innovation in other sectors. From this point of view mining, iron-smelting and the railways are successive candidates for the dominant role. Perhaps one of the most important ways in which the cotton industry affected the rest of the economy was by undercutting the domestic textile industry, forcing people to find other sources of income.

The attempt to industrialize by transplanting individual pieces of modern technology into underdeveloped countries is beset with difficulties. As we have seen, technology designed for production and use in an industrial context is unlikely to fit a pre-industrial one. This method of development would only be

[1] W. W. Rostow, *The Stages of Economic Growth*, 2nd ed. (Cambridge, 1971), pp. 53-5.

practical if it were possible to arrange the elements of industrial technology in a transplanting order ensuring that each element would be consistent and profitable in the context of the preceding elements. The first element would have to be workable in the context of the unaltered pre-industrial economy, the next element on the basis of that economy plus the first element, and so on. (This comes close to the problem of triangularizing a detailed input–output table.) Of course there is no reason why it should be possible to order industrial technology in this way: it did not develop like that – there were intermediate stages which have disappeared. It may sometimes simplify problems of technical consistency if closely interlocking industrial complexes are introduced as a unit, but the best strategy is difficult to analyse. If a new industry fits in too easily it does little to stimulate the rest of the system. Profitability may be reduced, but it will be more stimulating if the new technology stretches the old to its limits. In the example of the establishment of a diesel engine plant in India it was clear how 'problems of procurement' could (and did) force the company to adopt a policy of 'vendor development', so that fewer components had to be imported. The difficulties the company faced are some measure of its potential developmental impact on the economy.

The advantages of following in the wake of the early industrializers are not unmixed. Although problems of invention are avoided, it is unlikely that the technology will be as sensitive to local conditions as it was in the countries where it was invented. Invention is not just a matter of pure conceptualization: it is also a problem of reducing the concept to a realizable form given the existing state of the technology, i.e. of dealing with problems of technical consistency at the design stage. The crude appearance of early machinery is not an indication of the limitations of the inventor's mind. Newcomen could easily have imagined perfectly fitting pistons and cylinders just as Henry Ford could have imagined streamlined curves for his car bodies, but their ability lay in allowing their inventiveness to be disciplined by practical realities.

A particularly satisfying example of the kind of sensitive adaptation of established technology which is needed comes from an irrigated area of Vietnam.[1] In the Mekong Delta a pump was needed to raise water one or two metres from the canals for irrigation. American aid workers had recommended diesel centrifugal pumps of 10 to 20 horsepower, but on short lifts these were more expensive to run and had a lower delivery rate than the traditional pedal driven waterwheels. A Vietnamese who farmed a hectare of rice and ran a small motorcycle repair shop developed a much simpler and cheaper pump. A propeller on the end of a long drive shaft was used to pump water up the short length of piping in which it was housed. The pump could be made locally and could be powered by a smaller and cheaper engine. The whole thing could be bought for about the same price as a pig and was light enough to move from one field to another. Within three years the use of this pump had enabled rice output in the upper delta to be increased by 40 per cent. The American experts familiar with working in a different technological and economic context remained extremely sceptical about its merits even after the invention began to prove successful.

Having discussed the technical development of pre-industrial countries in terms of a movement towards modern industrial technology and resource-base, it should be pointed out that this may be a shortsighted policy. Predictions of when the resources which modern industrial technology depends on will run out are usually within the same time scale as the predictions of when many underdeveloped countries may reach industrial maturity. The industrial nations cannot avoid having to change their whole resource-base and technology for a second time, but some of the pre-industrial nations might manage to avoid making more than one change. More of the research and technical development effort could be directed towards improving ways of exploiting lasting resources. The exploitation of nuclear power and solar energy, a concentration on artificially structured organic cycles, and the use of the more plentiful minerals are worth stressing.

[1] Robert L. Sansom, 'The motor pump: a case study in innovation and development', *Oxford Economic Papers*, XXI (1969), pp. 109–21.

Postscript

Many people will be unhappy with the overall impression they have gained of man's economic development from the ecological model. In particular the attitude of neutrality towards the place of progress in development and the general framework of cultural evolution are likely to meet opposition. The theory will be called a mechanistic one, leaving no place for human creativity or imagination, a theory which reduces man to the level of other animals in a Darwinian universe. Paradoxically, others will complain equally that the model usurps the economic calculus of efficiency, profit and loss from its traditional role. Although such criticisms reflect likes and dislikes instead of raising more important questions of truth and falsity, they are worth mentioning because they would also reflect a misunderstanding of the role of the theory. Development is of course a process of human creativity and imagination, just as it is of the economics which is usually used to explain it. But just as it is little more than a truism to say that a new machine was introduced because it was profitable, so it is a truism to say that a new invention is the product of human creativity. Human actions are not free of – in the sense of divorced from – reality; the forms they take, their reasons and purpose are all related to the world in which they take place. To understand the characteristically human qualities it is particularly important to examine them in the context in which living people actually express them rather than in some detached idealized form. While the economist must show what it is about the productive circumstances which makes an innovation profitable in one period rather than another, the person interested in man's creative genius must show why man has chosen to exercise it in one direction in one period and another in the next. The task of showing the changing circumstances to which people have had to tailor their actions is of course what the ecological model sets out to achieve. But for those who would dissociate themselves and all that is 'holy' from nature, the discovery that man is part of nature – instead of above it – will inevitably seem to degrade rather than enrich their view of human life.

Unlike many theories of economic development which confine analysis to highly impersonal and often abstract forces, the ecological model shows clearly how people are subject to the impersonal forces which characterize the particular period and society in which they live. We can often recognize our own attitudes in the ambivalence which our predecessors showed towards the changes which they were caught up in. As our understanding of the forces of change grows, we are no longer left to wrestle with confused and contradictory feelings: we can see what elements of change really are inevitable, when opposition to change really is 'holding up essential progress' and which are the most hopeful ways of maintaining the features of our lifestyles and surroundings which we value. Environmentalists who have already opted for stabilization policies must not weaken their case by ignoring the urgency of modern forms of poverty. If poverty is not to be alleviated by growth, then it must be alleviated by a redistribution of income. But whatever our views, we must expunge the fatalist belief that the great unplanned forces and unintended pressures which shape our society and technology have been, and will remain, magically benevolent. Too often they command our unthinking but reluctant compliance; instead we must make conscious planning decisions about the quality of our lives, hopefully gaining the initiative needed to make man the master of change rather than change the master of man.

Index

Index

abortion:
  animals, 25
  humans, 28, 30, 33, 36
Adam and Eve, 53, 67
adaptive problem situation, 12–13
  creation of new problems, 15–16
agricultural development:
  America, 162–4, 167–8
  examples, 59, 60, 62–3, 76–8
  general course of, 92–9
agriculture, beginnings of, 15, 67,
  83, 100–1
air pollution, 191
alienation from work, 108
alkali manufacture, 131–2
animal population limitation, 24–7
Australian aborigines, 46

Boserup, Ester, 92–6
breastfeeding, effect on fertility,
  37–8
building materials, 126–7

canals:
  America, 155–6
  England, 122–4
capital, 212
  accumulation, 202, 206–7
  laboursaving, 204–6
  shortage theories, 201–7
capitalist institutions, development
  of, 63, 87–8, 198–9
Carr-Saunders, Sir A., 31–2, 41

carrying capacity, 16, 21
  population limitation in relation
  to, 43–50, 51
cars, 178, 184
chemical industry, 131–2
Christianity, see missionaries
class structure, 61, 63, 82–3, 87–8,
  109–11, 198–9
climax communities, 21, 91
clothing materials, 4, 127–9, 151,
  157, 186
coal, substituted for wood:
  America, 153–5, 170
  England, 114–18, 126
communal economic institutions,
  breakdown of, 110, 113
community, see neighbours
competition:
  for scarce resources, 48–50
  in evolution, 23–4
consumption (see also needs, development of new):
  in industrial societies, 174–85,
  194–5
cost of living, rising real, 185,
  194–5
costs, rising real, 189–91
cotton industry, 127–30
cultural adaptation, 10–11, 14, 19,
  104
cultural determination of behaviour, 9, 13–14
cultural evolution, chapter 2

cultural pride, 89

demonstration effect, 86
disease, 29–30, 42–3, 72–3
domestic (rural) industries,   59,
    79–80, 82, 157

ecological equilibrium, chapter 3:
    and leisure preference, 85
    breakdown of, chapter 4
    defined, 21–2
    examples of breakdown in small-
        scale societies, 58–67
    in class societies, 67–83
ecological model, summarized, 4–6
ecological niche, 10, 19
economic base of culture, 11
economic development (*see also*
        economic efficiency):
    general course of, chapter 5
    national and local, 58
    need for, *see also* poverty; 63, 197,
        208
    pre-industrial, in England, 76–81
    qualitative   and   quantitative
        change in, 3, 76, 203
economic efficiency (*see also* labour
        productivity), 54
    and economic development, 54–
        6, 83–5, 91–2, 105–7, 140–2,
        146
    and prices, 189–91
economic growth models, 203–4
    mathematical, 1–2
education, 178, 200
engineering, mechanical, in under-
        developed countries, 211–13
entertainment, 181–2
environmental exploitation, inten-
        sification   of,   54–6,   90–2,
        101–3
evolutionary adaptation, 12
    group versus individual selec-
        tion, 23–4
    progress in, 11–12

exchange systems:
    in primitive societies, 48–9
    elsewhere, 87
extra-cultural model, 8

factors of production, 201
fallow period, 93–6
fertility of soil, *see* soil fertility
food preservation, 131, 177
food supplies:
    adequacy of in primitive societies
        (*see also* starvation), 41–2, 46–7,
        50, 65
    and leisure preference, 85, 200
frontier, American, 148

gas lighting, 133–4
geographical mobility, 180–1
GNP, *see* national income

'hand to mouth' existence, 47
holidays, 179
horse feed, scarcity of, 123–6
hunters and gatherers, 15, 41–2,
    44–7, 50

industrial labour force, creation of
    (*see also* urban migration), 59–
    62, 63, 80, 107, 151–2, 157–8
industrial revolution, 101, chapters
    6 and 8
inequality, 110, 199n
infanticide:
    animal populations, 24, 25
    humans, 33–7, 39, 73, 74n
inflation, 72, 114, 207–8
innovation, 56, chapter 7, 199–200,
    209–16
    the need for, 54–5, 134
interdisciplinary approach to de-
    velopment, 2
investment (*see also* capital):
    opportunities for, 140, 145, 209
iron-smelting:
    America, 154–5
    England, 116–17

Japan, 82–3

Kent, Connecticut, 149–50
Kenya, Pakot, 88–9
Koran, 68

labour (*see also* workload):
    hours of, 42, 92–3, 96, 102, 106,
        135–6, 168–9, 173, 187–8,
        191–2, 200
    productivity, 92–9, 135–6, 168
laboursaving innovations, 105, 107,
    135, 188–9
land:
    scarcity of, 149–50
    subdivision of holdings, 61–2,
        80, 149–50
'leading sector', 214
leisure activities, 181
leisure preference (*see also* labour,
    hours of), 84–5, 173–4
Lowell mills, Massachusetts, 158,
    161

Malthus, 22–3, 50–1, 69, 70, 148
marriage:
    population limitation and, 33,
        60, 64, 66, 75
    age at, 74
media, mass, 182–3
migration, among animals, 27
mining, technical problems in, 118–
    20
missionaries, 33, 60, 64–5, 68
moving house, *see* geographical
    mobility

Napoleonic Wars, 124, 125, 136
national income, 4, 185, 195
needs, development of new, 86,
    174–85
neighbours, 180–1
neolithic revolution, *see* agriculture,
    beginnings of
New England, 149–53

New Guinea, Siane, 49, 85
New York, 150–1
'noble savage', 24

oil, 171, 185–6
Orissa, 61

papermaking, 132–3
plastics, 185–6
ploughing, 94–5
    prairies, 168
poor relief:
    in America, 150
    in England, 136
population growth:
    America, 148
    England, 70–6
population limitation (*see also*
    abortion, infanticide, mar-
    riage):
    among animals, 24–7
    and age at marriage, 74
    and carrying capacity, 43–50
    cultural checks, 30–40, 64–6,
        72–5
    ideology affecting, in class
        societies, 67–8
    in England, 69–76
    in Japan, 82
    need for in relation to resources,
        22
    physiological checks in humans,
        28–30
    superstitions affecting, 39–40
poverty, 174–6, 184–5, 194–5
    in America, 149–51, 157–8, 164,
        166
power, additional sources of, 95,
    102–5, 143, 188–9
pre-contact societies, 31
prices (*see also* inflation):
    real and scarcity, 189–91
    relative, 143–5, 208
    trends in England, 70–2, 114,
        207

progress, the dilemma of, 83–5, 105–9, 146, 172, 193–6, 218

quality of life (*see also* industrial labour force *and* progress), 105–9, 172, 174–5

railways, 124–5
rationality, 197–8
refrigerators, 176, 184
refuse disposal, 176–7
relations, contact with, 183–4
resource management in primitive societies, 20–1, 44–6
resources:
  and class structure, 109–11
  destruction of, in America, 165–6
  England's dependence on land-based, 112
  renewable and non-renewable, 20, 216
  scarcity of, 54, 169–70, 192–3, 216
  substitution of (*see also* building materials, clothing, coal, gas, plastics), 101–2, 170–1, 185–6
riverboats, *see* steam-engine
roads, 121–3

savings (*see also* capital), 202
self-sufficiency, 58, 80–1, 151–2, 157
sewage disposal, 176
slash-and-burn agriculture, 92
soil fertility, 92, 94–6, 152–3, 162–4, 166–7
stability, conditions for, chapter 3
starvation, 22, 23, 27, 28, 30, 32, 50, 51, 82
steam-engine, 120, 142, 144, 158–61
  mills, 120–1, 160–1
  pumping, 119–20
  railways, 124–5
  riverboats, 159–61

surplus, production of (*see also* capital *and* savings), 47

Taiwan, 58–9
technical change, *see* innovation
technical consistency, chapter 7:
  and underdevelopment, 209–16
technology, 11, 109
  increasing complexity of, 102–5 188–9
telephone, 184
television, 181–2
territorial behaviour among animals, 26–7
Thailand, 62
Tikopia, 64–5
timber, *see* wood
totemism, 46
towns, growth of (*see also* urban migration), 80, 82
tractors, 210–11
trade, development of:
  in America, 155–6
  in England, 81, 121–2
transport, development of:
  and communications, personal use of, 184
  in America, 155–6
  in England, 81, 121–6
  to work, 178
Trobriand Islanders, 49–50

underdevelopment, obstacles to development, chapter 10
urban migration, 59, 60–1, 82

Vietnam, irrigation pump, 216
Vunamami, 66–7

wages (*see also* consumption in industrial societies):
  trends in England, 70–2
water power, shortage of, 120, 161
water supplies, domestic, 176
weeding, 92, 94, 95

wheat, British trade in, 114
wood:
  clearance of in America, 165
  prices in England, 114
  shortage of in America, 153,
    170
  shortage of in England, 114–16

work, *see* labour
workload, 101–7, 135–6, 167–8,
  186–9, 191–2
Wynne–Edwards, V. C., 21, 26–7
  48

Zulus, 60–1